THE CONDOMINIUM CONCEPT

*A Practical Guide for Officers, Owners and
Directors of Florida Condominiums*

12th Edition

Peter M. Dunbar, Esq.

Pineapple Press, Inc.
Sarasota, Florida

This publication is designed to provide accurate and authoritative information in regard to the subject matter covered. It is sold with the understanding that the publisher is not engaged in rendering legal, accounting, or other professional services. If legal advice or other professional assistance is required, the services of a competent professional person should be sought.
—From a *Declaration of Principles* jointly adopted by a Committee of the American Bar Association and Committee of Publishers and Associations

Inquiries should be addressed to:

Pineapple Press, Inc.
P.O. Box 3889
Sarasota, Florida 34230

www.pineapplepress.com

Library of Congress Cataloging-in-Publication Data

Dunbar, Peter M.
The condominium concept : a practical guide for officers, owners and directors of Florida condominiums / Peter M. Dunbar. -- 12th ed.
    p. cm.
Includes index.
ISBN 978-1-56164-480-3 (hb : alk. paper) -- ISBN 978-1-56164-481-0 (pb : alk. paper)
1. Condominium associations--Law and legislation--Florida. I. Title.
KFF114.C6D86 2010
346.75904'33--dc22
                                        2010023358

Twelfth Edition
Hb 10 9 8 7 6 5 4 3 2 1
Pb 10 9 8 7 6 5 4 3 2 1

Printed in the United States of America

About the Author

Peter M. Dunbar is a partner in the law firm of Pennington, Moore, Wilkinson, Bell and Dunbar, P.A. For a period of almost three years before joining the firm he served in the Office of the Governor of the State of Florida as General Counsel and later as Chief of Staff. In private practice, he has specialized in the areas of condominium and real property law. He is an Adjunct Professor at the College of Law at Florida State University on condominium law, and he has taught and lectured on condominiums and the law governing condominiums since 1974. Mr. Dunbar is a member of the Community Associations Institute and he served on its National Board of Trustees and was a Director and Vice President of Florida-Suncoast Chapter. He is a member of the Florida Bar, the American College of Real Estate Lawyers, and an honors graduate from the College of Law at Florida State University.

Mr. Dunbar served as a member of the Florida House of Representatives for ten years. During his legislative career he served as a member of the House Judiciary Committee and sponsored or co-sponsored every major new law affecting condominiums during his decade of service in the Legislature. He served two terms as a member of Florida's Condominium Advisory Council.

Contents

3 MEMBERSHIP MEETINGS: PRACTICE AND PROCEDURES 44

4 THE BOARD OF ADMINISTRATION AND MEETINGS OF THE BOARD 89

5 OFFICERS AND COMMITTEES 125

6 RULES OF PROCEDURE — A SHORT-HAND GUIDE 145

9

PROMULGATING RULES, AMENDING THE DOCUMENTS AND MODIFYING THE CONDOMINIUM PROPERTY 219

10

THE ASSOCIATION AUTHORITY AND RESPONSIBILITY 244

11

RIGHTS AND RESPONSIBILITIES OF THE UNIT OWNER 263

12

THE CONDOMINIUM DEVELOPER AND TRANSITION 278

13

ENFORCING THE DOCUMENTS AND RESOLVING DISPUTES 299

14 DISPUTE RESOLUTION AND THE DIVISION OF FLORIDA CONDOMINIUMS, TIMESHARES AND MOBILE HOMES 331

Forms Index

OFFICER AND COMMITTEE FORMS

RULES OF PROCEDURE FORMS

BUDGET AND FINANCIAL REPORT FORMS

ASSESSMENT FORMS

AMENDMENT FORMS

MANAGEMENT FORMS

FORMS GOVERNING UNIT OWNERS

TRANSITION AND DEVELOPER FORMS

ENFORCEMENT FORMS

DIVISION FORMS

Introduction

The purpose of *The Condominium Concept* is to provide a practical guide for officers and board members of residential condominiums. It is not designed as a legal treatise for lawyers. The manual will, however, refer frequently to provisions of the law helping its user understand the requirements that the law imposes on the operation of condominiums in Florida. Those familiar with prior editions of *The Condominium Concept* will find new references to the law that are presented by footnote in this edition, and the references have been expanded to include key decisions from Florida courts. This new feature expands the foundation for the operational guidelines in the book, and it will allow the reader the option to research further on points discussed here.

Condominiums are "creatures of statute." The Florida Condominium Act governs their creation and their ongoing activities. The Act also addresses the rights of unit owners and the responsibilities of those who govern the condominium on their behalf. This twelfth edition of the *Concept* includes the changes to the Florida Statutes through the 2010 legislative session.

Almost 20 percent of the state's population lives in a condominium governed by individuals selected from within the community and serving on a voluntary basis. The association is not like an advisory homeowners association and the authority and responsibility assumed by the volunteer officers is substantial and real. This manual is designed to assist them in understanding the responsibility they have assumed and to guide them in the exercise of the authority they have been given.

There are forms and sample documents to help association officials comply with the procedural requirements regulating their duties. There is a short-hand guide to the rules of parliamentary procedure and forms to assist in conducting association meetings. Finally, there are frequent references to sections and paragraphs of the *Florida Statutes* (F.S.) and the *Florida Administrative Code* (F.A.C.) to give foundation to the commentary and to direct the reader to other source material if there is need for more information.

The Condominium Concept will serve as a quick and easy reference source to answer many of the questions that confront officers and board members. On other occasions it will point out the need for assistance from the association's attorney.

Condominium living is unique. It is designed to create a lifestyle where joint ownership of property promotes the common welfare. This manual is offered in support of that goal and the author hopes that each user will find it helpful and effective.

1

The Condominium and the Condominium Documents

MISCELLANEOUS CONDOMINIUM DOCUMENT FORMS

1.1   History. The condominium form of ownership of real property has its earliest foundations during the Roman Empire. The term "condominium" is a derivative from the language of the time, meaning common ownership by two or more people. Reference can be found to condominiums through the Middle Ages and the concept was first put into law in 1804 in the Napoleonic Code of France.[1] The condominium concept in Florida, however, is relatively new and began when the 1963 Legislature enacted Chapter 711, Florida Statutes (F.S.), providing the basic legal authority for the creation of condominiums.[2]

In 1974 and 1975, major revisions to the Condominium Act added significant consumer protections for individual unit owners and established comprehensive requirements for the operation and management of condominium communities by their associations. All of these changes were designed for the ultimate benefit and protection of the condominium unit owner. In 1976, Chapter 711, F.S., was renumbered as Chapter 718, F.S., which is now known and cited as the "Condominium Act" in Florida.[3] Significant changes were added to the Condominium Act in both 1991 and 1992, and in each subsequent year, including a series of major revisions in 2010, modifications have been enacted that affect the operations in Florida's condominium communities.

1.2   Condominium Concept. The condominium concept is a form of joint ownership of real property. It is distinguished from other types of joint or common ownership because of the three distinct parts that make up the condominium. The first part is the exclusive ownership of a single unit; the second part is joint ownership, as tenants-in-common with others, of common areas; and the third part is an agreement or scheme among owners for the management and administration of the total condominium property.[4]

In more formal terms, "condominium" means the form of ownership of real property that is created under the Condominium Act and is comprised

---

[1] *Sterling Village Condominium, Inc. v. Breitenbach,* 251 So.2d 685, 688 (Fla. 4th DCA 1971), citing 38 St. John's L. Rev. 3; 15 Am. Jur. 2d, Condominiums, Etc., § 3; and Coke on Littlejohn, quoted in 39 Yale L.J. 621.

[2] "In Florida, condominiums are creatures of statute and as such are subject to the control and regulation of the Legislature." *Century Village, Inc. v. Wellington Condominium Ass'n,* 361 So.2d 128,133 (Fla. 1978).

[3] § 718.101, F.S.

[4] § 718.104, F.S.

of units owned individually by one or more persons together with joint ownership of an undivided share in the common elements.[5] Each of the three parts is essential to the condominium and a condominium cannot exist if all three elements are not present. The creation is formally accomplished when the parts are defined as required in the Condominium Act and a declaration of condominium is recorded with the Clerk of the Circuit Court in the county where the condominium property is located.[6]

1.3 Understanding the Parts. In general discussion the terms "condominium," "condominium unit," and "condominium association" are often used interchangeably. At times, however, to interchange one term with another can be not only confusing, but is inaccurate and inappropriate. A "condominium" is not the unit that is lived in, and it is not the entity which has a board of administration. "Condominium" refers to the entire grouping of all three parts together and includes the condominium unit, the common elements and the condominium association. The "condominium association" is the governing entity for the community and each unit owner is a member of the association.[7] The association is governed by a board of administration and the board is elected by the members.[8]

The unique interrelationship between the parts of a condominium distinguishes it from other similar forms of joint ownership, such as a cooperative or townhouses. A cooperative does not have a unit that is individually owned and the occupants only receive an exclusive right to occupy the apartment unit. Legal title to the property in a cooperative remains in the name of the association.[9]

In a townhouse style development, residents own their home but there are no "common elements" jointly owned with others.[10] The common property is either titled to a homeowners' association or is made available to residents through a long term lease. Only the condominium form of ownership has the "unit," the "common elements" and the "association" as separate and distinct pieces that combine to form the total "condominium."

---

[5] § 718.103 (11), F.S.

[6] § 718.104 (2), F.S.

[7] § 718.103 (2), F.S.

[8] § 718.103 (4), F.S.

[9] § 719.103 (12), F.S.

[10] The declaration of restrictions for single-family lots does not create a condominium form of ownership. See *Raines v. Palm Beach Leisureville Community Ass'n, Inc.,* 413 So.2d 30, 32 (Fla. 1982) and *Department of Business Regulation, Div. of Land Sales v. Siegal,* 479 So.2d 112 (Fla. 1985).

1.4 Compromise and the Common Scheme. The benefits of condominium living are many. They include a sharing of maintenance responsibilities and the expenses for quality recreation facilities. They promote a concept of community stability and security and provide an organization with central responsibility for efficient and quality operation of the property.[11]

Along with the benefits of the condominium concept, however, there are also some compromises which must be made and each individual unit owner gives up a certain degree of freedom which otherwise might be enjoyed in a separate single family home. The common elements of the condominium are not owned by an individual unit owner and they are to be shared and enjoyed by all.[12] (See 1.6).

The concessions and compromises of condominium living have been succinctly described by Florida's Fourth District Court of Appeal in the following passage:

"Every man may justly consider his home his castle and himself as the king thereof; nonetheless his sovereign fiat to use his property as he pleases must yield, at least in degree, where ownership is in common or cooperation with others. The benefits of condominium living and ownership demand no less. The individual ought not be permitted to disrupt the integrity of the common scheme through his desire for change, however laudable that change might be." *Sterling Village Condominium, Inc. v. Breitenbach,* 251 So. 2d 685, 688 (4th DCA, 1971.)

The overriding principle in the condominium concept is the promotion of the health, happiness and peace of mind of the majority of unit owners. In accomplishing this goal, there will be some compromises of individual rights. It is the association and the board of administration which continually face the responsibility of maintaining the delicate balance between individual rights of unit owners and preserving the common scheme for the benefit of all the owners.[13]

1.5 Unit and the Unit Owner. The "unit" is that portion or part of

---

[11] *Holiday Out in America at St. Lucie, Inc v. Bowes,* 285 So.2d 63, 65 (Fla. 4th DCA 1973).

[12] § 718.103 (8) and § 718.108, F.S.

[13] *Hidden Harbour Estates, Inc. v. Basso,* 393 So.2d 637, 640 (Fla. 4th DCA 1981).

the condominium property which is subject to exclusive ownership. The boundaries and the description of each unit must be specifically set forth in the declaration creating the condominium,[14] and ownership of a unit entitles the owner to its exclusive use. Once the real property has been submitted to condominium status, all the individual units become separate parcels of real property.[15]

The use of the unit must be consistent with the regulations and restrictions in the declaration of condominium, and the association has an irrevocable right of access to each unit when it is necessary to maintain, repair, or replace a portion of the common elements or any portion of the unit to be maintained by the association pursuant to the declaration of condominium. The association also has the right of access to each unit when it is necessary to make emergency repairs in a unit to prevent further damage to common elements or to another unit.[16]

When an owner receives title to a condominium unit, the title also includes the ownership of an undivided share of the common elements that are assigned to the unit by the declaration. The unit, together with its undivided share in the common elements, is known as the "condominium parcel."[17] A "unit owner" or "an owner of a unit" means the owner of a "condominium parcel," and title includes ownership of both the unit and a portion of the common elements assigned to it.[18]

In order for property to be subject to exclusive ownership in a condominium, it must be created and identified as a unit and it must have an undivided portion of the common elements assigned to it. A room or area of the condominium property called a unit but not assigned a percentage

---

[14] § 718.103 (27), F.S.
[15] § 718.109, F.S. See *Hyde Park Condominium Ass'n v. Estero Island Real Estate, Inc.*, 486 So.2d 1 (Fla. 2d DCA 1986) and *Estancia Condominium Ass'n, Inc. v. Sunfield Homes, Inc.*, 619 So.2d 1008 (Fla. 2nd DCA 1993) concerning "phantom units and contrast with *RIS Investment Group, Inc. v. Department of Business and Professional Regulation Division of Florida Land Sales Condominiums and Mobile Homes,* 695 So. 2d 357 (Fla. 4th DCA 1997).
[16] § 718.111 (5), F.S.
[17] § 718.103 (12), F.S.
[18] § 718.103 (28), F.S.

of ownership in the common elements has been classified by the courts as common elements and its owner's claim to exclusive ownership was disallowed.[19]

1.6   Common Elements. The portion of the condominium property jointly owned by all of the owners is defined as "common elements" and it includes all of the condominium property that is not located within the defined boundaries of the individual units.[20] The property legally described in a declaration of condominium must be one of two kinds—it must be a "unit," specifically described with a percentage of common element ownership assigned to it, or it will be common elements and jointly owned by all of the unit owners. No portion of the common elements is subject to exclusive ownership for so long as it remains a part of the condominium.[21]

The common elements are, however, subject to exclusive use by a particular unit or units to the exclusion of others if the declaration of condominium permits it. Common elements set aside for exclusive use by the declaration are known as "limited common elements" and examples include balconies, patios, storage lockers and assigned parking spaces.[22] Except for these limited common elements, all other portions of the common elements are for use by all of the unit owners, although an individual owner's use must not hinder or encroach upon the lawful rights and use by other owners.[23]

In addition to an assigned percentage of the common elements and the right to use them, each unit also has additional accessory rights or "appurtenances" which are inherent with the ownership of a condominium parcel. The appurtenances to a unit include the right to share in the common surplus (see 7.13) and the exclusive right to use the designated limited common elements.

Appurtenances include rights to use, and have access to, all of the easements and easement rights available to the condominium association. They also include various membership rights available to unit owners[24] and

---

[19] *Daytona Development Corp. v. Berquist,* 308 So.2d 548, 550 (Fla. 2d DCA 1975); see also *Sauder v. Harbour Club Condominium No. Three, Inc.,* 346 So.2d 556 (Fla. 2d DCA 1977).

[20] § 718.103 (8), F.S.; *Village of Doral Place Ass'n, Inc. v. RUA Real, Inc.,* 22 So.3d 627 (Fla. 3rd DCA 2009).

[21] *Daytona Development Corp. v. Berquist, supra* note 19 and *Mayfair Engineering Co. v. Park,* 318 So.2d 171, 173 (Fla. 4th DCA 1975).

[22] § 718.103 (19), F.S.; *Brown v. Rice,* 716 So.2d 807, 808 (Fla. 5th DCA 1998).

[23] § 718.106 (3), F.S.

[24] *Scott v. Sandestin Corp.,* 491 So.2d 334 (Fla. 1st DCA 1986).

the use and benefit from all property owned directly by the association. All supplemental rights or privileges which accompany the ownership of the unit, including membership in the condominium association, are considered "appurtenances" to the unit.[25]

1.7 Association. The third part of a condominium is the corporate entity which is responsible for the management and operation of the condominium property. It is referred to as the condominium association or simply as the "association."[26] The board of administration (directors) is the governing body of the association, and the board is responsible for administration of the association.[27]

Current provisions of Florida's Condominium Act require that the association be either a corporation for profit or a corporation not-for-profit. As a general rule, most condominium associations fall into the not-for-profit category. Prior to January 1, 1977, unincorporated associations were permitted and some can still be found operating in Florida.[28]

All unit owners are members of the association as an appurtenance to their ownership of a condominium parcel, but no owner may act for the association simply by virtue of being a member.[29] Through the board of administration it is the association's responsibility to administer to the shared facilities of the condominium property, to promote harmony and uniformity within the condominium community and to enforce the restrictive covenants contained in the declaration of condominium and other documents which regulate the condominium.

Unit owners in some condominiums may have a membership in more than one "association." In addition to the corporation responsible for management of the condominium, other corporate entities may also be an "association" under the terms of the Act. These might include a master association or a recreation association, and such association is governed by the Condominium Act when (1) it operates or maintains real property in

---

[25] § 718.106 (2), F.S.
[26] § 718.103 (2), F.S.
[27] § 718.103 (4), F.S.
[28] §718.111 (1)(a), F.S.
[29] § 718.111 (1)(c), F.S.

which unit owners have use rights, (2) where membership in the entity is composed exclusively of unit owners, and (3) where membership by unit owners is required by the condominium documents.[30]

1.8   Association Property. Traditionally, the condominium association does not own or lease property as a part of the general scheme for the condominium. The association does, however, have the power to acquire title to property and to otherwise hold or lease property for the use and benefit of its members.[31] When it does, the property is identified as "association property." "Association property" includes all real and personal property which is owned or leased by or is dedicated by a recorded plat to the association for the use and benefit of its members.[32] Technically, the property owned by the association is not common elements, but it is an appurtenance to the units and is treated for all practical purposes as if it were common elements.

The association will occasionally acquire title to real property when a recreation lease is purchased or when property is added to the community by purchase or gift. All personal property such as lawn maintenance equipment, pool furniture and similar types of personal property are considered "association property," and should be titled accordingly. This will allow the property to be disposed of and replaced by the board of administration as time and wear necessitate. If the property is owned as common elements or is defined as common elements, it cannot be sold or disposed of without the unanimous approval of the owners.[33]

1.9   Assessments. To fund the non-profit association's operations and special needs, each unit owner is required to contribute a proportionate share. The proportionate share required to fund the annual budget and general operations of the association is known simply as an "assessment."[34] The funds required from a unit owner, other than the assessments required to fund the annual budget, are referred to as "special assessments."[35]

Collectively, the assessments and special assessments must be enough to cover the payment of all of the association's capital obligations

---

[30] § 718.103 (2), F.S.
[31] § 718.111 (7), F.S.
[32] § 718.103 (3), F.S.
[33] § 718.110 (4), F.S.
[34] § 718.103 (1), F.S.
[35] § 718.103 (24), F.S.

and operating expenses. A unit owner may not avoid the responsibility for assessments by waiving the use or enjoyment of all or part of the condominium property,[36] and an owner delinquent in assessment obligations is not eligible for membership on the board of directors.[37] (See 4.7).

"Common expenses" include all of the expenses for the operation, maintenance, repair, and replacement of the common elements and association property; the costs of carrying out the powers and duties of the association; and any other expenses defined as common expenses by the Condominium Act, the declaration of condominium or the other documents creating the condominium.[38] Expenses for services or items mandated to be installed on the condominium property by federal, state, or local government, such as fire safety equipment or water and sewer meters, are deemed to be a common expense. Common expenses may additionally include reasonable transportation services, in-house communication services, and security services if they were provided from the time that control of the board was transferred from the developer.[39] Common expenses may also include hurricane shutters when their installation has been approved by a vote of the unit owners.[40] (See 9.14).

The definition of common expense allows the board of administration wide latitude for its fund raising depending on the character and nature of the condominium community. However, the expenses are always subject to challenge if they result from an abuse of the board's discretion or when they are not within the proper business scope of the association.[41]

1.10 Unity of the Parts. The parts of the condominium—the unit, the common elements and the condominium association—create the unique character of the condominium, and they cannot be separated from one another for as long as the condominium exists. The undivided share in the

---

[36] § 718.116 (2), F.S.
[37] § 718.112 (2)(d) 1. and § 718.112 (2)(n), F.S.
[38] § 718.103 (9), F.S.; *Rothenberg v. Plymouth #5 Ass'n,* 511 So.2d 651 (Fla. 4th DCA 1987).
[39] § 718.103 (9) and § 718.115 (1)(a), F.S.
[40] § 718.115 (1)(e), F.S.
[41] § 617.0830, F.S.; see also *B & J Holding Corporation v. Weiss,* 353 So.2d 141, 143 (Fla. 3rd DCA 1978).

common elements which is appurtenant to a unit passes automatically with a deed to the unit whether or not it is separately described.[42]

The common elements cannot be separated from a unit, nor can they be separately conveyed or mortgaged except as a part of the unit.[43] Governmental agencies may not separately assess property taxes against the common elements and tax bills must be sent to individual unit owners with each owner paying a portion of the taxes for the common elements.[44]

Membership in the condominium association is an appurtenance to unit ownership, and it is a right which cannot be denied to any unit owner.[45] Membership also places restrictions and mandatory financial obligations upon a unit owner that cannot be avoided by waiving use of the common elements. When title to a unit is transferred, membership in the condominium association is also transferred and vested in the new owner. Collectively all of the parts make up the condominium and to eliminate any one of the parts from the others destroys the condominium concept.

1.11 Democratic Sub-Society. The character of condominiums has emerged from its basic beginnings in 1963 to a sophisticated and well-ordered housing concept. The uniqueness of condominium living has resulted in a greater degree of control and limitation over the rights of individual unit owners and their use and occupancy of a condominium unit.[46] The concept has also allowed for owners to share in benefits and recreational amenities which would not otherwise be available to them as a single family homeowner. The sub-society of condominium unit owners, while more restrictive on some individual rights, is also an open quasi-government which is run in almost a purely democratic fashion.[47]

The assessments of the condominium association can be compared to the taxes of a city, and the ability of the board of administration and membership to develop and modify rules and regulations is similar to the

---

[42] § 718.107 (1), F.S.

[43] § 718.107 (2) and (3), F.S.

[44] § 718.120 (1), F.S.

[45] § 718.106 (2)(d), F.S.

[46] *Sterling Village Condominium, Inc. v. Breitenbach, supra* note 1.

[47] "Condominium unit owners comprise a little democratic sub-society of necessity more restrictive as it pertains to use of condominium property than may be existent outside the condominium organization." *Hidden Harbour Estates, Inc. v. Norman,* 309 So.2d 180, 182 (Fla. 4th DCA 1975).

ability of a municipality to pass and amend ordinances. The condominium association also possesses the authority to act as an enforcement body to fine its members and to enforce by court action the restrictions and regulations which govern the community.[48]

Tempering the exercise of the association's authority is the right to democratically elect the board of administration and to recall any member at any time when their performance is not satisfactory.[49] The condominium sub-society has the equivalent of a city charter in the form of its declaration of condominium. This foundation document spells out the mutual rights and obligations of the unit owners,[50] and it cannot be amended or changed to alter the rights and protections given to each unit owner unless an extraordinary majority vote is obtained or the affected owner consents. The basic property rights of the individual unit owner are protected by the community's governing documents and the owner's voice in the association affairs is assured by the Condominium Act.

1.12 Covenants Running with the Land. A covenant is a commitment, agreement or contract which grants a right or imposes a liability. Each declaration of condominium includes many such rights, liabilities and commitments governing the use and occupancy of the condominium property. They are an accepted part of condominium living and are recognized by a specific provision in the law.[51] The restrictions and covenants contained in the declaration of condominium "run with the land" as permanent restrictions governing its use[52] and will remain effective until the condominium itself is terminated.[53]

Covenants may range from the obligation to pay a portion of the common expenses, to restrictions on the age of permanent residents and the number of people that may live in a particular condominium unit. In essence, all of the provisions of the declaration of condominium and its exhibits are considered covenants running with the land and are permanent restrictions affecting the property. The covenants impose limitations on the use of the property by requiring the performance of certain duties or by

---

[48] § 718.303 (1) and (3), F.S.
[49] § 718.112 (2)(j), F.S.
[50] *Woodside Village Condominium Ass'n, Inc. v. Jahren*, 806 So.2d 452, 456 (Fla. 2002).
[51] § 718.104 (5), F.S.
[52] *Woodside Village Condominium Ass'n, Inc. v. Jahren*, *supra* note 50.
[53] § 718.104 (7), F.S.

guaranteeing certain rights to owners of the property.[54] Each unit owner in the condominium and the condominium association has the right to enforce these covenants running with the land against any other owner or the association when a violation of the covenants occurs. (See 13.1).

When covenants run with the land, a person who assumes ownership of a portion of the land also assumes ownership with the presumed knowledge of the covenants. In other words, each new unit owner is presumed to know and understand the content of the declaration of condominium and its exhibits. It is the responsibility of the board of administration to maintain copies of the condominium's documents for prospective purchasers, and to ensure that this knowledge is actually in place as new unit owners join the condominium community.[55]

1.13 Prospectus. Knowledge of the condominium documents and the covenants and restrictions that govern both the rights and limitations of condominium living is the responsibility of every owner of a condominium parcel. The "prospectus," or offering circular, is the introductory synopsis to the entire set of condominium documents governing the community.[56] The prospectus is initially prepared by the developer of the condominium at the beginning of the project and it must be distributed to each new purchaser of a condominium unit.[57]

The prospectus sets forth in outline form a summary of all the restrictions, financial obligations and liabilities of an owner in the condominium. It also sets forth the commitments and promises made by the developer, and the responsibilities which must be kept and maintained by the condominium association.[58] The prospectus must be accompanied by a copy of the annual financial report, governance form, and a separate summary sheet entitled "Frequently Asked Questions and Answers" informing each owner about key provisions in the condominium documents relating to use restrictions, voting rights, individual financial responsibilities and other important matters. (See 7.14 and 12.5).

---

[54] *White Egret Condominium, Inc. v. Franklin,* 379 So.2d 346, 350 (Fla. 1979).

[55] § 718.111 (12)(c), F.S.

[56] § 718.504, F.S.

[57] § 718.503 (1), F.S. Each purchaser may cancel the purchase agreement within 15 days after receipt of the prospectus or any material amendment to the prospectus. *BB Landmark, Inc. v. Haber,* 619 So.2d 448, 449 (Fla. 3rd DCA 1993).

[58] § 718.504 (1)-(27), F.S.

The "Frequently Asked Questions and Answers" sheet must be maintained by the association (§718.111 (12)(d), F.S.).[59] Under most circumstances, neither the prospectus nor the "Frequently Asked Questions and Answers" are recorded in the public records like the balance of the condominium documents.

1.14 Declaration of Condominium. In Florida, condominiums are established under the Condominium Act by recording a declaration of condominium in the public records of the county where the land is located.[60] The declaration of condominium is the document or the set of documents that actually creates the condominium. It establishes the covenants and restrictions which will affect the property and govern the residents during the entire existence of the condominium.[61]

The declaration of condominium includes within its definition any amendments which may be made to it, and all exhibits which are attached to the foundation document and incorporated into it by reference.[62] The combined parts of the declaration of condominium create an elaborate set of covenants and restrictions and establish the basic rights and responsibilities for the residents and guests of the property.

A valid declaration of condominium must contain or provide for the name of the condominium, the legal description of the condominium property, an identification of each unit by letter or number, and the percentage by which each unit will own the common elements and will share in the common expenses. The declaration must establish easements for ingress and egress to all units and to the common elements. It must contain a survey and plot plan giving a graphic description of the condominium property. Finally, the declaration must also include the articles of incorporation and the bylaws for the condominium association.[63]

The declaration defines and identifies all of the parts of the condominium property and establishes the nature of the relationship which each has to the other. Following the recording of the declaration of condominium, a description of a condominium parcel by number or letter

---

[59] § 718.111 (12)(d), F.S.
[60] § 718.104 (2), F.S.
[61] *Woodside Village Condominium Ass'n, Inc. v. Jahren, supra* note 50; *Brickell Bay Club Condominium Ass'n, Inc. v. Hernstadt,* 512 So.2d 994, 996 (Fla. 3rd DCA 1987).
[62] § 718.104 (14), F.S.
[63] § 718.104 (4), F.S.

becomes the permanent, formal legal description for the property, and is a sufficient legal description for all purposes.[64] With the recording of the declaration, the real property loses its traditional ownership characteristics and it becomes a condominium.

1.15 Plot Plan and Survey. The plot plan and survey are traditionally found attached to the declaration of condominium as an exhibit, most often as Exhibit "A." This part of the declaration of condominium is also the most often overlooked. Yet, it is an essential requirement of the declaration, and it is frequently a helpful problem-solving tool when questions of boundaries between units and common elements arise.[65] The plot plan and survey must show the boundaries for all units and will identify visually each unit, by number or letter.

On many occasions parking space assignments, parking locations, and the identification of limited common elements will also be shown on the plot plan together with the actual boundaries of the condominium units. The Clerk of the Circuit Court may use a separate plat book for display of these condominium plot plans and surveys and the location for this separate book should not be overlooked. It usually contains a larger version of the plot plan and survey attached to the declaration, and the boundaries and dimensions will be clearer and easier to read and understand.

The plot plan and survey of the lands contained within the condominium must show all of the easements and must give a graphic description of all of the improvements on the condominium property. The plot plan, together with the written declaration of condominium, must be in sufficient detail to identify all of the common elements, each of the units, their respective locations, and their approximate dimensions. A surveyor must certify that the plot plan and survey are an accurate representation of all of these improvements, including the drainage retention areas, walkways, driveways, parking areas, recreational improvements and the other common elements.[66]

---

[64] § 718.109, F.S.

[65] The survey, graphic description and plot plan must be in sufficient detail to identify all units and the common elements. *Ackerman v. Spring Lake of Broward, Inc.,* 260 So.2d 264, 266 (Fla. 4th DCA 1972).

[66] § 718.104 (4)(e), F.S.

1.16 Articles of Incorporation. The articles of incorporation, or corporate charter, is the document which establishes that part of a condominium responsible for the maintenance, management and operation of the common elements and the condominium property.[67] The declaration of condominium must make provision for the articles of incorporation within its own text or as an exhibit. The articles themselves must define the membership rights of each unit and the voting rights which each unit owner has in the association's operation.[68]

The term "articles of incorporation" includes the original document creating the association and all amendments to it and any other documents which define the existing form, membership and responsibility of the association. For example, the definition also includes articles of consolidation or articles of merger if several condominium associations have been combined into a single organization.[69] The articles of incorporation may permit the association to operate more than one condominium, either in their original form, or by amendment, merger or consolidation.[70]

The articles of incorporation may establish a corporation for profit or a corporation not-for-profit to operate the condominium. Under most circumstances, the articles of incorporation establish a "corporation not-for-profit" under Chapter 617 of the Florida Statutes to govern the condominium. A corporation not-for-profit is not tax exempt but it is a corporation where no part of the income may be distributed to the members, directors or officers of the association.[71]

The articles of incorporation for a corporation not-for-profit may contain all of the powers traditionally granted to profit-making corporations in Florida, except as restricted by the Condominium Act or by the articles of incorporation themselves. The articles of incorporation become effective and the association may begin to operate when they are filed with the Division of Corporations of the Department of State.[72]

---

[67] § 718.103 (2) and § 718.111 (1), F.S.; see also *Juno By The Sea North Condominium Ass'n, Inc. v. Manfredonia,* 397 So.2d 297, 302 (Fla. 4th DCA 1980).
[68] § 718.104 (4)(i) and (j), F.S.
[69] § 617.01401 (1), F.S.
[70] § 718.111 (1)(a), F.S.
[71] § 617.01401 (5), F.S.
[72] § 617.0203 (1), F.S.

1.17 Bylaws. The articles of incorporation of the association define its basic structure and its areas of responsibility. The bylaws establish the procedures for carrying out these responsibilities. They define the powers and the manner for exercising those powers by the board and by each of the association's officers. Stated differently, the operation of the association is governed by the bylaws of the association.[73] A copy of the actual bylaws must be attached to the declaration of condominium as an exhibit in order for a valid condominium to be created at the time of recording. Technical defects in the bylaws themselves, however, will not affect the validity of the condominium's creation.[74]

When creating the bylaws, there is a substantial amount of discretion available to establish the specific procedures which the association will follow. There are some required provisions that the Condominium Act mandates for the bylaws and if they are not actually set forth in writing, the Condominium Act states that they shall be deemed to be included.[75] Among these requirements are restrictions on the use of proxies, the requirement that all board meetings be open to the members of the association, and the requirement that notice be posted for all board meetings.

The law requires procedures for the election of board members, adopting the budget and a requirement that all records of the association be open to unit owners. The bylaws must provide for at least three officers, a president, a secretary and a treasurer, and there must be a provision for mandatory nonbinding arbitration of disputes involving unit owners and the association. Because a portion of these mandatory requirements may not physically be within the bylaws, the board of administration and the association officers must be aware that portions of the bylaws may be found in the Condominium Act and not as a part of the bylaws actually attached to the declaration. The procedural rights established by the bylaws are for the benefit of association members, and non-members do not have standing to require that an association abide by its bylaws.[76]

1.18 Rules and Regulations. The supplemental restrictions authorized by the bylaws and promulgated by the board of administration are traditionally

---

[73] § 718.112 (1)(a), F.S.
[74] § 718.104 (4)(l), F.S.
[75] § 718.112 (2), F.S.
[76] *Backus v. Smith,* 364 So. 2d 786, 787 (Fla. 1st DCA 1978)

referred to as the "rules and regulations." The bylaws of the association may provide for the authority to adopt the rules and regulations, and may set out the procedures to follow when adopting them.[77] The rules and regulations of the association are similar to the restrictions and covenants contained within the declaration of condominium, but they are not clothed with the strong presumption of validity and enforceability that accompany restrictions actually found in the declaration.

The rules and regulations promulgated by the board of administration are best described as supplemental to the covenants and restrictions in the declaration of condominium. These rules and regulations cannot contradict or contravene those in the declaration or its attached exhibits. The standard of reasonableness for rules and regulations of the board must be carefully applied to ensure enforceability.[78] The rules and regulations must also be within the scope of the board of administration's authority, as described in the bylaws, to be valid.

Some supplemental rules and regulations may be attached to the declaration of condominium as an exhibit at the time of recording, while others consist of unrecorded rules adopted by the board of administration. Under either circumstance, the rules and regulations are supplemental to the main covenants and restrictions governing the condominium.

1.19 Policy Statements and Resolutions of Procedure. Statements of policy and resolutions of procedure outline and clarify existing standards of conduct for unit owners and their guests.[79] They also establish standard forms for providing warning notices to unit owners in violation of rules and as reminder correspondence to unit owners late or delinquent in maintenance payments.[80] Every condominium community has some established policies and standard procedures for carrying out the regulatory functions of the condominium association.

In many communities, "policy statements" and "resolutions of

---

[77] § 718.112 (3)(a), F.S.; see also *Neuman v. Grandview at Emerald Hills, Inc.,* 861 So.2d 494, 497 (Fla. 4th DCA 2003).

[78] *Hidden Harbour Estates, Inc. v. Norman, supra* note 47.

[79] The board is empowered to implement the broad statements of general policy contained in the declaration of condominium to address day-to-day problems of operations. See *Beachwood Villas Condominium v. Poor,* 448 So2d 1143, 1145 (Fla. 4th DCA 1984).

[80] See *Chattel Shipping and Investments, Inc. v. Brickell Place Condominium Ass'n, Inc.,* 481 So2d 29, 30 (Fla. 3rd DCA 1985), holding that uniform policy created an enforceable standard in the condominium.

procedure" are not written or formally codified as a part of the governing documents. To preserve consistency in the community's policies and practices, the standard operating procedures of the board of administration should be reduced to writing. These formal statements of policy and resolutions of procedure are then readily available for examination by all unit owners and will ensure consistency in both practice and procedure from one board to another.

Resolutions of procedure may provide for temporary assignments in the use of common elements, or may include a procedure for the use of a recreation room or a recreation hall. The range of subjects to be covered by policy statements and resolutions of procedure covers all aspects of condominium living. When the board of administration and the association take the time to reduce these policies and procedures to a written format, it helps to ensure that the procedures are tailored to the need of the individual association, and that they will be applied in a uniform, consistent manner for the benefit of all owners.

1.20   Priority and Consistency of Documents. Each of the documents which make up the declaration of condominium and support its operation and implementation are designed to interrelate and compliment each other for the benefit of the community.[81] Each of these documents should be consistent with all of the others and should be interpreted to carry out the common scheme of the condominium.[82] When an apparent inconsistency is identified, the provisions of the two documents should be interpreted in such a way as to leave both provisions in effect and consistent with one another. When it is not possible to resolve an inconsistency between two different documents governing the condominium, then the provision in the highest priority document will prevail.[83]

The document with the highest priority in the community is the

---

[81] "(T)he whole declaration must be considered and the general intent of the contract should prevail." *Raines v. Palm Beach Leisureville Community Ass'n, supra* note 10.

[82] "When interpreting the meaning of these documents, every part of the instrument must be given effect." *Sweetwater Oaks Condominium Ass'n, Inc. v. Creative Concepts of Tampa, Inc.,* 432 So.2d 654, 656 (Fla. 2nd DCA 1975).

[83] *Sans Souci v. Division of Fla. Land Sales and Condominiums,* 421 So.2d 623 (Fla. 1st DCA 1975).

declaration of condominium itself and its provisions will prevail over inconsistent provisions in other documents.[84] In descending order, the articles of incorporation have the next highest priority after the declaration.[85] They are followed in descending order by the bylaws of the association, the rules and regulations attached to the recorded declaration of condominium, the rules and regulations promulgated by the board of directors, and finally, the policy statements and resolutions of procedure.[86]

When inconsistency between the documents cannot be resolved by any reasonable interpretation between the apparent conflicting provisions, the provision in the document of the highest priority will prevail.[87] If the conflict arises in the same document between a provision specifically dealing with a particular subject and a provision only generally dealing with the subject, the specific provision is controlling.[88] When a provision in any of the documents is inconsistent with state, federal or local laws, the inconsistency in the community documents will be invalidated in favor of the law.

---

[84] "The articles and bylaws must be consistent with the superior document, the Declaration." *S & T Anchorage, Inc. v. Lewis,* 575 So.2d 696, 698 (Fla. 3rd DCA 1991).

[85] The bylaws may not be inconsistent with the articles of incorporation. See §617.0206, F.S.

[86] See *Woodside Village Condominium Ass'n, Inc. v. Jahren, supra* note 50, for discussion on categories of restrictions governing the use of condominium property.

[87] *Koplowitz v. Imperial Towers Condominium, Inc.,* 478 So.2d 504 (Fla. 4th DCA 1985).

[88] *Island Manor Apartments of Marco Island, Inc. v. Division of Florida Land Sales, Condominiums and Mobile Homes,* 515 So.2d 1327 (Fla. 2nd DCA 1987).

WATERFRONT XX CONDOMINIUM ASSOCIATION, INC.
A Corporation Not-for-Profit

STATEMENT OF ASSOCIATION POLICY

EFFECTIVE DATE: January 10, 2010

SUBJECT: FUNCTIONS INVOLVING LARGE NUMBER OF VISITORS AND GUESTS ON THE CONDOMINIUM PROPERTY.

PROBLEM: Uncontrolled and unlimited use of the common elements may interfere or infringe on the rights of other owners to use the common elements and other facilities of the condominium.

STATEMENT: The operation and control of the condominium property and the common elements is the responsibility of the Association. All unit owners are entitled to the quiet enjoyment of their unit and reasonable use of the common elements. When an owner or group of owners holds a function with a large number of visitors and guests, it is the desire of the Board to permit the function and also preserve the community's security and the rights of the non-participating owners to use the common elements without unnecessary interference and inconvenience.

POLICY:

1. No owner shall hold an activity or function at which more than twenty-five (25) persons will be invited unless it shall first be approved by the board of administration.

2. The request to hold an activity or function shall be in writing and state the nature of the event, the approximate number of guests, and other information pertinent to the event.

3. The consent of the board shall not be unreasonably withheld; however, the board may impose reasonable conditions and restrictions on the use of the condominium property to insure that non-participating owners are not unreasonably hindered.

WATERFRONT XX CONDOMINIUM ASSOCIATION, INC.
A Corporation Not-for-Profit

STATEMENT OF ASSOCIATION POLICY

EFFECTIVE DATE: January 10, 2010

SUBJECT: UNAUTHORIZED ENCLOSURE OF BALCONY AREAS IN VIOLATION OF DECLARATION OF CONDOMINIUM AND THE BUILDING AND ZONING CODES OF THE COUNTY.

PROBLEM: Prior to transition of the Association from the control of the developer, the balcony areas adjacent to certain units were enclosed contrary to the provisions of the Declaration of Condominium.

STATEMENT: The operation and maintenance of the common elements and the maintenance of a uniform exterior appearance of the buildings is the responsibility of the Association. Certain exterior modifications have been made by unit owners by enclosing balcony areas during the period the developer controlled the board of administration. The enclosure of balcony areas is in violation of the ordinance of the County and Article XI of the Declaration of Condominium.

POLICY:
1. No owner shall enclose any portion of the balcony area adjacent to any condominium unit.
2. Each owner shall be furnished a copy of this policy by personal delivery or by regular U.S. mail.
3. The board of directors shall further provide written notice to any unit owner commencing any improvements described in this policy statement directing that such work cease immediately and that the exterior of the building be restored immediately. Enforcement proceedings shall be commenced immediately if the owner fails to comply with the demands of the board.

A RESOLUTION OF THE BOARD OF ADMINISTRATION ESTABLISHING PROCEDURES FOR THE COLLECTION OF DELINQUENT ASSESSMENTS.

BE IT HEREBY RESOLVED by the Waterfront XX Condominium Association, Inc., as follows:

Section 1.   THAT all assessments, or assessment installments, not received by the Association by the 15th day of the month shall be deemed delinquent and the manager shall notify the owner of the delinquency by regular U.S. Mail. A copy of the notification shall be placed in the Association records for the unit and provided to the Association's legal counsel.

Section 2.   THAT any assessment, or assessment installment, not paid within thirty (30) days from the date when due, shall be enforced as provided in the Condominium Act. The manager shall notify legal counsel and instruct counsel to provide to the delinquent owner by certified mail a notice of the association's intent to file a lien to collect the delinquent monies if the assessment, together with all costs, is not paid within thirty (30) days.

Section 3.   THAT legal counsel shall be, and is hereby, authorized to provide such notice, and thereafter to commence foreclosure proceedings against any unit owner who remains delinquent after receiving the notice provided for in Section 2.

ADOPTED by the Board of Administration this 30th day of September, 2011.

By:_____
        Secretary of the Association

2

The Condominium Act and the Law Governing Condominiums

2.1 **General.** Condominiums are "creatures of statute."[1] They are created, operated, regulated, terminated and exist by operation of law and under the standards established by Chapter 718 of the Florida Statutes, known simply as the "Condominium Act."[2] It is the foundation statute for all condominiums and it is referred to frequently in the practical application of the provisions of this manual. There are six distinct parts to the Condominium Act, and some of the parts have far greater applicability to a mature condominium community than others.

The Act grants jurisdiction over residential condominiums to the Division of Florida Condominiums, Timeshares, and Mobile Homes, and gives to the Division the authority to promulgate rules and regulations which regulate condominiums and their operation.[3] (See 14.2). The rules of the Division found in the Florida Administrative Code expand the law governing condominiums beyond the provisions of Chapter 718, F.S., but the rules and the Act are only part of the law that govern condominium residents and their community.

The laws and regulations affecting condominiums and condominium associations range from Chapter 617 of the Florida Statutes, regulating non-profit corporations, to Chapter 119 of the Florida Statutes, relating to Florida's public records. The State and Federal Constitutions have applicability to condominium living, as do the ordinances of the county or municipality where the condominium property is located. The most significant laws are discussed in this Chapter, but the discussion is not intended to be an exhaustive or comprehensive treatment of all the laws and their parts.

2.2 **Condominium Act—Part I.** The general provisions for the creation and operation of condominiums are contained in Part I of the Condominium Act. Part I mandates the content of each declaration of condominium,[4] and outlines the basic authority that each condominium association possesses.[5] Part I sets forth the basic legal definitions which

---

[1] *Woodside Village Condominium Ass'n, Inc. v. Jahren,* 806 So.2d 452, 455 (Fla. 2002),
[2] § 718.101, F.S.
[3] § 718.501, F.S.
[4] § 718.104, F.S.
[5] § 718.111, F.S.

apply to condominiums,[6] it specifies the mandatory content for the bylaws of condominium associations,[7] and it establishes the responsibility for the payment of common expenses and the liabilities for the failure to pay them.[8] Part I of the Act contains most of the provisions frequently used and relied upon in the day-to-day operations of the condominium.

The general provisions of the Condominium Act contained in Part I establish the authority to lien a condominium unit, the procedures to be followed when amending the condominium documents, a definition of the common elements and appurtenances for each condominium unit, the basic rights for each unit owner, and the requirements for the termination of a condominium. For members of the board and for the officers of the association, a general familiarity and working knowledge of Part I are essential. This part of the act will be referred to and relied upon in disputes between individual unit owners and the association. More than any other part of the Condominium Act, it will govern the exercise of the board's responsibilities in the management of the condominium.

2.3   Condominium Act—Part II. The rights and obligations of developers are set forth in Part II of the Condominium Act, and this part has limited application to the mature condominium community. Among its provisions, Part II of the Act establishes specific escrow requirements and provides other protections for purchasers during the construction period of new condominium communities.[9]

For the owners of condominium units, the most significant portion in this part of the Act is the section relating to the quality of construction and the implied warranties of fitness and merchantability. The statutory warranties benefit each individual unit owner and the association membership collectively.[10] Recognition of these statutory warranties is important at the time of transition from developer control and during the initial years of unit owner control of the association.

The warranties in Part II of the Condominium Act are not the only ones that apply to residential construction. The board of administration should consult its legal advisor when a potential construction defect arises

---

[6] § 718.103, F.S.

[7] § 718.112, F.S.

[8] § 718.116, F.S.

[9] § 718.202, F.S.

[10] *Rogers & Ford Construction Corp. v. Carlandia Corp.,* 626 So.2d 1350, 1353 (Fla. 1993).

to make sure that both common law and statutory warranties have been pursued. The maximum statutory warranties extend for a period of three (3) years from completion of the building, or for a period of one (1) year from the time that the unit owners assume control of the association. Under no circumstances do these warranties extend for more than five (5) years from the date of completion of the building and improvements.[11] (See 12.11). Part II of the Condominium Act defines "completion," and extends manufacturers' and sub-contractors' warranties from the developer to each individual unit owner.[12] The warranties are extended to the new unit owner and to each subsequent owner. The warranties are specifically conditioned upon proper maintenance by the association, whether controlled by the developer or the unit owners. Part II of the Condominium Act is particularly significant to a condominium community in the early stages of its development, but it loses its significance as the condominium community matures and the warranty terms expire.

2.4   Condominium Act—Part III. Part III of the Condominium Act outlines certain specialized rights and obligations relating to the condominium association. The mandatory requirements for transition in control of the board from the developer to the unit owners are set forth in Part III,[13] as well as the rights of the association to cancel agreements entered into by the developer-controlled board.[14] Beyond the point of transition, Part III also mandates the standards and the elements of enforceable maintenance and management agreements for condominium properties.

The provisions of Part III relating to maintenance and management require that services be specifically identified and that the obligations and responsibilities of the manager be clearly delineated. They require that agreements specify the cost for each service, the frequency of its performance, and the number of persons that will be employed to provide the service or services. The management agreement must disclose any relationship that the manager or maintenance contractor has with the developer, and each of these requirements must be met or the agreement is not enforceable.[15]

Part III establishes the requirement that certain contracts for

---

[11] § 718.203 (1), F.S.
[12] § 718.203 (2) and (3), F.S.
[13] § 718.301, F.S.
[14] § 718.302, F.S.
[15] § 718.3025, F.S.

materials, equipment and services to be furnished to the condominium be in writing. It also requires certain contracts with the association requiring payments in excess of 5% of the total annual budget of the association be competitively bid by the board of administration.[16]

One of the other significant general provisions of the Condominium Act is also contained within Part III. It provides that the prevailing party shall be entitled to recover court costs and reasonable attorney's fees when enforcing the provisions of the Condominium Act, the condominium documents or the rules and regulations which have been promulgated under the condominium documents.[17]

The right to recover fees and costs in an enforcement action extends to each unit owner in the condominium community as well as to the board of administration. The ability to recover costs and attorneys' fees is a significant tool in preserving the condominium concept, and in enforcing the covenants and conditions that are imposed by the declaration of condominium.

2.5   Condominium Act—Part IV. Part IV of the Condominium Act describes the special types of condominiums which may be created under the law. In addition to the traditional form of condominium ownership, Part IV allows condominiums to be created by leasehold estate,[18] by conversion of existing buildings, and by adding new phases to an existing condominium. It also establishes requirements for condominiums that mix commercial and residential units in a single community,[19] and provides for the creation of multi-condominium communities governed by a single association.[20]

The conversion method of condominium creation is authorized by Part IV of the Act, but the comprehensive requirements of conversion are listed in Part VI.[21] Leasehold condominiums are severely restricted by Part IV which grants the right to unit owners to purchase the leased property, and

---

[16] § 718.3026, F.S.
[17] § 718.303 (1), F.S.
[18] § 718.401, F.S.; *Ackerman v. Spring Lake of Broward, Inc.* 260 So.2nd 264 (Fla. 4th DCA 1971).
[19] § 718.404, F.S.
[20] § 718.405, F.S.
[21] § 718.402, F.S.

prohibits the enforcement of rent escalation clauses that are based upon a consumer price index or other similar provision.[22]

The restrictions, prohibitions and protections relating to leasehold condominiums in Part IV of the Act did not become effective until June 5, 1975. Efforts to apply the restrictions in Part IV to leases created prior to June 5, 1975, have met with limited and narrow success. When a declaration of condominium written prior to the effective date of Part IV incorporates the Condominium Act by reference "as amended from time to time," then the protections and restrictions in Part IV will apply to the leasehold condominium.[23] Under other circumstances, the protections and prohibitions against escalations in rent will not apply.

The phasing of a condominium community allows the developer to create the condominium and begin its operation with only a small number of the actual units that will ultimately make up the entire community. Part IV of the Act establishes the standards that must be defined in the original declaration of condominium, including the interrelationship between the units in each phase, the recreational facilities to be constructed, the percentage of common element ownership which each unit will have, and the other specific aspects that will ultimately result in a completed condominium community.[24]

In a multi-condominium community, the association operates two or more separate condominiums. Pursuant to Part IV, the documents must provide for the manner of sharing assets, liabilities, common surplus and common expenses of the association. The use rights to the common elements and recreational amenities must be set out, and the voting rights of unit owners in the election of the board and in other multicondominium association affairs must be established.[25]

Careful examination of the condominium documents will establish whether or not a community is a phased condominium. There is an important distinction between a phased community, managed by a single association, and several condominiums managed by the same association. When the condominium is a phased community, only one set of records

---

[22] § 718.401, F.S.
[23] *Kaufman v. Shere,* 347 So.2d 627 (Fla. 3rd DCA 1977).
[24] § 718.403, F.S.
[25] § 718.405 (1), F.S.

must be kept under the law, while a separate set of records must be kept for each condominium when multicondominiums are managed by a single association.[26]

2.6   Condominium Act—Part V. Regulation by the Division of Florida Condominiums, Timeshares, and Mobile Homes is established and authorized under Part V of the Condominium Act. The Division of Florida Condominiums, Timeshares, and Mobile Homes is part of the Department of Business Regulation.[27] It is the administrative agency designated to enforce and ensure compliance with the provisions of Florida's Condominium Act and the rules which are promulgated under it. The Division's authority extends to the construction, sale, lease, ownership, operation and management of residential condominiums, and it has the ability to enforce many of the consumer elements of the Act.[28]

The authority of the Division begins with the development of a condominium and extends through the construction phase and the ultimate operation and management of the condominium. The Division divides the implementation of its authority into three bureaus: the Bureau of Compliance, the Bureau of Standards and Registration, and the Customer Service Bureau. A separate section of the Department has been established to handle the arbitration of disputes. (See 13.9).

Part V of the Act mandates the specific disclosure requirements which must be made for all new condominiums created in Florida, and requires that they be properly filed and approved by the Division before units can be sold.[29] The documents filed by the developer with the Division are maintained on file and are part of the public records of the Division. Copies of these records are available to the condominium upon request and upon payment of the costs necessary to copy them.[30]

The Division of Condominiums, Timeshares, and Mobile Homes is funded by fees from those who benefit from its regulation. Each condominium association is required to pay a fee for each unit in a condominium operated by the association before January 1st of each year. If an association fails to make the required payment, it can be assessed a penalty and it is not

---

[26] § 718.111 (1) and (2), F.S.
[27] § 718.103 (17), F.S.
[28] § 718.501, F.S.
[29] *Id.*
[30] § 119.07 (1)(a), F.S.

permitted to maintain any action in the courts of Florida.[31]

The Division is required to furnish each association that pays its fees a copy of the Condominium Act and the rules that are promulgated under it. The Division must also provide the association with a summary of the Declaratory Statements and formal legal opinions that it renders.[32]

2.7   Condominium Act—Part VI and Part VII. Part VI and Part VII of the Condominium Act address developer rights, responsibilities, and regulatory oversight in special circumstances. Part VI of the Act is devoted exclusively to condominiums which are created when existing improvements are converted to a residential condominium. This part of the Act provides protections to the existing renters in the building and to prospective purchasers of the converted condominium units. Renters are entitled to written notice of the proposed conversion and an option to extend their current lease. Each tenant has the right of first refusal to purchase the unit and the developer must provide basic background information to assist each tenant in evaluating the potential purchase.[33]

For new prospective purchasers and the ultimate owners of converted condominium units, the developer must provide the same basic disclosures that are required in all condominium developments, and must additionally provide certain specific information which relates directly to the conversion. This additional information includes a statement on the condition, structural soundness, age, and estimated useful life of all of the buildings being converted. The disclosure must contain a substantiation of these representations by an architect or an engineer authorized to practice in Florida.[34]

The developer of a conversion must post a bond, give the same statutory warranties as new condominiums, or establish specific conversion reserve accounts for the structural components of the existing buildings.[35] The application of Part VI is limited to converted residential condominium properties, but for communities which fall into this conversion category, the special protections and rights which are granted to residents should not be overlooked by the board of administration.

---

[31] § 718.501 (2)(a), F.S.
[32] § 718.501 (1)(h) and (i), F.S.
[33] § 718.604 through § 718.622, F.S.
[34] § 718.616 (3)(b), F.S.
[35] § 718.618 (1), F.S.

Part VII of the Act provides the regulatory framework for failed or failing condominium projects.[36] It provides the opportunity for a bulk purchaser of units in a distressed community to step into the shoes of the original developer, but it provides for the responsibilities and obligations that a bulk buyer or bulk assignee has to the existing unit owners in the community.[37] Sales and marketing activities by a bulk buyer must comply with traditional disclosure requirements,[38] and the Division retains jurisdiction over the activities of a bulk buyer or bulk assignee.[39] (See 14.2).

2.8 Chapter 617, F.S.—Florida Not for Profit Corporation Act.

The Condominium Act requires that the condominium association be a corporation for profit or not-for-profit. Condominium associations not-for-profit are organized under the provisions of Chapter 617, F.S. A corporation created under this not-for-profit chapter cannot distribute any part of its income to individual members, directors or officers of the association, although it is permitted to pay reasonable compensation to officers, directors and agents if the articles of incorporation or the bylaws permit.[40]

Chapter 617, F.S., outlines the provisions that must be included in the articles of a non-profit corporation. These requirements include the manner in which the articles can be amended, the purpose for which the corporation was organized and the limits on the corporation's authority.[41] Chapter 617, F.S., also outlines the full range of the corporate powers that are granted to not-for-profit corporations in Florida. This authority ranges from the ability to operate and manage the condominium property, to the borrowing of funds and the mortgaging of association property.

The provisions of Chapter 617, F.S., require the corporation to maintain a registered agent and registered office, and specify that the board of administration will carry out the powers and duties of the corporation. It allows for the indemnification of the officers and directors when they act in good faith and in the normal course of their duties on the corporation's behalf.

The provisions of Chapter 617, F.S., permit not-for-profit corporations

---

[36] § 718.702, F.S.
[37] § 718.704 and § 718.705, F.S.
[38] § 718.706, F.S.
[39] § 718.501, F.S.
[40] § 617.01401 (5), F.S.
[41] § 617.0202, F.S.

to merge or consolidate their operations and it specifies the procedures which must be followed when such a merger or consolidation occurs. The Chapter basically confers upon the association the full authority necessary to carry out the duties of a not-for-profit corporation for the purpose that the corporation was organized.[42]

2.9   Chapter 607, F.S.—Florida General Corporation Act. The Florida General Corporation Act applies to corporations that are organized for profit. For those communities governed by a for-profit corporation, the provisions of Chapter 607, F.S., control the organization and operation of the condominium association. The Florida General Corporation Act is similar in content and format to the Florida Not for Profit Corporation Act. It prescribes the content for the association's articles of incorporation and specifies the corporate powers of the association. The corporate law establishes the perimeters for the association's creation, existence and termination, and it is an important element of the law governing condominium living.

2.10   Florida Administrative Code. The Condominium Act grants to the Division of Condominiums, Timeshares, and Mobile Homes the authority to promulgate administrative rules under the provisions of Chapter 120, F.S. The Division must determine that the proposal is necessary in order to implement, enforce or interpret the provisions of Chapter 718, F.S., and it may then enact it into a rule. Once the rule has been promulgated, it is incorporated into the Florida Administrative Code (F.A.C.) as part of Chapter 61B-15 through 61B-24, or in Chapters 61B-45 or 61B-50, which are the chapters of the Code dealing with condominiums and the arbitration of disputes.

The rules contained in the Florida Administrative Code amplify or clarify the provisions of Chapter 718, F.S. They delineate the authority of the Division to accept and investigate complaints, as well as providing the form and format for the various types of documents used by condominium communities. The Florida Administrative Code provides a recommended budget format and establishes the procedure for including and waiving reserves in the budget. The Code contains forms for proxies, for petitions

---

[42] § 617.0302, F.S.

and for complaints to be filed before the Division, and the format and rules to be used in the arbitration of disputes.

The Administrative Code also contains the organization for the Division. It authorizes and establishes an educational component which provides periodic seminars for condominium residents and distributes educational materials and other information to communities throughout Florida. A copy of the chapters of the Florida Administrative Code relating to condominiums, as well as a copy of the Condominium Act, are available from the Division of Condominiums, Timeshares, and Mobile Homes. They are provided without charge for all condominium associations that have paid their annual filing fee.[43]

2.11 Chapter 120, F.S.—Administrative Procedure Act. The Administrative Procedure Act sets the standards which govern the day-to-day activities of all state agencies, and it regulates the way each carries out the authority conferred upon it by law. Chapter 120, F.S., governs the rule-making for all agencies, and allows both notice and the right to participate by all substantially affected parties.[44]

The Administrative Procedure Act requires each agency, including the Division of Condominiums, Timeshares, and Mobile Homes, to maintain a rule allowing for the filing and disposition of petitions requesting declaratory statements from the agency. The declaratory statement may request the Division's opinion on the applicability of the Condominium Act, the administrative rules or any orders of the Division to factual circumstances in the petitioner's condominium.[45]

Chapter 120, F.S., requires that all final agency orders contain findings of fact and conclusions of law when disposing of complaints or enforcement actions. These findings and conclusions serve as a guide to other boards and individuals in similar circumstances, and allow all parties affected by the order the opportunity for judicial review in Florida's District Courts of Appeal.[46] The Administrative Procedure Act also requires that a uniform indexing procedure for all agency rules and regulations be maintained, and the compilation becomes the Florida Administrative Code.

---

[43] § 718.501 (1)(h), F.S.
[44] § 120.54, F.S.
[45] § 120.59, F.S.
[46] § 120.68, F.S.

The provisions of Chapter 120, F.S., provide the protection to ensure that all practices of the Division of Condominiums, Timeshares, and Mobile Homes, both formal and informal, will be properly documented, and that the results will be readily available to all affected and interested parties. The Division must make copies of all orders and rules available at cost to anyone wishing to have them. When seeking advice or assistance from the Division on a particular condominium community, Chapter 120, F.S., and the rules of procedure promulgated under it, benefit and protect the association and the condominium residents.

2.12 Chapter 119, F.S.—Public Records. Since each condominium community is substantially affected by both the law and the public agencies which implement the law, access to the records and proceedings of government agencies can often be significant. The Public Records law is part of the State's policy of open government. It imposes upon the Division of Condominiums, Timeshares, and Mobile Homes and other agencies of state and local government similar requirements to those imposed upon condominium associations by the Condominium Act. The policy extends to all records of state, county and municipal governments, and to the inspection of those records at all reasonable times.[47]

The term "public records" means all documents, papers and other materials received by an agency of government, under law or ordinance, in connection with the official business of the governmental agency. For the condominium association, this extends to all actions of the Division of Condominiums, Timeshares, and Mobile Homes and to all of the documents filed with the Division by the developer or its successor.[48]

Inherent in the right of access to public records is the right to examine them at all reasonable times, under proper supervision, by any person desiring to make the inspection. The custodian of the records is required to furnish copies upon request, and upon payment of the standard fees or the actual costs of duplication.[49]

When a question arises about the official version of the documents governing the condominium community and the commitments initially made

---

[47] § 119.01 (1), F.S.
[48] § 119.011 (1), F.S.
[49] § 119.07 (1)(a), F.S.

by the condominium developer, access to the records and filings with the Division is a significant statutory protection and can provide the necessary answers. Access to local public records helps ensure that a community is being treated consistently and fairly by the local governing body.

2.13 Chapter 721, F.S.—Florida Vacation Plan and Timesharing Act. Chapter 721, F.S., addresses a narrow scope of special condominiums or special parts of condominiums. Timesharing of residential properties is not limited to the condominium form of ownership, but if it does exist within a condominium, the timeshare scheme must comply fully with the provisions of the Timesharing Act. Timeshare estates are not permitted in a condominium community unless they are created under specific provisions of the declaration of condominium which permits their existence.[50]

In a manner similar to the disclosure requirements of Part V of the Condominium Act, Chapter 721, F.S. mandates disclosure requirements, escrow protections and management standards for all time-share communities. If a condominium is also a timeshared community, or if a portion of the community is available for timeshared estates, the board of administration must be prepared to comply with the separate standards of Florida's Timesharing Act. Chapter 721, F.S. mandates specific standards for management, insurance, record keeping, exchange programs and auditing of the financial accounts.

For the board of administration faced with managing and operating a condominium that consists entirely or partially of timeshare estates, the challenges for complying with the law are both complicated and unique. Chapter 721, F.S., is designed to provide consumer protection for each timeshare owner in a parcel of real estate that involves as many as fifty-two separate owners instead of just one. The board of administration is faced with the task of record keeping for this large number of owners and with the dual requirements of both the Condominium Act and the Florida Vacation Plan and Timesharing Act.

2.14 Residential Manager's Law. The management companies and managers of residential condominiums having ten (10) or more units or

---

[50] § 718.1045, F.S.

having an annual budget of $100,000.00 or more are required to be licensed by the Department of Business and Professional Regulation.[51] To be certified as a residential community manager, an individual must demonstrate good moral character and pass an examination administered by the Department prior to obtaining a license.[52] A licensed residential community manager must additionally have up to ten (10) hours of continuing education each year to be eligible for renewal of the license.[53]

The Division of Professions exercises jurisdiction over the community manager and management company licensing process for the Department. By law, the Division sets the standards for the application, examination and revocation of the licenses for those who wish to serve as managers of residential communities in Florida.[54] Any person or company desiring to provide these types of services for residential communities in Florida must comply with the manager's licensing law through the offices of the Division,[55] and comply with the limitations placed on the services by the Florida Supreme Court.[56]

For members of the board of administration of a condominium association, their fiduciary duty to the unit owners requires the board to employ only a licensed community manager where licensure is required.[57]

2.15 Resort Condominiums, Fire Sprinklers and Swimming Pools. "Resort condominiums" are regulated under Chapter 509, Florida Statutes, the state's public lodging law. A condominium is a "resort condominium," or public lodging establishment, when individual units are rented to the public more than three (3) times a year for periods of less than a month.[58] In such circumstances, special licensure requirements apply

---

[51] § 468.431, F.S.
[52] § 61B-55.004, F.A.C.
[53] § 468.433, F.S.
[54] *Id.*
[55] § 468.432, F.S.
[56] *The Florida Bar re Advisory Opinion—Activities of Community Ass'n Managers,* 681 So.2nd 1119 (Fla. 1996).
[57] § 61B-23.001 (6), F.A.C.
[58] § 509.242 (1)(c), F.S.

to the unit owners or their agents. Also under the provisions of Chapter 509, Florida Statutes, resort condominium buildings with three (3) stories or more may be required to install complete central fire sprinkler systems. Basically, the law requires installation of a fire sprinkler system in units and in the common elements of buildings where more than 50% of the units are advertised or available to the public for "transient occupancy."[59]

In a similar fashion, communities having minimum rental periods of sixty (60) days or more are exempt from most of the swimming pool regulations imposed by the Department of Health and Rehabilitative Services. Communities having rental periods of less than sixty (60) days must comply with all of the swimming pool requirements. Exempt communities, however, are subject only to one annual inspection to check the quality of the water and the life-saving equipment for the swimming pool facility. Initial construction standards for swimming pools must still be met in the community but other Department rules, including life guard restrictions, do not apply to condominiums having rental periods of more than sixty (60) days.

2.16   Penny-ante Gambling and Bingo. Limited gambling is permitted in the common elements or recreation areas of the condominium or in an individual condominium unit. Games permitted include poker, pinochle, bridge, rummy, canasta, hearts, dominoes and mahjongg. Jackpots are limited to $10 per game, the host must be present during the game and cannot receive any commission. Participants may not be solicited to play and all must be over eighteen (18) years of age. No debt incurred in a game is legally enforceable. The condominium association or an owner participating in the game shall not have any civil liability for damages if the restrictions of the law related to penny-ante gambling are properly followed.[60]

Condominium associations are among a group of not-for-profit and charitable organizations authorized to conduct bingo games in Florida.[61] Any association desiring to do so must comply with the restrictions enumerated in the law.[62] These include restrictions on the location of the game, size of the prizes and the persons authorized to both conduct and participate in the games.[63]

---

[59] § 509.215 (5), F.S.
[60] § 849.085, F.S.
[61] § 718.114, F.S.
[62] § 849.093 (2) and (4), F.S.
[63] § 849.093, F.S.

2.17 Constitutional Provisions. Because condominiums in Florida are creatures of statute, they are also subject to many of the basic constitutional standards which govern the validity of the statutes themselves. The authority to make the laws, and the standards the laws must meet, comes from the grant of authority found in the United States Constitution and the Constitution of the State of Florida. As the board of administration undertakes its responsibilities, it will encounter the application of constitutional principles on frequent occasions.

The most common of these encounters will be with the rights to equal protection and due process of law that are guaranteed to each of the community's residents. The protection of contract rights and obligations is also a basic constitutional principle that arises frequently.[64] Since the declaration of condominium and all of its exhibits constitute a contract among the many individuals who share the real property, application of the principle is obvious.

The equal protection that is guaranteed by both the State and Federal Constitutions prevents the board from selectively enforcing its covenants and restrictions. It also prohibits the use and enforcement of arbitrary, unreasonable or capricious rules and regulations.[65] The standards of due process, including the rights of an individual to have notice and the opportunity to be heard in matters affecting an owner's rights, are basic constitutional protections. Due process guarantees fairness and it is applicable to the restrictions and covenants of the declaration of condominium and their enforcement.

The constitutional protection of basic contract rights prevents a community from modifying or denying rights of owners by amendments to the condominium documents or regulations. However, when applying the principles which prohibit the impairment of contracts, it must be remembered that most declarations provide for a method of amendment. Individuals assuming the rights and protections of the declaration of condominium also assume them with the knowledge that they are subject to change and amendment under the circumstances set forth in the declaration.[66] (See Chapter 9).

---

[64] U.S. Const., art. I, § 10; Fla. Const., art. I, § 10; *Cohn v. The Grand Condominium Ass'n, Inc.*, 26 So.3 8 (Fla. 3rd DCA 2009).

[65] *White Egret Condominium, Inc. v. Franklin*, 379 So.2d 346 (Fla. 1979).

[66] *Woodside Village Condominium Ass'n, Inc. v. Jahren, supra* note 1.

2.18 County and Municipal Ordinances. The Condominium Act prohibits local ordinances from discriminating against the condominium form of ownership and it requires county and municipal ordinances to be applied uniformly, without regard to the form of ownership of the real property.[67] Chapter 718, F.S., overrides local ordinances that attempt to modify or regulate the form of condominium ownership or the procedures that govern a condominium association and its operation. However, ordinances governing the health, safety and welfare of residents, and the standards that govern the construction of buildings and the improvements that serve the condominium community are enforceable.

Building codes, ordinances governing safety standards for exterior improvements such as swimming pools, and fire safety codes are typical of the local ordinances with which the condominium community must comply. Repairs, alterations and modifications to the condominium buildings and other improvements must be done in accordance with local building codes. The board of administration must be aware of the benefits and obligations of local ordinances and be prepared to comply with the safety standards that are imposed to protect the community and its residents.

Ordinances relating to fire safety and to the equipment and improvements that protect residents from the hazards of fire can present the board with its most difficult encounter with local regulations. The overriding public policy concern for health and safety permit amendments to the fire code, upgrading fire protection standards within existing structures, to be imposed retroactively upon existing buildings under some circumstances. When local fire officials or enforcement officers begin implementation of new protection standards, the community is often faced with the burden of substantial improvements and the need to raise substantial assessments to complete the improvements. The Condominium Act does provide opportunities for the association to exempt the condominium from some of the requirements to retrofit existing buildings for certain upgrades upon the approval of the association membership. (See 10.14 and 10.15).

2.19 Administrative Decisions. Decisions from the Division of Condominiums, Timeshares, and Mobile Homes affecting condominiums

---

[67] § 718.507, F.S

serve as a guide and a reference source to other condominiums facing similar problems. These formal administrative decisions from the Division come in one of three forms. They appear as a declaratory statement interpreting a part of the Act, as an order rendered in the exercise of the Division's enforcement authority, or from decisions handed down in disputes submitted to arbitration.[68]

The final administrative orders that are rendered in matters relating to enforcement of the Act or the rules, or when a dispute has been decided by arbitration, must appear in writing or must be stated in the formal record with findings of fact and conclusions of law.[69] As do declaratory statements, final orders serve as a guide when a condominium association finds itself in a similar set of factual circumstances as those described in the order. Administrative decisions may serve as a foundation for appropriate board or community action if circumstances dictate.

The Division of Condominiums, Timeshares, and Mobile Homes annually provides each condominium association with a summary of its declaratory statements and formal legal opinions relating to the operation of condominiums rendered by the Division during the previous year.[70] As these summaries become available, the board of administration should index them and keep them for a permanent reference source.

2.20 Judicial Decisions and Precedents. The primary function of our court system is to resolve disputes between the parties in a court action. There is a by-product to this problem-solving which is an important benefit when the court decisions are written and codified. The written decisions by the appellate courts embrace the findings of fact and the application of the law in a particular case, and provide an interpretation upon which the ultimate decision is based. These interpretations may resolve conflicts between different parts of the law or the condominium documents or the covenants and restrictions governing use of the property.[71]

The applicability of the court's decision technically relates only to the parties involved in the law suit. The "case law" developed from the

---

[68] § 718.501, F.S.

[69] § 120.59, F.S.

[70] § 718.501 (1)(i), F.S.

[71] Jurisdiction to interpret conflicting or ambiguous provisions of condominium documents is vested in the courts. *Peck Plaza Condominium v. Division of Florida Land Sales and Condominiums,* 371 So.2d 152, 154 (Fla. 1st DCA 1979).

written interpretation of the facts and the law of the individual case becomes precedent, however. It guides future court decisions and other boards of administration and their legal advisors in similar circumstances. The precedent established by "case law" through court decisions must be used and applied with caution though, since the facts and the application of law may vary in each separate case.[72]

2.21 Priority of the Law. With the many laws and regulations which govern condominium living, at times there will be conflicts, or apparent conflicts, in determining what part of the law is applicable. From among the many laws and regulations, there is a system of priorities with which the board of administration should be familiar.

The provisions of the State and Federal Constitutions have the highest priority and the rights they grant and protect are of the highest dignity. The state and federal statutes are next in priority, and they establish and define public policy and its relationship to the private rights of individuals. The administrative rules are next in order of priority, followed, finally, by the local ordinances of counties and municipalities.

There is a priority among the many types of opinions and decisions which are rendered for the benefit of condominium communities and their residents. Court decisions from the Supreme Court of Florida take precedent over those rendered by Florida's District Courts of Appeal. The decisions from the Courts have a higher priority than the administrative interpretations and decisions which are rendered by the Division of Condominiums, Timeshares, and Mobile Homes.

Opinions and rulings under local municipal ordinances are next in priority, followed by the written opinions from the community's legal advisor. Each of these sources has its place for the benefit of the community, and each has its priority in relation to the others.

2.22 Application and Interpretation of the Law. The application and interpretation of the law comes to bear when the board of administration seeks to resolve disputes in the community or when it is determining what restrictions are applicable to the condominium's current operation.

Standards of interpretation: (1) favor a resolution of apparent inconsistencies with consistency and based upon the ordinary meaning of

---

[72] *Woodside Village Condominium Ass'n, Inc. v. Jahren, supra* note 1.

the words in the documents whenever possible;[73] (2) require that ambiguities in the declaration and its exhibits be construed against the author of the declaration;[74] (3) provide that the express language of the declaration is controlling and is to be expressly constued;[75] and (4) that construction and interpretation of the law be governed by principles of basic fairness.[76] Fairness includes an assurance to purchasers of condominium units that they will get the benefits and the property rights that they were promised at the time of purchase.

In the same manner that an inconsistency between the various condominium documents is resolved by applying the document of highest priority, an inconsistency in the law is also resolved by yielding to the standard with the highest priority. The retroactive application of the law presents different problems and will vary depending upon whether or not it is of such significant public policy so as to override the standards in existence at the time the condominium was created.[77]

The use and application of court decisions and administrative orders must be approached cautiously. The subtle differences in the facts of the case in the community may bring about a significantly different conclusion than the decision relied upon. In other circumstances, the factual similarities in the community and the interrelationship with the formal decision can make the application appropriate. The role of the association's legal advisor should never be overlooked when the board faces the application and interpretation of the law.

2.23   The Legal Advisor. With the law come the lawyers, and they can be an important advisor to every board of administration. Almost every condominium community has one or more retired lawyers, or one or more non-lawyers who have knowledge of the law governing condominiums, each of whom is willing to offer their advice and counsel to the board of

---

[73] *Schmidt v. Sherrill,* 442 So.2d 963 (Fla. 4th DCA 1983); *Sterling Village Condominium v. Breitenbach,* 251 So.2d 685 (Fla. 4th DCA 1971).

[74] *Kaufman v. Shere, supra* note 23.

[75] *Palm Beach Hotel Condominium Ass'n v. Rogers,* 605 So2d 143, 145 (Fla. 4th DCA 1992); *Brickell Bay Club Condominium Ass'n, Inc. v. Hernstadt,* 512 So.2d 994 (Fla. 3rd DCA 1987).

[76] *White Egret Condominium, Inc. v. Franklin, supra* note 65.

[77] The law in existence on the date of recording of the declaration of condominium is controlling. *Suntide Condominium Ass'n, Inc. v. Division of Fla. Land Sales and Condominiums,* 463 So.2d 314, 317 (Fla. 1st DCA 1984); see also *Pomponio v. Claridge of Pompano Condominium, Inc.,* 378 So.2d 774 (Fla. 1979).

administration without charge. Such advice may not be a bargain for the board receiving it. Relying on a wrong answer under such circumstances may be particularly hazardous to the board of administration, since its members are ultimately responsible for the consequences of the advice.

Each community should have a legal advisor knowledgeable in the Condominium Act and the law governing condominiums. When the need arises, the board should call upon its counsel to render opinions for clarity and for guidance on matters affecting the community. The board of administration has met its responsibilities and abided by its fiduciary relationship when it asks for and relies upon the opinions of its attorney.[78] When receiving legal advice and to ensure its permanency, the opinions should be in writing and should be made a part of the association's permanent records.

To avoid unnecessary expense, a recommended practice followed by many condominium communities is the maintenance of a book, or index, of legal opinions for use by future boards of administration facing similar problems. Written opinions also provide insulation for the board that has relied upon them, or has acted based on their direction. The condominium community and the board of administration will benefit from the skill and professional expertise offered by a competent attorney when the advice is appropriately sought and correctly followed.

---

[78] § 617.0830 (2), F.S. and § 61B-23.0025 (1), F.A.C.

3

Membership Meetings: Practice and Procedures

MEMBERSHIP MEETING FORMS

3.1   General. Membership meetings are an essential part of a successfully operating condominium community. The meetings provide an opportunity for association members to select their leaders, a forum to adopt and approve their financial policies, make changes in their governing documents, handle items of special business involving the membership and address other matters for the general welfare of the community.

If proper procedures are implemented and followed, membership meetings can deal with the most controversial subjects and still end with productive results. Unless the association bylaws otherwise provide, a majority of voting interests in the condominium community must be present at a meeting to constitute a quorum.[1] An election ballot returned by a voting member may not be counted for purposes of constituting a quorum. A voting interest must be represented in person or by proxy at a meeting to be considered present for purposes of establishing a quorum.[2]

In some circumstances owners may take action by written agreement, without a meeting, when it is expressly permitted by the declaration, the bylaws or the law requiring the action. In all other cases, actions requiring unit owner approval must take place at meetings that are properly called and conducted.[3] The practices and procedures for conducting the meeting can be found in both the association bylaws and the Condominium Act, and the essential elements are highlighted in this chapter.

3.2   Annual and Regular Meetings. All condominium communities are required to hold at least one regular membership meeting each year.[4] This meeting is referred to as the "annual meeting," and the date and time for it will likely be set forth in the bylaws of the association. The regular election of board members occurs at the annual members' meeting,[5] and often the annual meeting presents the only periodic opportunity that individual owners have to review the affairs of their association.

The annual meeting of the unit owners must be held at the location provided in the bylaws of the association. If no location for the meeting is identified in the bylaws, the site will be determined by the board of directors and must be at a location that is within forty-five (45) miles of the

---

[1] § 718.112 (2)(b), F.S.
[2] § 61B-23.002 (10), F.A.C.
[3] § 718.112 (2)(d), F.S.
[4] § 718.112 (2)(d) 1., F.S.
[5] § 718.112 (2)(d) 3., F.S.

condominium property.[6]

A well-planned annual meeting will maximize the opportunities to provide information to the members of the association and to receive their input, suggestions and complaints.[7] The bylaws for some condominium associations provide for more than one regular membership meeting in each calendar year. The bylaws should be consulted to determine when the regular or annual meetings of members should be held, and whether more than one is required in each calendar year.

3.3   Special Meetings. From time to time, members of the association or the board of administration may find it necessary to hold a special members' meeting. Special meetings are limited in their scope and purpose,[8] and in some circumstances a separate set of procedures must be followed when calling or conducting the meeting. The board of administration should anticipate, and be prepared to deal with, the special meeting procedures established in the community's documents and in the Condominium Act.

Examples of the purposes and procedures required for special meetings include those where a petition of 10% of the unit owners can call a meeting to change a budget when the budget of the board exceeds 115% of the previous year's budget;[9] where a petition by 10% of the members results in a meeting to recall the board of administration;[10] and when there is a meeting to waive the current year's budget reserves.[11]

Provisions for special meetings are additionally made in the Condominium Act for the cancellation of contracts made by the developer when unit owners no longer desire to maintain the contracts[12] and for the transition of association control from board members designated by the developer to board members elected by the unit owners.[13] Community leaders must always be prepared for the special needs of special meetings.

---

[6] § 718.112 (2)(d) 1., F.S.
[7] "Corporations must be allowed to function under majority control, so long as the majority does no actual wrong to the minority or to others." *Coleman v. Plantation Golf Club, Inc.*, 212 So.2d 806, 808 (Fla. 4th DCA 1968).
[8] "(A)t a special meeting no business at all can be transacted except that specified in the notice." Fletcher's Cyclopedia on Corporations, Corporate Meetings and Elections, § 2016.
[9] § 718.112 (2)(e), F.S.
[10] § 718.112 (2)(j), F.S.
[11] § 718.112 (2)(f), F.S.
[12] § 718.302 (1), F.S.
[13] § 718.301 (2), F.S.

In most circumstances they grant special rights to unit owners and proper procedures must be followed to protect those rights.

3.4   Proof of Notice. A membership meeting cannot be properly held without notice,[14] or when notice has only been provided to part of the association membership.[15] Under some circumstances notice of a meeting may be waived, but unit owners must do so in writing, and there must be authority for the waiver in the association's declaration or its bylaws, or in the statute under which the meeting is called.[16] In addition to actually giving notice to all members, the board must also preserve proof that the notice was given to each of the association members in written form.

The giving of notice to members may be accomplished in one of three ways. The notice may be provided by U.S. Mail to the unit owner at the last address furnished to the association, it may be hand delivered to the unit owner, or it may be given by electronic transmission when authorized by the association bylaws.[17] To ensure that "proof of notice" is properly preserved, a little planning can go a long way. A roster of unit owners for the current association membership must be maintained by the board of administration;[18] an extra copy of this roster can be used, and can ultimately become the proof of notice.

If the notice is to be given by U.S. Mail, an officer of the association, manager, or other person providing the notice must provide an affidavit or a "certificate of mailing" from the U.S. Post Office to be included in the association records, stating that the notice has been given to each owner. The roster of unit owners can be attached as an exhibit to the affidavit or certificate of mailing, and it becomes permanent and accurate evidence that notice was properly given.

In a similar fashion, the roster can be used as an exhibit for the hand delivered notices or notices given by electronic transmission. An affidavit of the secretary or other authorized agent of the association that the notice

---

[14] § 718.112 (2)(d) 2., F.S.
[15] Where notice was not provided as the law required, "(t)he action of the court . . . holding the . . . meeting . . . illegal and the action taken null and void . . . was warranted by the evidence. . . ." *Gentry-Futch Co. v. Gentry,* 90 Fla. 595, 608, 106 So. 473 (Fla. 1925).
[16] § 718.112 (2)(d) 5., F.S.
[17] § 718.112 (2)(d) 2., F.S.
[18] § 718.111 (12)(a) 7., F.S.

has been given by electronic transmission is, in the absence of fraud, prima facia evidence of the facts stated in the notice.[19]

3.5 Posting of Notice. In addition to mailing, delivering, or transmitting notice of each members' meeting to each unit owner, the notice for such meetings must also be continuously posted in a conspicuous place on the condominium property at least fourteen (14) days prior to the meeting. The board of administration is required to establish the specific location on the condominium property by a duly adopted rule.[20] Prior to establishing the specific location by rule, the board of administration must provide notice of the board meeting at which the decision will be made to all unit owners in the condominium. (See 4.17 and Form 4.03). If there is no condominium or association property upon which notices can be posted, the posting requirements for members' meetings does not apply.[21]

In lieu of or in addition to the physical posting of notice, the association may repeatedly broadcast the notice and the agenda on a closed-circuit cable television system serving the condominium. If broadcast notice is used in lieu of a notice posted conspicuously on the condominium property, the notice and agenda must appear at least four times every broadcast hour of every day that a posted notice is otherwise required, and it must appear in a manner so that an average reader may observe and comprehend the notice content. Broadcast notice may be implemented by rules adopted by the board of administration.[22]

3.6 Content of Meeting Notice. The notice for a membership meeting, whether annual or special, must contain the date, time and place at which the meeting will be held. The notice for an annual membership meeting must incorporate or include an agenda for the meeting.[23] If the meeting is a special meeting, the notice must state the specific purpose for which the meeting has been called. In addition to the mandatory content for the meeting notice, other items may also be included in the notice that are both advisable and helpful to the board and the membership.

In a well-run condominium community, the giving of notice will include, at minimum, the notice with the agenda of the business to be

---

[19] § 617.0141 (8), F.S.
[20] § 718.112 (2)(d) 2., F.S.
[21] *Id.*
[22] *Id.*
[23] *Id.*

covered, a voting certificate and a limited proxy form for the convenience of members who cannot attend in person. The annual meeting of members is the regular election for board members,[24] and the mailing may include appropriate election documents, such as the "second notice of election," the information sheet on each candidate and the election ballot for use by those who will not attend the meeting in person. (See 3.8, 3.16 and 4.4).

Additional items may be included in the notice mailing based upon the individual needs of the community. Each condominium association is required to give a financial report to its membership annually,[25] and including the report with the annual meeting notice can be both economical for the community and helpful to individual members. If the budget is to be adopted at the meeting, or at a board meeting in close proximity to the membership meeting, or if the community is going to consider waiving the reserves,[26] copies of the budget may accompany the meeting notice.

As a final option, the notice can be accompanied by reports of committees, reports by the association's president, or reports by the management company. If amendments to the documents are to be considered at the meeting, then copies of the amendments should be included with the notice. Finally, it may be helpful to include a general letter of explanation of the business to be discussed at the membership meeting and procedures to be followed during the course of the meeting.

3.7   Time of Notice. The Condominium Act requires that at least fourteen (14) days written notice be given for annual meetings of the membership.[27] To ensure compliance with this requirement, it is advisable to have the notices post-marked, hand delivered or electronically transmitted at least fourteen (14) days prior to the day on which the meeting is to be held. The notice must also be posted on the condominium property at least fourteen (14) continuous days preceding the annual meeting. While the fourteen (14) day notice requirement is the most common, there may be some variations in the length of notice required by the Condominium Act or by an association's own bylaws. If the notice for the annual meeting also includes the "second notice of election," the notice must be mailed or

---

[24] § 718.112 (2)(d) 3., F.S.
[25] § 718.111 (13), F.S.
[26] § 718.112 (2)(f) 2., F.S.
[27] § 718.112 (2)(d) 2., F.S.

delivered not less than fourteen (14) days nor more than thirty-four (34) days prior to the annual meeting.[28] (See 3.8).

Variations for the time of notice may result from the nature of the business to be discussed or the type of meeting being held. If a longer period of time is required by the bylaws, the board should be guided by the bylaw provision. If a shorter period of time is specified in the association's bylaws, then the time period in the Condominium Act should be followed.

Sometimes more than one notice may accompany the mailing to the membership. If the board adopts the annual budget, notice of the budget meeting of the board can be included with the notice for the membership meeting. The "second notice of election" for the board of administration may also be accompanied by the notice for the annual meeting of members. In cases where multiple notices are included in the mailing, the timing for each notice must be correctly calculated. If giving multiple notices at one time can be accomplished, then a single mailing will provide proper notice to the complete membership effectively and economically.

3.8   Notices for Board Elections. When an election for members of the board of administration is to occur simultaneous with the annual meeting, additional notices announcing the election are required. (See 4.4). The "first notice of election" must be mailed sixty (60) days before the scheduled election.[29] It announces the election to the membership and allows unit owners the opportunity to qualify for election to the board. The "first notice of election" must contain the name and the correct mailing address for the secretary or the name and correct mailing address of a person designated by the secretary.[30] At least fourteen (14) days and not more than thirty-four (34) days prior to the election, a "second notice of election" must be mailed or delivered to owners. The second notice contains the election ballot and an information sheet for each candidate who requests that a sheet be distributed.[31]

Each candidate for the board of administration may make a request that an information sheet be included with the "second notice of election" describing the candidate's background, education and qualifications. If

---

[28] § 718.112 (2)(d) 3., F.S.
[29] *Id.*
[30] § 61B-23.0021 (4), F.A.C.
[31] § 61B-23.0021 (8), F.A.C.

consented to in writing by the candidates involved, two (2) or more candidate information sheets may be consolidated into a single page. The information sheet must be furnished to the association not less than thirty-five (35) days before election by the candidate, and it cannot be larger than 8 1/2 inches by 11 inches.[32]

The association is not permitted to edit, alter or modify the content of the information sheet submitted by a candidate; however, the association has no liability for its content.[33] The association is permitted to print or duplicate the candidate information sheets on both sides of the paper to save costs. The expense for reproduction and mailing of the sheets to unit owners is born by the association.[34]

3.9   Agenda. The required agenda for the annual members' meeting in most condominium associations is specifically set forth in the bylaws of the association, and the Condominium Act requires that the agenda accompany the annual meeting notice given to unit owners.[35] The presiding officer of the meeting should follow the agenda correctly, and should depart from the established order of business only if the rules of procedure for the meeting have been waived by a vote of two-thirds of the members present.

The agendas for most association meetings have items of both substantive and procedural business. The procedural items are customarily disposed of early in the meeting. "Calling the meeting to order" is done by the simple act of the presiding officer; the "calling of roll and certifying of proxies" is procedural and done generally without difficulty; and "proof of notice" can be handled by simply delivering the appropriate documents to the secretary of the association. In most cases the procedural business items take little time, while other areas of the agenda, such as the "election of directors," "unfinished business" and "new business" take up the bulk of the meeting's time and attention.

It is both desirable and advisable for the board to consider creating sub-categories of the agenda where substantive business is to be discussed. By way of example, under "unfinished business" or under "new business," sub-categories may include, (i) matters relating to the budget, (ii) waiver

---

[32] § 718.112 (2)(d) 3., F.S.
[33] § 61B-23.0021 (7), F.S.
[34] § 718.112 (2)(d) 3., F.S.
[35] § 718.112 (2)(d) 2., F.S.

of reserves, (iii) approval for modifications or alterations to the common elements, (iv) consideration of amendments to the condominium documents, and (v) other matters which the board may wish to present to the membership for vote.

In the event that the meeting is a special members' meeting, the board should take careful note that both the notice of the meeting and the agenda may need special preparation. If the bylaws of the association do not establish an agenda for special meetings, then one should be prepared with sufficient detail to inform the members of the nature and the order of the business to be considered at the special meeting. If the meeting is being held to remove a member or members of the board, then both the agenda and the notice must state that the meeting is for purposes of considering the removal.[36] Agendas serve to prepare both the board and the membership for the business to be considered at the meeting and as a guide to carry out the meeting in an orderly manner.

3.10   Proxies. The bylaws for most condominium associations permit absent unit owners to participate and vote in membership meetings by proxy. The Condominium Act also authorizes the use of proxies by an owner, but places restrictions on the types of proxies and the purposes for which they must be used.[37] No proxy may be more than ninety (90) days old, and a proxy may be used only at the meeting for which it was given. The proxy may be general in nature or very specific, limiting the person designated to vote it and allowing little discretion when representing the absent member. No proxy may be used in the election of members of the board of administration, and voting in all board elections must be by ballot, unless the condominium association has authorized an alternative method of election in its bylaws. (See 4.6).

General proxies may be used only to establish a quorum and for other non-substantive matters where the use of limited proxies is not required by the Condominium Act. The Act requires the use of limited proxies for votes taken to waive or reduce reserves with special disclosure languge;[38] for votes to waive financial reporting requirements; for votes to amend the

---

[36] § 718.112 (2)(k), F.S.
[37] § 718.112 (2)(b), F.S.
[38] § 718.112 (2)(f) 4., F.S.

declaration of condominium, articles of incorporation or bylaws; and for other matters where a vote of unit owners is required or permitted by law.[39] A limited proxy effectively directs the holder of the proxy to vote in a specific way, the choice having already been made by the absent owner at the time the limited proxy is delivered.

To be valid, the proxy must identify the person who will vote the proxy at the meeting. The identification may be made by name, or by designating a specific officer of the association, such as the president or secretary.[40] The proxy must identify (1) the meeting for which the proxy is given, (2) the condominium parcel which the proxy represents, (3) the member who is granting the proxy, and (4) it must provide a signature block for all owners of record or the voting representative to sign and date the proxy.[41] The bylaws of most associations require that the proxies be returned to the secretary or other officer of the association prior to the meeting. Once the presiding officer has called the meeting to order, no further proxies may be accepted.

Some association bylaws limit the number of proxies which a single individual may vote. The most common restriction limits a member to no more than five (5) proxies, in addition to the member's own vote. If no limit is specified then there is no restriction on the number of proxies that a member may vote. The Condominium Act does not restrict members from soliciting proxies from other owners or otherwise campaigning for issues of their choice.

A proxy may be revoked at any time by an owner prior to or at the meeting. Unless the bylaws specifically require otherwise, the person designated by a proxy does not have to be a member of the association and an owner may designate a renter, his attorney or another non-owner to represent the unit. An attorney-in-fact under a power of attorney may designate himself or another person as the proxy of a unit owner so long as the proxy is in the required form and the person so designated is not precluded from acting as a proxy under the bylaws of the association.[42]

---

[39] § 718.112 (2)(b) 2., F.S.
[40] § 718.112 (2)(b), F.S.
[41] § 61B-23.002 (1) and (2), F.A.C.
[42] § 61B-23.002 (6), F.A.C.

3.11 Voting Certificate. Most condominium association bylaws provide for the designation of a voting representative for units which have multiple owners, or for units which have corporate owners.[43] This "voting certificate" or "designation of voter form" is sometimes overlooked by the board of administration and is often confusing to association members.

Failure to have such a voting certificate on file with the association is the most common reason why a unit is not permitted to participate at a membership meeting, especially when an issue to be voted upon is controversial and proper procedures are being closely followed. The bylaws of the association should be consulted for the need, the content, and the persons who are eligible to be named in the voting certificate.[44]

A voting certificate form should be on file in the association records from each jointly-owned and each corporate-owned unit in the community, and a roster of "designated voters" should be maintained by the association secretary. The voting certificate remains valid until the owners wish to change the designated person or until the condominium unit is sold.

Unlike a proxy that expires within ninety (90) days,[45] the term for the voting certificate is indefinite. The joint ownership by husband and wife should not be overlooked and a designation should be made by them as well. When selecting an individual to be the designated voter, it is advisable to select one of the owners of the unit to serve in that capacity if possible. Corporate owners should select an officer of the corporation owning the unit.

While the form and content of a voting certificate and a proxy are similar, they are designed to serve different purposes and in most cases one document cannot be a substitute for the other.[46]

A voting certificate cannot serve as a proxy if it does not identify the specific membership meeting at which it is to be used and if it survives for a period longer than ninety (90) days. A valid proxy by multiple owners may, on the other hand, serve as both a valid proxy and a valid voting certificate for a specific meeting. If the proxy has been signed by all of the owners of

---

[43] § 718.103 (29), F.S.

[44] § 61B-23.002 (5), F.A.C.

[45] § 718.112 (2)(b) 2., F.S.

[46] A proxy must conform to the requirements of the Condominium Act. See *Nettles Island, Inc. v. Ely,* 436 So.2d 278 (Fla. 4th DCA 1983).

record and if it appropriately designates a voter, the proxy may serve the dual purpose for the meeting at which it is presented. Upon final adjournment of the membership meeting, the proxy expires and it would not survive as a voting certificate for future meetings.

3.12 Check-In Procedures. Proper check-in procedures help to ensure an orderly and successful membership meeting that will begin on time. The initial key to a successful check-in process is a current roster of unit owners and a current roster of designated voters.[47] When the appropriate rosters are available, the proper meeting participant can be easily identified for admission to the meeting and as an appropriate recipient of a voting ballot. To insure complete and proper participation in the meeting, accountability for the voting membership should be assured at the time of check-in to the meeting place.[48]

Controlled entry of voting members enhances a successful check-in policy. Depending on the size of the condominium association and the number of voting members, a predetermined division of community should be made. The division or classification may be by unit number or by the alphabetical order of the owners. Each station should have a roster for owners and designated voters to confirm ownership and the voting representative for each condominium parcel. A balanced division of units by number, or by alphabetical grouping, helps to avoid delays, and allows each qualified member to be admitted to the meeting so it may begin on time.

Effective check-in procedures will allow for distribution of ballots to designated voters at the time of the check-in, eliminating the necessity of distributing ballots once the meeting has commenced. To insure that ballot distribution at the time of check-in is successful, it is important for the board to anticipate the contested issues that will come before the meeting and to have a ballot prepared which will address each issue appropriately.

3.13 Presiding Officer Selection. Selection of the proper individual to preside at a meeting of the membership is an important ingredient for a fair and orderly meeting. In almost every community, the bylaws designate the individual who will serve as chairman of the meeting, or they will establish

---

[47] A current roster of unit owners and voting certificates are a required portion of the association's official records. § 718.111 (12)(a) 7., F.S.

[48] Ballots, sign-in sheets, and all other papers relating to elections must be maintained for a period of one (1) year. § 718.111 (12)(a) 12., F.S.

the procedures by which the presiding officer or chairman is selected. The bylaws may specify the officer, generally the president, or they may provide for the election of a chairman from the meeting itself. The bylaws may allow the president or the board of administration to designate a chairman for the meeting. In addition to these three options, it is also possible for the membership to select another presiding officer by waiving the rules and designating a chairman. (See 6.10).

When the bylaws permit the board to appoint an individual to serve as chairman, the appropriate resolution should be passed by the board prior to the meeting. If the bylaws do not specifically allow for a designation and the board still wishes to have a particular individual serve as chairman, the members can be asked to give their consent (or a waiver of the rules) to permit the individual to serve.[49] Under most circumstances, a properly presented request to the membership will be approved, and the desired presiding officer can assume the chairmanship of the meeting without controversy.

While most membership meetings do not have major elements of controversy, on occasion, controversial issues and closely contested votes will arise. On such occasions, it is helpful to have an experienced individual presiding who is familiar with the issues before the meeting and the rules of procedure which govern the conduct of the meeting.

The presiding officer may not take part in the substantive debate, nor may the chairman make or second motions during the meeting.[50] If the president, or other officer who would normally chair the meeting, wishes to participate actively in the debate and business, another individual must preside over the meeting.

3.14   Pre-Meeting Preparations.
For the presiding officer, the board of administration and other leaders in the community, an analytical review of the agenda and other procedural aspects of the coming meeting should always precede the meeting itself. The procedures which guide an annual meeting are not complicated, but they can be a trap for the unwary. With pre-meeting preparation to ensure that the meeting will be properly conducted,

---

[49] *Roberts Rules of Order Newly Revised,* § 22.
[50] *Roberts Rules of Order Newly Revised,* § 58.

unexpected surprises and unnecessary delays can be easily avoided.[51]

It is helpful to have motions written down, and for the presiding officer to assign specific motions to designated individuals. By doing so, procedural items such as waiving the reading of minutes of the previous meeting can be disposed of in an orderly and efficient manner. The presiding officer and the board should also anticipate points of difficulty, and how such points will be dealt with, including the selection of sergeants at arms, and, if necessary, appropriate outside security.

Pre-meeting preparation may include preliminary remarks by the chairman prior to formally starting the meeting. This is helpful particularly when unusual or complicated business is to come before the meeting. In such preliminary remarks, the presiding officer can explain what business is expected at the meeting, the manner by which a member can be recognized to speak at the meeting and at what point each item of business may be properly brought before the meeting.

The Condominium Act allows each unit owner the right to participate with reference to all items on the meeting agenda. The association, however, may impose reasonable rules governing the participation by owners.[52] Brief remarks at the pre-meeting stage, and an assurance that all members will have the opportunity to be heard at the appropriate time, will often avoid shouting matches and major meeting disruptions during close votes or when controversial issues are being debated.

3.15 Ballot Preparations. The preparation of ballots will be governed, to a great extent, by the issues that will come before the membership meeting. At most meetings, there will be an election of board members, but in addition to that, there may also be votes for the waiver of reserves, votes for modification or alteration to the common elements, or votes on amendments to the condominium documents. These different votes will all be factors in determining how many different ballots will be used, and in what format they will appear. The ballots for board elections require special attention (see 3.16), and consideration should be given to using a separate ballot for other votes to be taken at the meeting. Votes by limited proxies for

---

[51] "(I)n absence of evidence to the contrary, it will be presumed that the meeting was held in accordance with the statutes, charter and bylaws." *Abbey Properties Co., Inc. v. Prudential Insurance Co.,* 119 So.2d 74, 77 (Fla. 2nd DCA 1960).

[52] § 718.112 (2)(d) 6., F.S.

the waiver of reserves require a specific statutory disclosure statement, and the appropriate language must appear on the limited proxy in capitalized, conspicuous type.[53] (See 7.9). Another element to consider in preparing ballots or limited proxies is how the voting interests are allocated among the membership and how the votes will be counted on the issues after the vote.

The majority of communities allow each unit a single vote, but some condominium associations provide that a unit's voting interest will be equal to its percentage of ownership in the common elements. Vote tabulation and ballot and proxy preparation where there is such a variation for the voting interest of each unit presents a unique type of problem. A similar situation affecting ballot preparation also arises when an association governs several condominiums.[54]

In a multi-condominium association meeting, matters of association business, such as election of board members, can be decided by the membership generally. Some matters, however, such as amendments to separate declarations of condominium and other votes relating directly to one condominium, will require tabulation by the condominium and not by the multi-condominium association.[55] When dealing with separate condominiums in a single meeting, or when dealing with different percentages of voting interests in the same meeting, the use of colored ballots should significantly improve the voting procedures and the tabulation of ballots.

The ballots should contain each item of business the board anticipates will come before the membership meeting for a vote. Each issue should be concisely stated with an appropriate "yes" or "no" alternative provided. While not prohibited by law, multiple choice answers should be discouraged and each issue should be framed so that there is a clear alternative.

Unlike a proxy which requires the identification of the unit owner, a ballot is not required to have, and should not provide for, an identification of the individual voting the ballot or the unit that it represents.[56] Ballot control should be handled at the check-in stage through the use of designation of voter lists and not at the actual time of voting.

---

[53] § 718.112 (2)(f) 4., F.S.
[54] § 718.111 (1)(a), F.S.
[55] § 718.110 (12), F.S.
[56] § 61B-23.0021 (9), F.A.C.

3.16 Ballots for Board Elections. Ballots for the election of members of the board of administration under the requirements of the statute must be prepared and distributed with a "second notice of election". To properly prepare the ballot, the association must first establish who will be the candidates. This is accomplished by mailing or delivering notice to each unit owner of the pending election at least sixty (60) days before the election occurs. This is known as the "first notice of election," and it may be delivered or mailed separately, or with another association mailing or delivery, such as a regularly published association newsletter.[57]

Any unit owner or other eligible person desiring to be a candidate for the board must notify the association, in writing, of his or her desire not less than forty (40) days before the scheduled election.[58] A written receipt must be provided by the secretary, or a person designated by the secretary, to all candidates responding in a timely fashion to the first notice of election.[59]

Once all potential candidates have been identified, the ballot for election is completed for distribution to the association members by listing each eligible candidate in alphabetical order by his or her surname. The ballots must be uniform in appearance and may not indicate which candidate or candidates are incumbents.[60] The ballot, together with information sheets and certification forms from the candidates, must then be mailed or delivered to each owner with a "second notice of election" not less than fourteen (14) days or more than thirty-four (34) days prior to the scheduled election.[61] The ballot and information sheets must be accompanied by an outer self-addressed envelope and a smaller inner envelope in which the completed ballot is to be placed.[62] The ballot shall not be accompanied by any communication by the board of administration which endorses, disapproves, or otherwise comments on any candidate.[63]

Once a ballot has been completed, the voter must insert the ballot in the smaller envelope, seal it and place the smaller envelope in the envelope self-addressed to the association. Each inner envelope may contain only

---

[57] § 61B-23.0021 (4), F.A.C.; § 718.112 (2)(d) 3. a., F.S.
[58] § 61B-23.0021 (5), F.A.C.
[59] § 61B-23.0021 (6), F.A.C.
[60] § 61B-23.0021 (9), F.A.C.
[61] § 718.112 (2)(d) 3., F.S.
[62] § 61B-23.0021 (8), F.A.C.
[63] *Id.*

one (1) ballot and if a member is entitled to cast more than one (1) vote, a separate inner envelope must be used for each ballot. The voting member must sign and identify the unit represented on the exterior of the outer envelope prior to returning it to the association by mail or hand delivery for tabulation.[64] (See 3.18).

Ballots for the board of administration must also be available at the meeting where the votes are tabulated. Voting members who have not returned ballots by mail may vote by ballot at the meeting.[65] A voting member casting a ballot at the meeting must mark his or her ballot and place it in the inner envelope. The inner envelope must then be placed in an outer envelope upon which the voting member affixes his or her signature and identifies the unit being represented. The sealed ballot is then turned in for tabulation.

3.17 Voting. The process of voting is the method of expressing the collective will of the membership. There are five basic ways for that voting process to take place: (1) by "general consent," (2) by "voice vote," (3) by "show of hands," (4) by "roll call," and (5) by "ballot" or voting machine.[66] Each type of voting has its appropriate place at a membership meeting, and each type can be used effectively at a well-run meeting of the members.[67] Use of an inappropriate voting method, on the other hand, can result in disruption or in an actual breakdown of the meeting.

Voting by "general consent" is most often used when there is no objection to an issue before the membership. The chairman of the meeting will simply ask if there is any objection to the motion on the floor and, if there is none, the chairman will declare that the motion is approved. "Voice voting" is used when an issue before the meeting is relatively non-controversial. The chairman of the meeting will ask for those in favor of the issue to say "aye," and for those who are opposed to the motion to say "no." The chairman will then rule on which group carried the motion. A voice vote should be taken only when the motion requires a majority vote, and if

---

[64] *Id.*

[65] § 61B-23.0021 (10)(a), F.A.C.

[66] *Robert's Rules of Order Newly Revised,* § 44.

[67] The procedural requirements governing the association's role on behalf of its members are appropriately political matters to be addressed within the organization and political framework of the association. *Eberwein v. Coral Pine Condominium One,* 431 So.2d 616, 618 (Fla. 4th DCA 1983).

a member disagrees with the ruling of the chairman on the voice vote, the member may request a count by one of the other voting methods.

Voting by "show of hands" is often a simple sight version of a voice vote, and does not necessarily require that an actual count of hands be made. An exact count of the hands can be made, but an exact count by either roll call, limited proxy, or by ballot is more correct. A "roll call" vote requires that the name of each member present be called, allowing for a response of "yes" or "no" to be made on the issue. Because a roll call vote is both time consuming and tedious, it is rarely used at association meetings.

Voting by "ballot," limited proxy, or voting machine is the preferred alternative when an exact vote tabulation is desired. Unless the association bylaws provide for an alternative method of election, voting by ballot or by voting machine is required in elections for board members.[68] Limited proxies are recommended on votes to waive or reduce reserves, to waive financial statement requirements, to waive building inspection reports, to amend the condominium documents, and in other votes where the law requires the use of limited proxies.[69] A vote by ballot is secret, and no owner may permit another to mark his or her ballot.[70] If a unit owner is blind, unable to read or otherwise disabled and needs assistance in voting, the unit owner may request and receive the necessary assistance.[71]

3.18 Vote Tabulations. The final result when voting by general consent, by voice vote, or by a show of hands, is determined by the chairman of the meeting. Tabulation of a roll call is a simple summation of the individual responses of members, while determining the results from a vote by ballot is by a separate, organized counting procedure which can be simplified significantly if the board has properly organized for the count. A majority of votes cast will decide most matters before the meeting, unless the condominium documents or the Condominium Act specify a different, extraordinary vote, such as when documents are being amended. (See 6.13). In the case of elections to the board, however, the decision will be based upon a plurality of the ballots actually voted. Candidates with the most votes will be declared the winners, although at least 20% of the eligible voters must

---

[68] § 718.112 (2)(d) 3., F.S.
[69] § 718.112 (2)(d) 2., F.S.
[70] § 718.112 (2)(d), F.S.
[71] § 61B-23.0021 (11), F.A.C.

cast a ballot in order to have a valid election.[72]

The envelopes containing ballots returned to the association for board elections must be collected unopened by association officials and transported to the meeting of unit owners where the votes are to be tabulated. As the first order of business at the meeting, ballots not yet cast shall be collected. Next, the signature and unit identification on each outer envelope must be checked, or "validated," against the list of qualified voting members.

Any exterior envelope not signed by the eligible voter must be marked "Disregarded," and any ballots contained in the envelope are not counted. As exterior envelopes are validated, voting members are checked off on the list of unit owners as having voted.[73]

Once the validation process has been completed, the inner envelopes are removed from the outer envelopes, and the inner envelopes are placed in a receptacle. When all the inner envelopes have been placed in the receptacle, the envelopes may be opened and the ballots removed for tabulation in the presence of the unit owners in attendance.[74]

If an inner envelope contains more than one (1) ballot, all of the ballots from the envelope shall be marked "Disregarded" and they shall not be counted.[75] When counting, a ballot containing votes for too many board members must be disallowed, while a ballot that does not vote for all available choices is counted for the choices made. Should it be determined that an owner permitted another to improperly vote his or her ballot, the ballot shall be considered invalid and disallowed.

When deciding who will actually serve as inspectors of election and validate and tabulate the ballots at a membership meeting, the board should keep in mind two basic considerations. The first consideration is the number of votes to be cast and the number of individuals that will be needed to insure a prompt and accurate tabulation of the votes. The second consideration is the nature of the election and whether other issues are involved. It is helpful to have representatives of both sides of controversial issues involved in the count to remove any doubt on the validity of the results.

---

[72] § 718.112 (2)(d) 3., F.S.
[73] § 61B-23.0021 (10)(a), F.A.C.
[74] *Id.*
[75] *Id.*

It is permissible for an association to verify outer envelope information in advance of the meeting provided that it occurs on the same day as the meeting. The board of administration must designate an impartial committee to conduct the verification, and its membership may not include current board members, officers, candidates for the board, or the spouses of board members, officers or candidates for the board. At the meeting of the committee and in the presence of unit owners in attendance, the signature and unit identification on each outer envelope must be checked against the list of qualified voters in the same manner as if the verification were occurring at the election meeting.[76]

All of the ballots from the election, including those "Disregarded" and all outer envelopes, are official records of the association[77] and must be retained for a period of one (1) year.[78]

3.19 Conducting the Meeting. Conducting a fair and successful meeting is the responsibility of the presiding officer or chairman.[79] The chairman must set and maintain the proper tenor for the meeting and, as chairman, must at all times be fair, impartial and neutral on each issue that comes before the meeting. The goal of the chairman should be to conduct an open and fair membership meeting, without regard to the outcome on specific votes or motions.

In addition to setting an example of basic courtesy and fairness, the chairman must also be familiar with the proper parliamentary procedures used for conducting the membership meeting. (See 6.1). While the law allows unit owners the right to participate at members' meetings, it also allows the association to impose reasonable rules governing the frequency, duration, and manner of unit owner participation.[80] Every unit owner who so desires may speak at any meeting, and no rule may contain a limitation on the total number of unit owners authorized to speak at a meeting. It is permissible, however, to limit each owner to a maximum of three (3) minutes or more, and to require unit owners wishing to speak to file or request with the association a reasonable time in advance of the meeting.[81]

---

[76] § 61B-23.0021 (10)(b), F.A.C.
[77] § 61B-23.0021 (10), F.A.C.
[78] § 718.111 (12)(a) 12., F.S.
[79] *Roberts Rules of Order Newly Revised*, § 58.
[80] § 718.112 (2)(d) 6., F.S.
[81] § 61B-23.0021 (7), F.A.C.

Debate or remarks by individual members should be limited or cut off only in extreme circumstances, or when they are being made at an improper point on the agenda. It is not unusual to find one or more individual members who will attempt to be disruptive, either intentionally or because they feel strongly on a particular issue. In such circumstances, the chairman must remain courteous, patient and composed. The disruptive member desiring to be heard should be guided to the correct part of the agenda for his remarks, and advised how to make them in an appropriate and dignified fashion. By following proper procedures, the chairman can allow the meeting to proceed with full participation of all members, but without argument or disruption.

Conducting a successful meeting requires the assurance that all members wishing to participate can do so, and that members wishing to make motions or debate an issue will have the appropriate opportunity. Particularly in large gatherings, it is helpful to have microphones available on the meeting floor to assist members wishing to participate.

The chairman should require members wishing to speak to stand or to come to the microphone and state their full name and their unit number before beginning their remarks. This allows the secretary to identify the speaker for record keeping purposes and it introduces the speaker to the balance of the membership. If a microphone is not available, the chairman of the meeting should be prepared to restate the motions or the remarks for the benefit of all of the meeting participants.[82]

3.20   Reports. The reports by officers and committees are often a part of the required meeting agenda and they provide an appropriate segment in the meeting for the membership to be updated on association affairs. Reports, however, may also lead to disruptive and unnecessary discussion if they are not properly presented and disposed of. Reports by officers and committees at the meeting should be basic summaries from written reports, and the written reports themselves should be available for separate distribution and a more complete analysis by members.[83]

Reports of a general nature, including the treasurer's report and reports by recreational and other committees are, by their nature, informational, and

---

[82] *Roberts Rules of Order Newly Revised,* § 6.
[83] § 718.111 (12)(c), F.S.; *Winter v. Playa del Sol, Inc.,* 353 So.2d 598 (Fla. 4th DCA 1977).

unnecessary questions and remarks from the floor of the meeting should be avoided or deferred since all of these records are available to unit owners at reasonable times.[84] Officers or committee chairmen should not request comments or questions at the conclusion of their reports, and if discussion is to be held on any portion of the reports presented to the meeting, it is appropriately brought up under the "unfinished business" portion of the agenda.

Occasionally, reports will require some special action by the membership meeting. Under such circumstances, the report should contain the specific recommendation being made and it can be acted upon at the time that the report is concluded or under "unfinished business." Examples of such recommendations include reports by a finance committee, the board, or the treasurer that recommend reserves in the budget be waived for the coming fiscal year.

3.21 Unfinished Business. The unfinished business portion of the agenda is for the discussion and consideration of matters that have previously come before a meeting of the membership, either earlier in the present meeting or at a previously scheduled meeting.[85] Business that has previously come before the meeting under reports by officers and by committees, and requiring membership action, should be taken up and disposed of under this part of the agenda.

Such unfinished business may include the waiver or reduction of budget reserves, the waiver of financial statement requirements, and other similar items of association business. To the extent possible, it is important for the board to identify, in advance, these matters of unfinished business. Items of unfinished business that can be identified in advance can be set aside under the unfinished business portion of the agenda as separate sub-categories.

The sub-categories will help to inform the members when specific items will arise within the general agenda category. The presiding officer will then be prepared to direct the members to the appropriate part of the agenda, and maintain an orderly flow to the meeting. Unfinished business is

---

[84] § 718.111 (12)(c), F.S.
[85] *Robert's Rules of Order Newly Revised,* § 40.

appropriately restricted to matters previously before the meeting, and matters not previously on the floor should be deferred until the consideration of new business.

3.22 New Business and General Discussion. The new business portion of the agenda obviously intends to deal with new matters not previously presented to the meeting. This part of the agenda is also the last, or one of the last, items to come before the meeting prior to its adjournment. As such, most required business has already been disposed of and more flexibility can be allowed by the presiding officer when permitting debate and discussion under the new business portion of the agenda.

Under new business, general discussion may be considered as an appropriate agenda sub-category. Additional tolerance and latitude can be allowed by the presiding officer towards the end of the meeting, and individual members can voice their objections or other concerns with association affairs at this time. In the unlikely event that the meeting and the discussion should become unreasonable and unruly, a motion to adjourn the meeting is always in order and can be voted upon without fear of leaving major unfinished business incomplete.

Other appropriate sub-categories of new business are items which require an extraordinary vote for approval by the members. Such items include proposed amendments to the condominium documents, cancellation of contracts entered into by the developer, approval of material alterations or modifications to the common elements and other issues where either the documents or the Condominium Act mandate an extraordinary vote.[86] Again, the reason for holding these items for consideration as sub-categories under new business is the proximity of new business on the agenda to adjournment of the meeting.

The bylaws of most associations permit a meeting to be adjourned and reconvened if the required quorum is not obtained. An extraordinary vote can be postponed when an insufficient number of members is present to reach the required extraordinary majority. The business requiring only a simple majority can be disposed of first before the question requiring the extraordinary vote is placed on the floor. A motion can then be made to adjourn the meeting, after tabulating votes towards the extraordinary majority, to reconvene at a later date for purposes of counting the additional

---

[86] § 718.110 (1), F.S.; § 718.302 (1), F.S.; § 718.110 (4), F.S.;

votes for the required extraordinary majority.[87] (See Form 6.03—Sample Motions).

While the new business portion of the agenda permits some creative options when seeking an extraordinary majority, it is important to consult the association bylaws for appropriate authority. The association's legal advisor should also be called upon to assist with the appropriate parliamentary steps. As under unfinished business, sub-categories for new business are recommended for an organized and complete presentation of the association business.

3.23   Adjournment. Adjournment concludes the proceedings and, in almost all cases, it occurs simply because there is no further business to come before the meeting. On rare occasions, a simple ending of the meeting may not be desired or may not be easily accomplished. Under such circumstances, the presiding officer must be prepared to deal with the unusual or unexpected. Since the motion to adjourn the meeting is the highest priority motion available from the floor, the presiding officer may need such a motion to be made if the meeting becomes disruptive or unruly. When made in simplest form, the motion to adjourn is not debatable and it may be made, seconded and voted on before control of the proceedings is lost.[88]

A different motion to adjourn will be used on occasions when the adjournment is to be followed by a reconvening of the meeting at a later time. Such a motion to adjourn and reconvene may be desired so that additional information can be brought to the membership, or because the meeting has lasted for an excessive length of time and members are tiring.[89] The motion to adjourn and reconvene may also be used when an item of business requires an extraordinary majority and an insufficient number of members are present to meet the extraordinary majority. The motion to adjourn and reconvene is debatable and, if made and approved, it will allow the meeting to be temporarily ended and reconvened at a later time for the purpose of

---

[87] "A majority of the stockholders in interest present at an annual shareholders' meeting may adjourn the meeting to another day when they see fit to do so for a proper purpose." 18A Am. Jur. 2d, Corporations, § 1013.

[88] *Robert's Rules of Order Newly Revised,* § 21.

[89] *Roberts Rules of Order Newly Revised,* § 17.

continuing the meeting business and counting additional votes present at the reconvened portion of the meeting.[90]

3.24 Minutes. Minutes of the membership meeting serve as the permanent record of the proceedings and are considered prima facia evidence of the business conducted at the meeting.[91] Their content should include a description of all pertinent items of business conducted at the meeting, and the disposition made of each item by the membership.[92] A complete meeting record does not require that a word-by-word transcript be kept or that an elaborate account of debate and general discussion be placed in written minutes. Proper minutes will confirm the time, place and presiding officer for the meeting. They will establish that proof of notice was given for the meeting and will state the exact quorum that is in attendance. These elements will provide a permanent record that a proper membership meeting was convened, and the minutes must be maintained as part of the official records of the association for at least seven (7) years.[93]

The minutes will include an account of each item of business that was brought before the meeting, and will contain a clear and concise record of the item's disposition. The use of exhibits in minutes provides a helpful way to organize a complete and accurate record of the proceedings. The proof of notice, copies of the notice and agenda, attendance and check-in sheets, reports and the actual vote tabulations can be included in the minutes by reference as attached exhibits. Exhibits can eliminate lengthy minutes while maintaining a complete record of the meeting events.

When the minutes of the meeting have been prepared and approved by the secretary, it is advisable to make them available to the membership for inspection and review. This procedure will help keep the membership informed and will also provide a basis for the waiver of the reading of the minutes at the next regular meeting. The minutes of all meetings must be available for inspection by unit owners or their authorized representatives at any reasonable time.[94]

---

[90] 18A Am. Jur. 2d, Corporations, § 1013.

[91] *Wimbledon Townhouse Condominium I, Ass'n, Inc. v. Wolfson,* 510 So.2d 1106 (Fla. 4th DCA 1987); *Gentry-Futch Co. v. Gentry, supra* note 15.

[92] § 617.1601 (1), F.S.

[93] § 718.111 (12)(b), F.S.

[94] § 718.111 (12)(a) 6., F.S.

If audio and video recordings are made by the board of administration or at the direction of the board, the recordings must be maintained at least until the minutes of the meeting have been approved. After approval of the minutes, the recordings may be discarded unless the board elects to preserve them as part of the official records of the association.[95]

3.25   Election Records. In addition to the minutes and minutes' exhibits, there are other records from the membership meeting which must be kept and maintained by the association. The voting certificates for units owned by more than one person or by corporate owners are kept and updated for continuing use at future meetings. The sign-in sheets, ballots, voting proxies and other papers relating to elections which have been used during the membership meeting must also be kept by the association for at least one (1) year.[96]

Unopened voting proxies received by the association do not become official records subject to inspection by members of the association until after the election for which the proxies were given. The existence of sealed proxies, however, may not be kept secret from association members, and the unopened proxies are available for inspection by members of the association as they are received. Proxies received by the association do not become voting proxies until they have been verified as legitimate and submitted for counting.[97]

---

[95] § 61B-23.002 (5)(b) 6., F.A.C.
[96] § 718.111 (12)(a) 12., F.S.
[97] *Id.*

WATERFRONT XX CONDOMINIUM ASSOCIATION, INC.
A Corporation Not-for-Profit

NOTICE OF MEMBERS' MEETING

NOTICE IS HEREBY GIVEN, in accordance with the Bylaws of the Association and Florida's Condominium Act, that the annual (special*) meeting of members will be held at the following date, time and place:

Date: January 15, 2011

Time: 7:00 p.m.

Place: Clubhouse
Waterfront XX Condominium
100 Waterfront Drive
Waterfront, Florida 33444

Agenda:

1. Calling of roll and certifying of proxies.

2. Proof of notice of meeting or waiver of notice.

3. Reading and disposal of any unapproved minutes.

4. Election of inspectors of election.

5. Election of board members.

6. Reports of officers.

7. Reports of committees.

   a. Recreation Committee.

   b. Audit Committee.

   c. Grounds Committee.

8. Unfinished business.

   a. Waiver of budget reserves.

   b. Adoption of budget.

9.   New business.

     a.   Consideration of amendments to declaration of condominium.

     b.   Consideration of covered parking installation.

     c.   General discussion by members.

10.   Adjournment.

WATERFRONT XX CONDOMINIUM
ASSOCIATION, INC.

By:_____
                  Secretary

Dated: This 15th day of December, 2010.

*(The notice for a special members' meeting must state the purpose for which the meeting is called.)

WATERFRONT XX CONDOMINIUM ASSOCIATION, INC.
A Corporation Not-for-Profit

PROOF OF NOTICE AFFIDAVIT

STATE OF FLORIDA   )
COUNTY OF PINELLAS   )

The undersigned Secretary of the Association, being first duly sworn, deposes and says that notice of the annual (special) membership meeting was mailed or hand delivered to each unit owner at the address last furnished to the Association in accordance with the requirements of Section 718.112 (2)(d) Paragraph 2, F.S., at least fourteen days prior to the annual (special) meeting.

Dated this 15th day of December, 2010.

By: _____
                    Secretary

The foregoing Affidavit was acknowledged before me this 15th day of December, 2010, by Nancy Thomas, the Secretary of Waterfront XX Condominium Association, Inc.

_____
            Notary Public

My commission expires:

WATERFRONT XX CONDOMINIUM ASSOCIATION, INC.
A Corporation Not-for-Profit

AGENDA
MEMBERSHIP MEETING
January 15, 2011

1. Calling of roll and certifying of proxies.

2. Proof of notice of meeting or waiver of notice.

3. Reading and disposal of any unapproved minutes.

4. Election of inspectors of election.

5. Election of board members.

6. Reports of officers.

7. Reports of committees.

   a. Recreation Committee.

   b. Audit Committee.

   c. Grounds Committee.

8. Unfinished business.

   a. Waiver of budget reserves.

   b. Adoption of budget.

9. New business.

   a. Consideration of amendments to declaration of condominium.

   b. Consideration of covered parking installation.

   c. General discussion by members.

10. Adjournment.

Agenda for Member's Meeting FORM 3.03

WATERFRONT XX CONDOMINIUM ASSOCIATION, INC.
A Corporation Not-for-Profit

PROXY
January 15, 2011
Membership Meeting

TO: Secretary
       Waterfront XX Condominium Association, Inc.
       100 Waterfront Drive
       Waterfront, Florida 33444

KNOW ALL PERSONS BY THESE PRESENTS, that the undersigned hereby appoints the Secretary of the Association or _____, attorney and agent with the power of substitution for and in the name, place and stead of the undersigned, to vote as proxy at the membership meeting of the Association, to be held at the Clubhouse, January 15, 2011, at 7:00 p.m, and any adjournment thereof, according to the number of votes that the undersigned would be entitled to vote if then present upon the matters set forth in the Notice of Meeting dated December 15, 2010, a copy of which has been received by the undersigned.

(In no event shall this proxy be valid for a period longer than 90 days after the date of the first meeting for which it was given.)

DATED this _____ day of January, 2011.

Unit Owner

_____

_____

Unit Number:_____

General Proxy   FORM 3.04

WATERFRONT XX CONDOMINIUM ASSOCIATION, INC.
A Corporation Not-for-Profit

PROXY
January 15, 2011
Membership Meeting

TO: Secretary
        Waterfront XX Condominium Association, Inc.
        100 Waterfront Drive
        Waterfront, Florida 33444

KNOW ALL PERSONS BY THESE PRESENTS, that the undersigned hereby appoints the Secretary of the Association, his or her designee, or _____, attorney and agent with the power of substitution for and in the name, place and stead of the undersigned, to vote as proxy at the membership meeting of the Association, to be held at the Clubhouse, January 15, 2011, at 7:00 p.m., and any adjournment thereof, according to the number of votes that the undersigned would be entitled to vote if then present in accordance with the specifications hereinafter made, as follows:

General Powers
_____   I hereby authorize and instruct my proxy to use his or her best judgment on all matters which properly come before the meeting as may be authorized by Sec. 718.112(2)(b)2, Florida Statutes.

Limited Powers
_____   I hereby specifically authorize and instruct my proxy to cast my vote in reference to the following matters only as indicated below.

1.   Should the reserves required by Section 718.112 (2)(f), F.S. be waived for the next fiscal year?
        Yes_____   No_____

WAIVING OF RESERVES, IN WHOLE OR IN PART, OR ALLOWING ALTERNATIVE USES OF EXISTING RESERVES MAY RESULT IN UNIT OWNER LIABILITY FOR PAYMENT OF UNANTICIPATED SPECIAL ASSESSMENTS REGARDING THOSE ITEMS.

2.   Should the audit of financial records by a certified public accountant be waived for the coming year?
Yes_____   No_____

The undersigned does ratify and confirm any and all acts and things that the proxy may do or cause to be done, whether at the meeting referred to above or at any change, adjournment, or continuation of it, and does hereby revoke all proxies previously executed.

Dated:_____   Unit Owner

_____

_____

Unit Number:_____

SUBSTITUTION OF PROXY

The undersigned, appointed as proxy above, does hereby designate _____ to substitute for me in the proxy set forth above.

Dated:_____   Proxy_____

(In no event shall this proxy be valid for a period longer than 90 days after the date of the first meeting for which it was given.)

Limited Proxy   FORM 3.05

WATERFRONT XX CONDOMINIUM ASSOCIATION, INC.
A Corporation Not-for-Profit

VOTING CERTIFICATE

TO: Secretary
        Waterfront XX Condominium Association, Inc.
        100 Waterfront Drive
        Waterfront, Florida 33444

KNOW ALL PERSONS BY THESE PRESENTS, that the undersigned is the record owner of that certain condominium unit in WATERFRONT XX CONDOMINIUM, a Condominium, shown below, and hereby constitutes, appoints and designates _____ as the voting representative for the condominium unit owned by said undersigned pursuant to the By-Laws of the Association.

The aforenamed voting representative is hereby authorized and empowered to act in the capacity herein set forth until such time as the undersigned otherwise modifies or revokes the authority set forth in this voting certificate.

DATED this 1st day of December, 2010.

Unit Owner

_____

_____

Unit Number:_____

BALLOT

1.   Should the reserves required by §718.112 (2)(f), F.S., be waived for the next fiscal year?

         Yes _____   No_____

WAIVING OF RESERVES, IN WHOLE OR IN PART, OR ALLOWING ALTERNATIVE USES OF EXISTING RESERVES MAY RESULT IN UNIT OWNER LIABILITY FOR PAYMENT OF UNANTICIPATED SPECIAL ASSESSMENTS REGARDING THOSE ITEMS.

2.   Should the bylaws of the Association be amended to restrict the rental of condominium units in accordance with the full text of the proposed amendment which accompanied the mailing of the meeting notice?

         Yes _____   No_____

3.   Should the audit by a certified public accountant required by §718.111 (13), F.S., be waived for the next fiscal year?

         Yes _____   No_____

FIRST NOTICE OF ELECTION

Notice is hereby given that the election to fill vacancies on the board of administration of Waterfront XX Condominium Association, Inc. will be held at 7:00 p.m. on January 15, 2011, at the Clubhouse located at 100 Waterfront Drive, Waterfront, Florida, 33444. Any unit owner (or other eligible person) desiring to be a candidate for the board of administration shall give written notice to the Secretary of the Association of such person's candidacy on or before December 6, 2010 (not less than 40 days before the election).

Written responses from individuals desiring to be a candidate for the board of administration should be directed to the secretary of the association at the following address:

Secretary
Waterfront XX Condominium Association, Inc.
101 Waterfront Street
Waterfront, Florida 33444

DATED AND MAILED: November 16, 2010 (not less than 60 days prior to the election)

WATERFRONT XX CONDOMINIUM ASSOCIATION, INC.

By:_____
Secretary

WATERFRONT XX CONDOMINIUM ASSOCIATION, INC.
A Corporation Not-for-Profit

101 Waterfront Drive
Waterfront, Florida 33444

December 5, 2010

Ms. Sara Harris
100 Waterfront Street, Unit 104
Waterfront, Florida 33444

RE: Receipt of Written Notice of Intention to be a Candidate for the
Board of Administration

Dear Ms. Harris:

This is to acknowledge receipt of your written notice to be a
candidate for the Board of Administration of Waterfront XX Condominium
Association, Inc. Your notice was timely received as required by the
Condominium Act and you are now a duly qualified candidate.

Respectfully,

WATERFRONT XX CONDOMINIUM
ASSOCIATION, INC.

By:_____
Secretary

BALLOT

The following are candidates who have qualified for election to the Board of Administration of the Association. There are three vacancies on the Board of Administration and you may vote for up to three individuals by placing a check mark next to their names. A ballot voting for more than three individuals will be disallowed.

Sara Harris   _____

Joseph A. Jones   _____

Matthew Marshall   _____

David Smith   _____

Marc Wesley   _____

INSTRUCTIONS FOR COMPLETING ELECTION BALLOT

Balloting for the board of Administration is secret. Eligible members of the association are entitled to vote on the day of the election by returning the enclosed ballot to the Secretary of the Association. An association member wishing to vote by using the enclosed ballot shall comply with the following instructions:

1. Mark the ballot for the candidates of the voter's choice. Do not place any identifying marks such as the voter's name or unit number on the ballot.

2. Place the completed ballot in the plain ("inner") envelope enclosed and seal the envelope securely. A separate envelope must be used for each ballot voted, if eligible.

3. Place the sealed plain envelope containing the marked ballot in the second envelope addressed to the association Secretary and seal securely.

4. The eligible voter shall sign the envelope and identify the unit which the voter represents adjacent to the signature.

5. Return the envelope to the Secretary of the Association prior to the time for tabulating the ballots.

Sample Ballot Instructions   FORM 3.11

SECOND NOTICE OF ELECTION

Notice is hereby given that the election to fill vacancies on the board of administration of Waterfront XX Condominium Association, Inc. will be held 7:00 p.m. on January 15, 2011, at the Clubhouse located at 100 Waterfront Drive, Waterfront, Florida, 33444. A ballot listing all candidates for the board of administration accompanies this notice. An information sheet on each candidate who has furnished information and requested its distribution on his or her candidacy is also enclosed with this notice.

The ballot is to be completed by the voting member in accordance with the enclosed instructions and returned to the Secretary of the Association at the following address:

> Secretary
> Waterfront XX Condominium Association, Inc.
> 100 Waterfront Drive
> Waterfront, Florida 33444

DATED AND MAILED: December 15, 2010 (not less than 14 days nor more than 34 days prior to the election)

WATERFRONT XX CONDOMINIUM ASSOCIATION, INC.

By:_____
    Secretary

CANDIDATE INFORMATION SHEET

NAME:_____   UNIT NO:_____

PERMANENT ADDRESS: EDUCATION:

_____   _____

_____   _____

PERSONAL BACKGROUND:

_____
_____
_____
_____

PRIOR CONDOMINIUM EXPERIENCE:

_____
_____
_____
_____

COMMENTS ABOUT BOARD CANDIDACY:

_____
_____
_____

WATERFRONT XX CONDOMINIUM ASSOCIATION, INC.
A Corporation Not-for-Profit

ANNUAL MEMBERS' MEETING MINUTES

The meeting was called to order at 7:00 p.m., Monday, January 15, 2011, in the clubhouse by the President. The President announced that the first order of business was the calling of the roll and the certifying of the proxies. Upon its completion, it was announced that 100 units were represented in person and 50 units were represented by proxy. The President declared that a quorum of the 200 units was present.

The President next called upon the Secretary to present the affidavit for proof of notice, and directed it to be annexed to the minutes of the meeting and made a permanent part of the Association's official records. The President stated that the next item of business was the reading of the minutes from the last members meeting. Upon a motion made by Mr. Jones and seconded by Mr. Smith, and upon discussion, it was unanimously carried by voice vote, that the reading of the minutes be waived.

The next item of business was the appointment of inspectors of election. The President appointed the Association's Vice President Susan Harris, and Mr. Campbell to serve as inspectors of election, and directed that all ballots be turned over to the inspectors for tabulation. The President then stated that, without objection, the meeting would stand in recess until the tabulation of the ballots was completed.

Upon reconvening the recessed meeting, the President called upon the Vice President to announce the results of the election. The Vice President then stated that the following individuals were elected to serve for a term of one year on the Board of Administration:

Sara Harris

David Smith

Marc Wesley

The next order of business was the reports of officers and committees. The President recognized the Treasurer who gave the financial report for the preceding twelve months. Upon completion of the presentation, the President directed that it be annexed to the minutes of the meeting and distributed to the membership.

Under reports of committees, the President recognized the chairman of the recreation committee, Mr. Johnson, who presented the schedule of functions and events planned for the coming calendar year.

The President next asked for items of unfinished business. Mr. Anderson moved that the reserve requirement for Section 718.112 (2)(f), F.S., be waived for the coming fiscal year of the Association. The motion was seconded and at the conclusion of the discussion the motion was unanimously passed by a voice vote. The President declared that the motion was adopted.

The President then stated that the next item on the agenda was consideration of new business. There being no new business to come before the meeting and no further member seeking recognition, upon a motion duly made, seconded and unanimously carried, the President stated that the meeting was adjourned at the hour of 8:30 p.m.

_____
Secretary

Minutes of Members' Meeting   FORM 3.14

WATERFRONT XX CONDOMINIUM ASSOCIATION, INC.
A Corporation Not-for-Profit

ROSTER OF UNIT OWNERS

UNIT NO.	UNIT OWNER	DESIGNATED VOTER
101	Joseph A. Jones Ann Marie Jones 101 Waterfront Drive Waterfront, FL 33444, Tel. #(111) 999–7101	Joseph A. Jones
102	Matthew Marshall 102 Waterfront Drive Waterfront, FL 33444, (no telephone)	Matthew Marshall
103	William Dunbar Lindsey Ann Dunbar 103 Waterfront Drive Waterfront, FL 33444, (telephone no. unknown)	Lindsey Dunbar
104	David R. Smith Nancy H. Smith 104 Waterfront Drive Waterfront, FL 33444, Tel. #(111) 999–7104	David R. Smith
105	Marc Wesley 105 Waterfront Drive Waterfront, FL 33444, Tel. # (111) 999–7105	Marc Wesley
106	ABP Corporation 113 Main Street Waterfront, FL 33444, Tel. #(111) 999–7106 Attn: David Dodd, Pres.	David Dodd

4

The Board of Administration and Meetings of the Board

BOARD OF ADMINISTRATION FORMS

4.1   General. The condominium association operates and manages the affairs of the condominium.[1] The board of administration, or board of directors, is responsible for carrying out the duties and responsibilities of the condominium association.[2] The "board of administration" is synonymous with the "board of directors" in a condominium association and the terms may be used interchangeably.

To the extent that the association has control of the affairs and the property of the condominium, the board has the responsibility to implement that authority.[3] An individual member of the association has no authority to act for the community or for the board simply by virtue of being a member.[4]

Members of the board of administration serve without compensation unless the bylaws of the association provide to the contrary.[5] Their authority is comprehensive and includes all of the powers and duties enumerated in Chapter 617, Florida Statutes, (Florida Not For Profit Corporation Act), as long as the powers are not inconsistent with the provisions of the Condominium Act and the documents governing the community.

4.2   Developer Board Members. The developer creates the association and appoints the first complete board of administration at the time that the condominium is created. The developer board maintains and operates the condominium until the community matures and control of the board of administration passes to the unit owners. During the period of developer control there are some specific restrictions on the board's authority which are designed to protect and preserve the rights of purchasers of the units in the condominium. (See Ch. 12).

The developer board cannot start, compromise or settle disputes involving construction defects in the community. A developer-controlled board cannot compromise commitments or promises that the developer has made to the community for existing or proposed facilities to be used by the unit owners.[6] When a developer-controlled board of administration exercises

---

[1] § 718.111 (1)(a), F.S.
[2] § 718.103 (4) and § 617.0801, F.S.; *Eberwein v. Coral Pine Condominium One,* 431 So.2d 616, 617 (Fla. 4th DCA 1983).
[3] § 617.0801, F.S.
[4] § 718.111 (1)(c), F.S.
[5] § 718.112 (2)(a), F.S.
[6] § 718.111 (3), F.S.

its power to make contracts for the maintenance, management or operation of the condominium, the authority to do so is subject to reconsideration by the unit owners when they assume control of the board.[7]

During the time when the board of administration is controlled by the developer, violations of the Condominium Act or rules promulgated under the Condominium Act by the association are the responsibility of the developer.[8] Florida's appellate courts have also recognized that inaction by a developer-controlled board does not prejudice future boards and their ability to enforce the condominium documents.[9] The distinction between the developer-controlled board and the owner-controlled board must be recognized and understood by the owner-controlled board if the full benefits for the unit owners are to be achieved.

4.3 Transition from Developer Control. As the developer sells the individual condominium units, the owners become entitled to a voice on the board of administration under the schedule established by the Condominium Act. When 15% or more of the units have been sold, the owners are entitled to elect at least one-third of the members of the board of administration. The owners are entitled to complete control of the board within three (3) months after 90% of the units have been sold, when all of the units have been completed and none of the remaining units owned by the developer are being offered for sale, when a developer is in receivership or files for bankruptcy protection, or seven (7) years after the initial recording of the declaration of condominium.[10] (See 12.7).

Within seventy-five (75) days from the time that the owners are entitled to control the board of administration, a meeting of the membership must be called by the developer to allow the owners to elect the new owner-directors.[11] Notices for the meeting and the procedures for the transition election are the same as those required for the regular elections for the board of administration.[12] (See 3.8). Once the owner board members have been

---

[7] § 718.302 (1), F.S.

[8] § 718.301 (5) and (6), F.S.

[9] *Ladner v. Plaza Del Prado Condominium Ass'n, Inc.*, 423 So.2d 927 (Fla. 3rd DCA 1982).

[10] § 718.301, F.S. A court may determine that transition after the appointment is detrimental to the community and stay the transition.

[11] § 718.301 (1) and (2), F.S.

[12] § 61B-23.0021 (1), F.A.C.

elected, the developer must provide the Division of Florida Condominiums, Timeshares, and Mobile Homes with the name and mailing address of each of the unit owner members of the board.[13]

When the time comes for transition, the developer must transfer, and the unit owners must accept, control of the board together with all of the property and records of the association. The developer never relinquishes his responsibility as developer at the time of transition. The responsibilities for warranty defects and other obligations remain with the developer even when control of the board is relinquished to the unit owners.[14]

The board of administration is the legal entity representing all of the owners and by assuming control of the board, the owners can pursue claims against the developer in an organized and efficient manner. It is a common mistake for owners to refuse control of their own association because they feel claims against the developer remain. In reality, their claims are best made through a board of administration controlled by the unit owners.

After control of the board passes to the owners, the developer remains entitled to at least one representative on the board as long as the developer continues to sell units in the ordinary course of business and continues to own at least 5% of the total units in the community. If the condominium has five hundred (500) units or more, the right of the developer to have at least one (1) member on the board continues as long as the developer owns at least 2% of the total units in the condominium.

The members of the board of administration serving as representatives of the developer are not subject to recall by the unit owners.[15] They may be removed only by the developer or under the requirements for the transition of control of the board.[16]

4.4   Election and Selection. There are two methods for selecting and electing members for the board of administration. The first, and most common, is by election to the board by members of the association at an annual or special meeting. Unless an alternative method of election is provided in the bylaws of the association, the election procedures that must be followed are specifically set forth in the Condominium Act and they require that the regular election for board members be held on the same date

---

[13] § 61B-23.003 (5), F.A.C.
[14] § 718.203, F.S.
[15] § 61B-23.0026 (1)(a), F.A.C.
[16] § 718.301 (1), F.S.

as the association's annual meeting.[17] The second method of selection is by appointment to the board of administration. The appointment may occur by the developer if the developer is still entitled to representation or it may be by the remaining members of the board of administration when a vacancy on the board occurs between meetings of the membership.[18]

When members of the board are to be selected by election, the Act requires that the election be preceded by the qualification of candidates. The association is required to mail or deliver the first notice of election to all unit owners sixty (60) days before a scheduled election. Any unit owner or other eligible person desiring to be a candidate may do so after this "first notice of election" by giving written notice of his or her candidacy to the association not less than forty (40) days before the scheduled election. (See 3.16).

Balloting is not necessary to fill a vacancy unless there are two (2) or more eligible candidates for the vacancy. If there are no candidates to fill vacancies or only one (1) candidate for a vacant position, not later than the date of the scheduled election, the association shall call and hold a meeting to announce the names of the new board members, or shall notify unit owners that one or more board positions remain unfilled. In the alternative, the announcement may be made at the annual meeting.[19]

If more candidates qualify for election than there are vacancies on the board, an election must be held and each candidate must be listed on the ballots that are distributed to unit owners.[20] The ballots must be provided to unit owners not less than fourteen (14) days nor more than thirty-four (34) days prior to the scheduled election. (See 3.16). The vote is by secret ballot, and when the ballots are tabulated on the day of the election, a plurality of the ballots cast shall decide the election. There is no quorum requirement for the election; however, at least 20% of the eligible voters must cast a ballot in order to have a valid election. (See 3.18). The voting interests in the condominium association also have the right to petition the condominium ombudsman to appoint an election monitor to attend the meeting and conduct the election.[21] (See 14.6).

When a new member is elected or appointed to the board of

---

[17] § 718.112 (2)(d) 3., F.S.
[18] § 617.0809 (1), F.S.; § 718.112 (2)(d) 8., F.S.
[19] § 718.112 (2)(d), F.S.
[20] § 718.112 (2)(d) 3., F.S.
[21] § 718.5012 (9), F.S.

administration, the new member is required to certify in writing to the secretary of the association that he or she has read the condominium documents, will work to uphold the documents and policies of the community, and will faithfully discharge his or her fiduciary responsibilities to the community.[22] In the alternative, a certificate of satisfactory completion of a condominium education course approved by the Division of Florida Condominiums, Timeshares, and Mobile Homes may be provided in lieu of the certificate to the secretary. A board member who fails to timely file the required written certification or education certificate within ninety (90) days of being elected or appointed is suspended from service on the board until the member complies with the certificate requirement. The certificate provided by each new board member must be retained in the association records for at least five (5) years.[23]

When a vacancy arises on the board between meetings of the membership, the remaining board members may select a new member by appointment to fill the unexpired term, unless the bylaws of the association provide otherwise.[24] Vacancies on the board, other than those created by recall, may be filled by the remaining members even if the remaining members are less than a majority of the full board.[25] (See 4.9).

The term of a board member appointed to fill a vacancy will continue until the next meeting of the membership, when a replacement member to the board can be elected. If the unexpired term of a member is for longer than one year when the appointment is made, the appointed member will serve for the balance of the unexpired term unless the bylaws specifically provide otherwise.[26]

4.5   Runoff Election. Unless another method is provided for in the bylaws of the association, the rules of the Division of Florida Condominiums, Timeshares, and Mobile Homes provide for a runoff election to resolve a tie vote for the board of administration.[27] Within seven (7) days of the election at which the tie vote occurred, the board is required to mail or personally deliver a notice of the runoff election to the voting members of the association. Only the candidates who received the tie vote are eligible to

---

[22] § 718.112 (2)(d) 3. b., F.S.

[23] *Id.*

[24] § 61B-23.0021 (13), F.A.C.

[25] § 617.0809 (1), F.S.; § 718.112 (2)(d) 8., F.S.

[26] § 718.112 (2)(d) 8., F.S.

[27] § 61B-23.0021 (10)(c), F.A.C.

participate in the runoff election.

Notice of the runoff election must inform the voters of the date scheduled for the election, and the notice must be accompanied by a ballot for the election and any candidate information sheet previously provided by the runoff candidates. The runoff election must be held not less than twenty-one (21) days nor more than thirty (30) days after the date of the election at which the tie vote occurred.[28]

4.6   Alternative Method for Election. Under the 2008 amendments to the Condominium Act, a condominium association of ten (10) or fewer units may provide for an alternative method of electing members to the board of administration. The alternative method may provide for elections to be conducted by limited or general proxy, but whatever alternative voting and election procedures the community selects must be included in the bylaws of the condominium association.[29] Amendments to the bylaws adopting an alternative method of election must be approved by the affirmative vote of a majority of the total voting interests of the association. (See 9.5–9.9).

4.7   Eligibility. The bylaws of the association will specify and provide the eligibility requirements for the members of the board of administration.[30] Florida's law does not require individual board members to be members of the association to be eligible for election to the board, but most association bylaws do impose a membership requirement for eligibility. While bylaws may prohibit non-members from serving on the board of administration, they cannot prohibit a member desiring to be a candidate from qualifying with the secretary of the association and seeking election to the board, whether or not the member is a permanent resident. No individual who has been suspended or removed by the Division of Condominiums, Timeshares, and Mobile Homes,[31] no individual who is delinquent more than ninety (90) days in the payment of regular assessments,[32] and no individual convicted of a crime that is considered a felony under Florida law is eligible to serve as a member of the board of administration.[33]

When eligibility is limited to ownership and a unit is owned jointly,

---

[28] *Id.*

[29] § 718.112 (2)(d), F.S.

[30] § 718.112 (2)(a), F.S.

[31] § 718.501 (1)(d) 4., F.S.

[32] § 718.112 (2)(n), F.S.

[33] If civil rights have been restored for no less than five (5) years, a member convicted of a felony is eligible for election. § 718.112 (2)(d) 1., F.S.

only one of the owners is eligible to serve on the board at one time unless the owners own more than one unit or unless there are not enough eligible candidates to fill the vacancies on the board.[34] When a unit is owned by a corporation or another type of artificial person, determining the eligibility for a representative of the unit to serve on the board of administration presents a unique dilemma.

If the bylaws permit, the designated voting representative of the corporation may be eligible serve as a member of the board. If eligibility is contingent upon association membership, however, then the unit may be effectively excluded from offering a candidate for the board since a corporation cannot sit as a member of the board of administration.[35] When eligibility is contingent upon association membership, a person acting for a unit owner under a power of attorney would similarly be precluded from serving on the board.[36]

An exception to this eligibility standard is made when the condominium unit is owned by a trust. If a unit is owned by a trust and the grantors or beneficiaries of the trust occupy the condominium unit, then the occupants are considered members of the association and are eligible for service on the board of administration.[37]

Membership in the association passes with ownership of a condominium unit. When a unit is sold the membership in the association is also transferred to the new owner. When ownership is an eligibility requirement for service on the board, transfer of a unit will terminate the eligibility of an individual to serve on the board of administration and create a vacancy on the board at the time of sale.[38]

4.8   Term. Unless the association bylaws permit staggered terms of no more than two (2) years, all members of the board of administration serve for a one (1) year period and their terms will expire at the annual meeting of the association where their successors are elected. The law does not provide for term limits and board members may stand for reelection, but if no one seeks the position of a board member whose term is expiring, the board

---

[34] In an association of ten (10) or fewer units, both owners are eligible to serve on the board at the same time. The restriction does not apply to timeshare condominiums. § 718.112 (2)(d) 1., F.S.

[35] § 617.0802, F.S.

[36] § 61B-23.001 (5), F.A.C.

[37] § 617.0802 (2) and 607.0802 (2) F.S.

[38] § 617.041 (4), F.S.

member is automatically reappointed to the board of administration and does not need to stand for reelecton.[39]

Every association should consider the option of multiple-year terms. Staggered two-year terms are permitted and help assure continuity and experience on the board of administration. In order to allow for two-year staggered board terms, the authority must be provided in the association bylaws and the two-year terms must be approved by a majority of the total voting interests of the association.[40]

4.9   Number. The number of members on the board of administration must be fixed in the bylaws or in the articles of incorporation of the association, or these documents must state how the number will be set by the members of the association.[41] In the event that a specific number for the board is not established by one of these methods, then the board of administration shall consist of five (5) members. If the condominium has five (5) or fewer units, the board of administration may consist of as few as three (3) members.[42]

Documents in many condominium communities permit the members of the association to vary the number of members on the board of administration within certain limits. At the discretion of the community, this option in the documents allows the membership to select a size for the board that will maximize the representation of unit owners and the efficient operation of the condominium property.

When members of the community are given the opportunity to set the size of the board, consideration should appropriately be given to the type and number of buildings, the categories of unit owners, the overall size of the condominium community, and the length of board terms when selecting the number of board members that will best serve the community. It is important to remember that while the number on the board may be increased or decreased in the manner established in the bylaws, the term of a sitting member of the board of administration cannot be decreased or shortened by changing the number of board members.[43]

---

[39] § 718.112 (2)(d) 1. and § 617.0806, F.S.
[40] *Id.*
[41] § 617.0803 (1) and (2), F.S.
[42] § 718.112 (2)(a), F.S.
[43] § 617.0806, F.S.

4.10 Removal and Resignation. Under some circumstances, removal from the board of administration may be automatic as a result of changes in circumstance. For example, if eligibility for the board of administration is contingent upon membership in the association, a sale or transfer of the board member's unit will terminate the rights of membership, including the right to serve on the board. Removal from the board of administration would be automatic at the time of sale.[44] Likewise, if a member of the board of administration is convicted of a felony, charged with felony theft or embezzlement of association funds, or removed by the Division of Condominiums, Timeshares, and Mobile Homes, the right to continue to serve as a member of the board is terminated.[45] Also, when a director is more than ninety (90) days delinquent in the payment of any monetary obligation due to the association, he or she is deemed to have abandoned the office and removal is automatic, creating a vacancy on the board.[46]

Any new member of the board who is otherwise eligible to serve but fails to timely file with the secretary of the association the written certification that is required under the Condominium Act is suspended and is not eligible to return to board service until the certification requirement is met.[47] (See 4.7).

Removal may also occur by recall, and any member of the board of administration is subject to recall or removal at any time, with or without cause, by a vote, or an agreement in writing, by a majority of the voting interests of the association. A special meeting for a recall vote must be held when 10% of the voting interests in the community request the meeting and provide written notice to the other members of the meeting.[48] Electronic transmission of notice is not authorized for a special meeting when a recall vote is scheduled rule.[49]

If the recall is approved at the meeting, it is effective immediately upon concluding the recall vote. When the recall is made by written agreement of a majority of the voting interests, the written agreement or a copy of the written agreement must first be sent to the association by certified mail.

---

[44] § 617.0802, F.S.
[45] § 718.112 (2)(d) and (o) and § 718.501 (1)(d) 4., F.S.
[46] § 718.112 (2)(n), F.S.
[47] § 718.112 (2)(d) 3. b., F.S.
[48] § 61B-23.0027 (1) and (2), F.A.C.
[49] § 718.112 (2)(j) 2., F.S.

The board must call a meeting within five (5) business days of receiving the written agreement to certify the recall. The recall and removal is effective immediately upon certification by the board of administration.[50]

Notice of any meeting to recall a member of the board must be accompanied by a dated copy of the petition containing 10% of the voting interests. The list must state specifically that the purpose for the signatures is to recall a member or members of the board. The notice must state that the meeting is to recall one or more members of the board, list the name of each member sought to be recalled, and specify the person who will preside at the meeting. Where a majority or more of the board is sought to be recalled, the notice must also include a list of eligible persons willing to serve on the board.[51] When the actual vote is taken at the meeting, it must be decided on each board member that is subject to recall. The recall vote may not be taken on more than one board member at a time and a separate motion is required for each board member.[52]

If a vacancy occurs on the board as a result of a recall and less than a majority of the board is removed, the vacancy may be filled by a majority vote of the remaining board members. If vacancies occur on the board as a result of a recall and a majority or more of the board members are removed, the vacancies shall be filled by election at the recall meeting at which the vacancies are created. The voting interests may vote in person or by limited proxy for replacement board members to fill each vacancy.[53]

4.11   Failure to Fill Vacancies. Without a board of administration, the management and operation of the association would normally just cease. To avoid the complete paralysis in operation of a condominium association, the Condominium Act makes special provision for operating the association when vacancies on the board of administration are not filled. When an association fails to fill vacancies in sufficient numbers to constitute a quorum as required by the bylaws, any unit owner may apply to the Circuit Court for appointment of a receiver to continue the management of the affairs of the association.[54]

An owner seeking appointment of a receiver must use the form

---

[50] § 61B-23.0028 (3), F.A.C.
[51] § 61B-23.0027 (2)(b), F.A.C.
[52] § 61B-23.0027 (3)(d), F.A.C.
[53] § 61B-23.0027 (3)(e) 1. and 2., F.A.C.
[54] § 718.1124, F.S.

provided by the Act[55] and give thirty (30) days notice to all other owners by certified mail or personal delivery prior to filing suit by mailing notice and posting a copy in the community.[56] If the remaining owners do not take the thirty-day opportunity to fill the vacancies, the court may appoint the receiver to run the affairs of the condominium.

The expenses of the receivership, including the receiver's salary, court costs and attorney's fees become common expenses of the association and will be shared by all the owners.[57] The receiver will assume all of the authority that would otherwise be exercised by the board of administration, and the receivership will continue until a proper quorum of board members is elected.

4.12 Fiduciary Relationship. The members of the board of administration, each officer of the association, and any licensed manager employed by the association have a fiduciary relationship with the unit owners in the condominium.[58] This fiduciary relationship imposes obligations of trust and confidence in favor of the association and its members. It requires the members of the board and licensed managers to act in good faith and in the best interests of the unit owners.[59] It means that board members and managers must exercise due care and diligence when acting for the community, and it requires them to act within the scope of their authority.[60] It is not permissible for a member of the board or any officer or manager to accept anything of value from any person or company providing goods or services to the association. (See 5.10).

The fact that the association is a corporation not for profit, or that the members of the board are volunteers and unpaid, does not relieve them from the high standards of trust and responsibility that the fiduciary relationship requires.[61] When a member accepts a position on the board of administration, he or she is presumed to have knowledge of the duties and responsibilities of a board member. Board members cannot be excused from improper action on the grounds of ignorance or inexperience, and liability of board members

---

[55] § 718.1124 (1), F.S.
[56] § 718.1124 (2), F.S.
[57] § 718.1124 (5), F.S.
[58] § 718.111 (1)(a), F.S.; *B & J Holding Corp. v. Weiss,* 353 So. 141 (Fla. 3rd DCA 1977).
[59] § 718.111 (1)(d), F.S.
[60] *Flight Equipment & Engineering Corp. v. Shelton,* 103 So.2d 615, 626 (Fla. 1956); *Garcia v. Crescent Plaza Condominium Ass'n, Inc.,* 813 So.2d 925 (Fla. 2nd DCA 2002).
[61] § 617.0830, F.S.

for negligence and mismanagement exists in favor of the association and the unit owners.

Each board member must recognize the fiduciary relationship and the responsibilities that the board has to the condominium association and each of its members. Under the "business judgment rule," the board must act in a reasonable manner,[62] and its duties must be performed with the care and responsibility that an ordinarily prudent person would exercise under similar circumstances,[63] and the ultimate responsibilities cannot be delegated to a manager, a management company or other third party. Further, to be consistent with its fiduciary duty to unit owners, the board of administration must employ only a licensed community manager where licensure is required by Section 468.431, Florida Statutes.[64]

4.13 Bonding and Insurance. Florida's Condominium Act provides for two types of security for members of the board of administration. The first is the requirement that the association obtain and maintain insurance or fidelity bonding of all officers, board members and other individuals who control and disburse funds for the association. Those "persons who control and disburse funds of the association" include, but are not limited to, the individuals authorized to sign checks on behalf of the association and the president, secretary and treasurer of the association.[65]

The fidelity bond or insurance must be in an amount that covers the maximum funds that will be in the custody of the association or its management agent at any one time, and special attention should be given to increases in the bonding amount when the association receives insurance proceeds following a significant casualty loss involving the condominium property. The association assumes the responsibility for the costs of the required insurance or fidelity bonding as a common expense of the condominium.[66]

Each association is additionally required to use its best effort to obtain and maintain adequate insurance coverage to protect the condominium property, the association, the association property, and the common

---

[62] *Farrington v. Casa Solana Condominium Ass'n, Inc.,* 517 So.2d 70 (Fla. 3rd DCA 1987).

[63] *Sonny Boy, L.L.C. v. Bhagwan Asnani, et, al.,* 879 So.2d 25, 27 (Fla. 5th DCA 2004); *Garcia v. Crescent Plaza Condominium Ass'n, Inc.,* 813 So.2d 975 (Fla. 2nd DCA 2002).

[64] § 61B-23.001 (6), F.A.C.

[65] § 718.111 (11)(h). F.S.

[66] *Id.*

elements.[67] Part of the adequate insurance coverage should appropriately include officers' and directors' liability insurance for all members of the board of administration and all officers of the association. The liability coverage for officers and board members provides a basic protection for those who have volunteered to serve in these positions of responsibility.

This insurance also provides a general blanket of protection for the members of the association who may ultimately have to indemnify the actions of the board. The articles of incorporation for most associations extend the right of indemnification to each member of the board against expenses actually and reasonably incurred when defending actions taken by them in the course of their duties.[68] Since all of the unit owners are indemnifying the directors, the errors and omissions coverage protects each unit owner from the costs that may result when the board must defend its actions.

4.14 Meetings of the Board. Actions of the board take place at meetings of the board. A meeting of the board of administration includes any gathering of a quorum of the members for the purpose of conducting condominium business.[69] Meetings may be either a regular or special gathering, and they may be called by the chairman, the president, or any other persons who are authorized to do so by the bylaws of the association.[70] A "workshop" of the board is considered a meeting of the board. Unless the bylaws place a restriction on the place of the meeting, it may be held wherever the board finds it necessary. The place may include the offices of the association's attorney, accountant, manager or other location deemed appropriate by the board.

Florida's corporate law permits the board of administration to take action without a meeting if all of the board members consent to the action in writing. The written consent will have the same effect as if a unanimous vote had been taken at a meeting.[71] The Condominium Act, on the other hand, requires that meetings take place only after notice of the meeting has been given for the benefit of unit owners, except in cases of emergencies.[72] (See 10.15). The board should be guided by the priorities of the Condominium

---

[67] § 718.111 (11)(a) and (b), F.S.
[68] § 617.0831, F.S.
[69] § 61B-23.001 (1), F.A.C.
[70] § 617.0831, F.S.
[71] § 617.0821, F.S.
[72] § 718.112 (2)(c), F.S.

Act, and actions by written consent of the board should only be taken in emergency circumstances.

4.15 Quorum and Absent Board Members. A majority of the full board of administration shall be a quorum for the board unless a greater number is required in the association bylaws. A majority of that quorum has the authority to act for the full board on all matters, unless some extraordinary majority is required by the association bylaws for a particular item of business.[73] Each board member present at a meeting is presumed to have assented to actions taken at the meeting unless he or she votes against the action or abstains from voting because of a conflict of interest.[74] Members of the board who are not present at a meeting in any way may join the results of the meeting by signing the minutes to concur with actions taken.

In most cases, absent members are excluded from partial or complete participation in the meeting and cannot be counted for purposes of establishing a quorum at the meeting.[75] An absent member may participate in a meeting of the board of administration by telephone, however, and can be counted towards a quorum.

When an absent member of the board is attending by telephone, a telephone speaker must be used so that the discussion may be heard by all board members and any unit owners who are present at the open meeting. If these requirements can be met, the absent board member participating by telephone is counted for all purposes, including the determination of a quorum and on roll call votes taken at the meeting.[76]

4.16 Notice to Board Members. There are two types of notices which must be given before a proper meeting of the board of administration can be held. The first is for the individual members of the board and the second is for the general membership. The notice to members of the board can be made by first-class mail, by personal delivery, by telegram or electronic transmission and must be given at least two (2) days prior to the meeting itself.[77] The provisions of the association's bylaws may provide for different notice requirements and for longer or shorter periods of time. The use of electronic transmission to

---

[73] § 617.0824 (1), F.S.; *Berkowitz v. Firestone,* 192 So.2d 298 (Fla. 3rd DCA 1966).

[74] § 718.111 (1)(b), F.S.

[75] § 718.112 (2)(b) 4., F.S.

[76] § 718.112 (2)(b) 5., F.S.

[77] § 617.0822 (2), F.S.

provide notice must be specifically set forth in the bylaws.[78]

The bylaws may dispense with notice for regular meetings of the board, or they may provide for the waiver of notice by board members. Waiver must be by written consent or by actual attendance at the meeting.[79] Notice, or the waiver of notice, for members of the board of administration is often misunderstood or ignored. Good practice will dictate that proper notice be given for each meeting of the board or that a proper waiver of notice will be obtained. The notice or waiver should become part of the records of the association.

4.17 Notice to Association Members. With the exception of meetings where litigation is being discussed with the association's attorney, all board meetings of the association must be open to the members of the association, and members are entitled to notice of all meetings of the board. The requirement for open meetings extends not only to meetings of the board, but to all committees of the board and executive councils which are carrying out a portion of the association's responsibilities.[80] (See 5.16).

Unit owners may be excluded from a meeting of the board of administration or a committee of the board when the association's attorney is present for purposes of providing legal advice concerning proposed or pending litigation. Such meetings, although closed to unit owners, must still be properly noticed in the same manner as all other meetings of the board or committees of the association. The only business properly discussed in a closed meeting is that which relates directly to the legal advice being provided by the association's attorney.[81]

Except in cases of emergency or when longer notice is required by law, notice of board meetings must be conspicuously posted on the condominium property at least forty-eight (48) continuous hours in advance of each meeting.[82] If there is no condominium or association property upon which notices can be posted, notices of board meetings must be delivered to each unit owner at least fourteen (14) days before the meeting. The notice must specifically incorporate an identification of the agenda items to be considered at the meeting.

---

[78] § 718.112 (3)(c) 2., F.S.
[79] § 718.303 (2) and § 617.0823, F.S.
[80] § 617.0825 (2), F.S.
[81] § 718.112 (2)(c), F.S.
[82] *Id.*

The place on the condominium property where notices are to be posted for all meetings of the board and the membership is determined by the board of administration. Upon notice to the unit owners, the board must do so by adopting a rule designating the exact location for posting of notices.[83]

Broadcast notice of board meetings by closed-circuit cable television may be used in lieu of or in addition to the physical posting of notice. Broadcast notice may be implemented by board rule, and if the broadcast method is to be used in lieu of posting, the notice and agenda must appear at least four times every broadcast hour of each day that the notice would have otherwise been required to be posted rule.[84]

When a special assessment is to be considered by the board of administration or when amendments to the rules regarding unit use are to be considered, notice of the meeting must be posted fourteen (14) days prior to the meeting. Written notice must additionally be mailed or delivered to each unit owner not less than fourteen (14) days prior to the meeting.[85] In the case of a special assessment, the notice must contain an additional statement that the special assessment will be considered. The statement must describe the estimated costs and the purposes for the special assessment.[86] When the budget is to be considered by the board, the notice of the board meeting must also be mailed to all of the members of the association not less than fourteen (14) days prior to the meeting, and a copy of the budget must be included with the notice.[87]

The notice requirement for members of the association is sometimes referred to as the "sunshine law" for Florida's condominium associations.[88] It is designed to ensure that the business of the association will be done for the benefit of the association members and that it will be open to their scrutiny. They may tape record or videotape the meetings and participate with reference to all designated agenda items. (See 11.6).

4.18 Agenda for Board Meetings. The bylaws of most condominium associations establish a set agenda for the board of administration, or adopt

---

[83] § 718.112 (2)(c) and (d) 2., F.S.
[84] § 718.112 (2)(d) 2., F.S.
[85] § 718.112 (2)(c), F.S.
[86] § 718.116 (10), F.S.
[87] § 718.112 (2)(e), F.S.
[88] § 718.112 (2)(c), F.S.

the latest edition of Robert's Rules of Order as the rules of procedure that will govern board meetings. If no agenda is provided for in the bylaws, and if no rules have been adopted by the board for an agenda, Robert's Rules of Order lists the following agenda:[89]

1.   Reading of minutes of previous meeting.

2.   Reports of standing committees.

3.   Reports of special committees.

4.   Special business.

5.   Unfinished business.

6.   New business.

7.   Adjournment.

Any item of business that is not included on the notice of the board meeting may only be taken up on an emergency basis after its consideration has been approved by an extraordinary vote of the board of administration. The extraordinary vote required is a majority of the board plus one member.[90] An emergency action taken by the board in this manner shall be noticed for the next regular meeting of the board and ratified at that meeting.

If twenty percent (20%) or more of the voting interests the condominium association petition the board of administration to address an item of business, the item must be placed on the agenda for the next regular meeting of the board or on the agenda of a special meeting at which the item will be addressed. Under either alternative, the item must be considered by the board of administration within sixty (60) days of the receipt of the petitition.[91]

4.19 Meeting Procedures. Proper parliamentary rules of procedure are to be followed throughout the course of all business meetings, and attending unit owners must be allowed to speak with reference to all agenda items.[92] Proper minutes of each meeting must be kept for inclusion in the permanent records of the association,[93] and the vote or abstention of each

---

[89] *Robert's Rules of Order Newly Revised,* § 40.

[90] § 718.112 (2)(c), F.S.

[91] *Id.*

[92] § 718.112 (3)(c), F.S.

[93] § 617.1601 (1), F.S.

board member present must be recorded in the minutes.[94]

When deciding matters before the board, each member may rely on the advice of the association attorney, certified public accountant, or other professional advisor.[95] When a member of the board of administration has a financial interest in a decision being made at a meeting, the board member involved has an affirmative obligation to disclose the financial interest to the remaining board members.[96] Under such circumstances, the board member may additionally choose to abstain from voting on the matter in which he has an interest.

Board members may only vote by secret ballot to elect officers of the association, otherwise board members may not vote by proxy or by secret ballot at board meetings. Each member of the board shall be presumed to vote "yes" on any action taken by the board of administration unless the member specifically votes "no" or abstains from voting because of a conflict of interest.[97] This includes the association president when the president is also a member of the board. A member of the board of administration cannot abstain on reasons of general principle, and may do so only when a conflict of interest actually exists. The nature of the conflict and the reason for abstaining must be disclosed to the remaining members of the board and recorded in the minutes of the meeting.[98]

4.20 Membership Participation. Members of the association do not have any authority to act for the association by reason of being a member,[99] but membership participation at meetings of the board is a right of each unit owner.[100] (See 4.17). Participation includes the right to speak with reference to all designated agenda items, and the right to tape record or videotape all meetings of the board. (See 11.6). It is also the right of not less than twenty percent (20%) of the members of the association to petition the board to include an item of business on the agenda of the next regular or special meeting of the board of administration.[101]

---

[94] § 718.111 (1)(b), F.S.
[95] § 617.0830 (2), F.S.
[96] § 617.0832 (1), F.S.; *Avila South Condominium Ass'n, Inc. v. Kappa Corp.*, 347 So.2d 599, 607 (Fla. 1977).
[97] § 718.111 (1)(b) and § 617.0824 (4), F.S.
[98] § 718.111 (1)(b), F.S.
[99] § 718.111 (1)(c), F.S.
[100] § 718.112 (2)(c), F.S.
[101] *Id.*

The right of unit owners to speak at meetings is subject to reasonable rules adopted by the association governing the frequency, duration and manner of unit owner statements. (See 6.12). The right to tape record or videotape is subject to rules adopted by the Division of Florida Condominiums, Timeshares, and Mobile Homes.[102] Each member of the association has the right to inspect and copy records from the meeting after its adjournment, and to initiate a petition for recall of members of the board if dissatisfied with their actions.

4.21   Minutes and Records. A record of all meetings of the board of administration must be kept in written form or in a form that is capable of being converted to a written form.[103] The minutes are the presumed, prima facia record of all of the official actions taken at the meeting.[104] If an audio or video recording of a meeting is made by the board, the recording must be maintained until the minutes of the meeting have been approved by the board.[105] The board of administration also has custody of all the official records of the association, and the board must ensure that they are properly maintained and available for inspection by the membership.[106] The minutes of the membership meetings, meetings of the board of administration and most other records of the association must be maintained for a minimum period of seven (7) years.[107]

The official records of the association must be maintained within the state of Florida and be available within forty-five (45) miles of the condominium property or within the county where the condominium is located.[108] The records must be available to a unit owner within five (5) working days after receipt of a written request to inspect the records, and the right to inspect the association records includes the right to obtain copies, although the association may charge a reasonable fee for the reproduction.[109] The association is not responsible for the misuse of any records, copies, or

---

[102] § 718.112 (2)(c), F.S.; § 61B-23.002 (10), F.A.C.

[103] "Ordinarily, the minutes of the corporate meetings are prima facie evidence, and usually held to be the best evidence of what they purport to show as to the corporate business." *Gentry-Futch v. Gentry,* 90 Fla. 595, 609, 106 So. 473 (Fla. 1925).

[104] *Wimbledon Townhouse Condominium I, Ass'n, Inc. v. Wolfson,* 510 So.2d 1106, 1108 (Fla. 4th DCA 1987).

[105] § 61B-23.002 (5)(b) 6., F.A.C.

[106] § 61B-23.002 (9), F.A.C.; *Winter v. Playa del Sol, Inc.,* 353 So.2d 598, 599 (Fla. 4th DCA 1977).

[107] § 718.111 (12)(a) and (b), F.S.

[108] § 718.111 (12)(b), F.S.

[109] § 718.111 (12)(c), F.S.

other information provided under the requirements of the Condominium Act.[110] In making the records available to the unit owners, the association has the option to do so electronically via the Internet or by allowing the records to be viewed in electronic format on a computer screen and printed upon request.[111]

The failure of the association to provide the records within ten (10) working days to a unit owner requesting them in writing is presumed to be a willful failure by the association to comply with the law. If a unit owner provides the Division of Florida Condominiums, Timeshares, and Mobile Homes with proof that the association has failed to provide the records after two (2) written requests, the owner is entitled to have the Division issue a subpoena for the requested records.[112] The willful failure of the association to provide the records as required by the Act entitles the unit owner to recover both damages and costs from the association.[113]

The Condominium Act places a special priority on the proper care and custody of the records of the association, and the Act provides sanctions for persons who fail meet the standards in the law.[114] Any officer, board member, or other person who intentionally defaces or destroys accounting records of the association is personally subject to civil penalties that include fines and removal from office.[115] The Division is also obligated to refer to local law enforcement authorities those persons that the Division believes have altered or destroyed association records to impair an investigation by the Division.[116]

Certain records of the association are considered privileged, and the association may preclude their inspection by a unit owner. Privileged records include attorney-client communications and other documentation relating to pending or imminent litigation, computer passwords and proprietary software, employee personnel records, e-mail addresses, telephone numbers, emergency contact information, unit owner medical records, and information obtained in connection with the transfer of a unit. Social security numbers, driver's license numbers, credit card numbers, and

---

[110] § 718.111 (12)(b), F.S.
[111] § 718.111 (12)(b), F.S.
[112] § 718.501 (1)(d) 5., F.S.
[113] § 718.111 (12)(c), F.S.
[114] § 718.501 (1)(d) 4., F.S.
[115] § 718.111 (12)(a) 1 and (c), F.S.
[116] § 718.501 (1)(n), F.S.

other personal identifying information of any person in the custody of the association are also considered confidential and are not accessible by unit owners.[117]

One part of the association records that deserves special attention is the roster of owners.[118] The requirement to maintain it and to keep it current is overlooked by many boards, even though it is frequently used and required by the Condominium Act. Condominium documents that provide for approval of sales allow the board to remain current with all new owners. If the roster of owners has become out-dated, or if there is no approval process provided for new owners, a current list of unit owners is readily available in the office of the County Property Appraiser.[119]

---

[117] § 718.111 (12)(c) 1. and 7., F.S

[118] § 718.111 (12)(a) 7., F.S .

[119] § 119.011 (1) and § 193.085 (1), F.S.

WATERFRONT XX CONDOMINIUM ASSOCIATION, INC.
A Corporation Not-for-Profit

NOTICE OF MEETING

TO: Members of the Board of Administration
1.   Joseph Jones
2.   Ann Jones
3.   David Smith
4.   Marc Wesley
5.   Matthew Marshall

NOTICE IS HEREBY GIVEN that a meeting of the Board of Administration of Waterfront XX Condominium Association, Inc., will be held at the following date, time and place:

Date: January 16, 2011
Time: 9:00 a.m.
Place: Clubhouse
Waterfront XX Condominium
100 Waterfront Drive
Waterfront, Florida 33444

Dated: January 10, 2011

_____
Secretary

WATERFRONT XX CONDOMINIUM ASSOCIATION, INC.
A Corporation Not-for-Profit

WAIVER OF NOTICE OF MEETING
OF BOARD OF ADMINISTRATION

We, the undersigned, being all of the members of the Board of Administration hereby agree and consent to the meeting of the Board to be held on the date and time, and at the place designated hereunder, and do hereby waive all notice whatsoever of such meeting and of any adjournment, or adjournments, thereof.

We do further agree and consent that any and all lawful business may be transacted at such meeting, or at any adjournment or adjournments thereof, as may be deemed advisable by the Board present threat. Any business transacted at such meeting or at any adjournment or adjournments thereof, shall be as valid and legal and of the same force and effect as if such meeting, or adjourned meeting, were held after notice.

Date of Meeting: January 16, 2011

Time of Meeting: 9:00 a.m.

Place of Meeting: Clubhouse
Waterfront XX Condominium
100 Waterfront Drive
Waterfront, Florida 33444

Dated: January 10, 2011

_____   _____

Member, Board of Administration   Member, Board of Administration

_____   _____

Member, Board of Administration   Member, Board of Administration

_____

Member, Board of Administration

Waiver of Notice by Board Members   FORM 4.02

WATERFRONT XX CONDOMINIUM ASSOCIATION, INC.
A Corporation Not-for-Profit

NOTICE TO ASSOCIATION MEMBERS OF
MEETING OF BOARD OF ADMINISTRATION

NOTICE IS HEREBY GIVEN that a meeting of the Board of Administration of Waterfront XX Condominium Association, Inc. will be held at the following date, time and place:

Date of Meeting: January 16, 2011

Time of Meeting: 9:00 a.m.

Place of Meeting: Clubhouse,
                     Waterfront XX Condominium
                     100 Waterfront Drive
                     Waterfront, Florida 33444

Agenda: The order of business for the regular meeting of the Board of Administration shall be as follows:

1.   Reading of minutes of the previous meeting.

2.   Comment and discussion by unit owners.

3.   Report of Manager.

4.   Report of Officers.

5.   Unfinished business.
     a.   Matters relating to grounds and buildings.
     b.   Matters relating to conduct of unit owners.
     c.   Matters relating to association financial affairs.

6.   New business.

7.   Adjournment.

_____
Secretary

Dated: January 2, 2011

Notice of Board Meeting for Association Members FORM 4.03

WATERFRONT XX CONDOMINIUM ASSOCIATION, INC.
A Corporation Not-for-Profit

PROOF OF NOTICE AFFIDAVIT

STATE OF FLORIDA   )
COUNTY OF PINELLAS   )

Comes now the undersigned Secretary of Waterfront XX Condominium Association, Inc., being first duly sworn, deposes and says that said Secretary has posted or caused to be posted, conspicuously on the condominium property and has mailed or delivered or caused to be mailed or delivered written notice of the meeting of the Board of Administration to be held on January 16, 2011, not less than 14 days prior to said meeting.

Dated this 2nd day of January, 2011.

_____
Secretary

The foregoing Affidavit was acknowledged before me this 2nd day of January, 2011, by Nancy Thomas, the Secretary of Waterfront XX Condominium Association, Inc.

_____
Notary Public

My commission expires:

RESOLUTION BY THE BOARD OF ADMINISTRATION OF WATERFRONT XX CONDOMINIUM ASSOCIATION, INC., ESTABLISHING LOCATION FOR POSTING OF NOTICE FOR MEETINGS OF THE BOARD OF ADMINISTRATION AND MEETINGS OF THE MEMBERSHIP.

THAT WHEREAS, Section 718.112 (2)(d), Florida Statutes, requires the posting of notice conspicuously upon the condominium property for all meetings of the membership, and Section 718.112 (2)(c), Florida Statutes, requires posting of notice for all meetings of the board of administration where non-emergency special assessments or rules regarding unit use will be considered, and

WHEREAS, said provisions of the Florida Statutes requires the association to designate the location for the posting of such notices by a rule adopted by the board of Administration.

NOW THEREFORE BE IT RESOLVED by the Board of Administration of Waterfront XX Condominium Association, Inc., that the rule for the posting of notice conspicuously upon the condominium property be as follows:

1.   Notice for all meetings of the membership and all meetings of the board of administration where non-emergency special assessments or rules regarding the use of units will be considered shall be posted on the bulletin board in the front entrance hallway of the recreation building for not less than fourteen (14) continuous days prior to any such meeting.

2.   The Secretary of the Association shall be responsible for the posting of all required notices in the designated location.

Adopted by the Board of Administration this 5th day of January, 2011.

By:_____
        Secretary of the Association

Rule Designating Location for Meeting Notice FORM 4.05

WATERFRONT XX CONDOMINIUM ASSOCIATION, INC.
A Corporation Not-for-Profit

AGENDA FOR REGULAR MEETING
OF THE BOARD OF ADMINISTRATION

The order of business for the regular meeting of the Board of Administration shall be as follows:

1. Reading of minutes of the previous meeting.

2. Comment and discussion by unit owners on all matters to be considered by the Board.

3. Report of Manager.

4. Report of Officers.

5. Unfinished business.
   a) Matters relating to grounds and buildings.
   b) Matters relating to conduct of unit owners.
   c) Matters relating to association financial affairs.

6. New business.

7. Adjournment.

WATERFRONT XX CONDOMINIUM ASSOCIATION, INC.
A Corporation Not-for-Profit

WRITTEN ACTION BY THE
BOARD OF ADMINISTRATION

The Board of Administration of Waterfront XX Condominium Association, Inc., determining that an emergency exists, and, by unanimous written action, adopts the following resolutions:

1.   RESOLVED, that the windstorm damage caused to the roof of Building 100 be repaired immediately to prevent further damage to the interior of the building.

2.   RESOLVED, that the President of the Association be and is hereby authorized and directed to obtain three bids and to accept the lowest responsible bid for the purpose of commencing the repairs to the roof of Building 100.

3.   RESOLVED, that sufficient monies be made available from the reserve fund for the roof for the purpose of paying for the repair to Building 100.

4.   RESOLVED, that a special meeting of the Board of Administration be called, after proper notice has been given and posted for the benefit of all the members, for the purpose of reviewing these written actions of the Board of Administration and for discussing further the wind damage to the condominium.

DONE by unanimous written consent this 16th day of January, 2011.

_____   _____
Member, Board of Administration   Member, Board of Administration

_____   _____
Member, Board of Administration   Member, Board of Administration

_____
Member, Board of Administration

Written Action by Board Members   FORM 4.07

WATERFRONT XX CONDOMINIUM ASSOCIATION, INC.
A Corporation Not-for-Profit

MINUTES OF MEETING OF THE
BOARD OF ADMINISTRATION

The meeting of the Board of Administration was held on the date, time and at the place set forth in the notice of meeting fixing such time and place, and attached to the minutes of this meeting. Notice of the meeting was posted on the bulletin board in the Clubhouse forty-eight (48) hours prior to the meeting.

There were present the following:

Joseph Jones	David Smith
Ann Jones	Peter Johnson
Matthew Marshall	

being all the members of the Board of Administration.

After the meeting was called to order, a motion was made, seconded and unanimously adopted waiving the reading of the minutes from the previous meeting. The President then declared that the floor was open for comment and discussion by any unit owner on any subject that was to be considered by the Board, or on any other subject concerning the condominium.

Mr. Wesley, owner of Unit 105, addressed the Board regarding safety in the swimming area. The President advised that the Board would review the matter in more detail. Mrs. Jones, the owner of Unit 101, next addressed the Board on the speed of vehicles passing along the main entrance road to the community. The President directed that the manager notify the city and request that the roadway area be more closely patrolled.

At the conclusion of comments by unit owners, the President called upon the property manager. The manager presented a report on the bids for insurance for the coming year and recommended that the lowest bid be accepted. Upon a motion duly made, seconded, and unanimously carried, it was

RESOLVED, that the bid of the Florida Insurance Company, being the lowest bid, be accepted, and that they be directed to provide the insurance for the condominium for the next calendar year.

The President stated that there were no reports of officers and no unfinished business. The President then asked if there was any new business to come before the meeting. There being no new business, and upon a motion duly made, seconded and unanimously carried, the President declared the same adjourned.

Dated: _____   _____
                                                        Secretary

OFFICIAL RECORDS LIST

1. Copy of the plans, permits, warranties and other items provided by the developer at the time of transition.

2. Recorded copy of Declaration of Condominium and all amendments.

3. Certified copy of the Articles of Incorporation of the Association and all amendments.

4. Recorded copy of the Association Bylaws and all amendments.

5. Copy of all current Rules and Regulations, Policy Statements and Resolutions of Procedure.

6. Book of Minutes for all meetings of the board of administration and of the membership for at least seven (7) years.

7. Roster of all unit owners, their mailing addresses, unit identification, voting certificates, and, if known, telephone numbers. (Records shall also include the e-mail addresses and fax numbers of unit owners electing to receive notice by electronic transmission.)

8. All current insurance policies for the Association and for all condominiums operated by the Association.

9. Management agreement, lease agreements and other contracts under which the Association is responsible.

10. Bills of sale, deeds, easements and other recorded documents.

11. ballots, sign-in sheets and other papers relating to elections, which shall be maintained for one (1) year from the date of the meeting to which the documents relate.

12. Accounting records for the Association, and separate accounting records for each condominium operated by the Association. The accounting records shall be maintained for at least seven (7) years and shall include, but are not limited to:

    (a)   Itemized, detailed records of all receipts and expenditures;

    (b)   A current accounting for each unit owner, with assessment amount, the amount paid and the balance due;

    (c)   All audits, reviews, accounting statements and financial reports of the Association and the condominium(s);

(d)   All contracts for work to be performed for the Association (bids shall also be considered official records and shall be kept for at least one year).

13. Budget and annual financial report to Association membership.

14. All rental records, when the Association serves as the rental agent for the condominium units.

15. A copy of the current "Frequently Asked Questions and Answers" summary.

16. A copy of the building inspection report.

17. Written certifications of new board members.

18. All other records of the Association which are related to the operation of the Association.

WATERFRONT XX CONDOMINIUM ASSOCIATION, INC.
A Corporation Not-for-Profit

RECALL PETITION

The undersigned members of WATERFRONT XX CONDO-MINIUM ASSOCIATION, INC., do hereby petition and demand that Matthew Marshall be recalled as a member of the Board of Administration of the Association in accordance with the provisions of Section 718.112 (2) (k), Florida Statutes, and do further demand that a membership meeting be called for the purposes of allowing for a vote upon the recall. If such vote is successful, to further allow for the election of a new member to the Board of Administration to replace Matthew Marshall.

The undersigned members have selected Marc Wesley, 105 Waterfront Drive, Waterfront, Florida 33444, to receive pleadings, notices or other papers on behalf of the petitioning unit owners in the event that the vote at the meeting is disputed and a petition for arbitration is filed.

Unit 101   **Unit 201**

Owner   Date   Owner   Date

Owner   Date   Owner   Date

Unit 102   **Unit 202**

Owner   Date   Owner   Date

Owner   Date   Owner   Date

Unit 103   **Unit 203**

Owner   Date   Owner   Date

Owner   Date   Owner   Date

Recall Petition   FORM 4.10

BOARD MEMBER CERTIFICATION

I, _____(print name of board member), certify that I have read the association's declaration of condominium, articles of incorporation, bylaws, and current written policies; that I will work to uphold such documents and policies to the best of my ability; and that I will faithfully discharge my fiduciary responsibility to the association's members.

Signed:_____(signature of board member)

Date:_____

5

Officers and Committees

OFFICER AND COMMITTEE FORMS

5.1 General. The condominium association can only carry out acts through its officers and agents. The board of administration makes the policies for the association but the officers and agents carry out these policies and administrative functions for the condominium community.[1] Some of the officers are merely clerical or ministerial, while others carry out substantive functions based on the policies established by the board. All of the officers have an affirmative obligation to act with utmost good faith towards the association with the care of an ordinarily prudent person,[2] and officers cannot deal in the funds or the property of the association to their own advantage or personally solicit or accept any item or service of value.[3]

Each condominium association must have a president, secretary and treasurer.[4] Unless the bylaws otherwise prohibit additional appointments, the board of administration may also appoint other officers and outline their duties and responsibilities.[5] Collectively, the officers will perform the duties established in the bylaws and carry out the management responsibilities of the corporation under the policies approved by the board of administration.

5.2 Election of Officers. The officers of the association are elected, or appointed, by the board of administration. They are not elected by the membership of the association unless the bylaws of the association specifically require a membership vote for a particular office.[6] Except in rare circumstances, the only officers that will be elected by the full membership are those individuals that are selected to serve as chairman of a membership meeting, or those who are selected as inspectors of elections to tabulate the ballots at membership meetings.

The remaining officers of the association are selected by the board of administration at the time, place and in the manner set forth in the bylaws. Like all meetings of the board of administration, the meeting of the board at which the selection of officers is made must be open to members of the association, however, board members are permitted to elect association

---

[1] "(T)he officers exercise the power of management under the policies and directives of the board of directors." *Flight Equipment & Engineering Corp. v. Shelton,* 103 So.2d 615, 623 (Fla. 1958).

[2] § 718.111 (1)(d), F.S

[3] § 718.111 (1)(a), F.S.; *B & J Holding Corp. v. Weiss,* 353 So.2d 141, 143 (Fla. 3rd DCA 1977).

[4] § 718.112 (2)(a), F.S.

[5] § 617.0804 (1), F.S.

[6] § 718.112 (2)(a) and § 617.0840 (1), F.S.

officers by secret ballot.[7] A majority vote of the whole board is generally required for election. In most circumstances, the election will take place at the annual or organizational meeting of the board. When a vacancy occurs in an office of the association, the successor may be elected or appointed at any subsequent meeting of the board of administration.[8]

5.3   President. The president of the association is vested with all the powers generally given to the chief executive officer of a corporation. While specific bylaw provisions may vary the president's duties, it is generally presumed that he will preside at all meetings of the board and the membership.[9] He will execute contracts and other documents in the name of the association as its agent. When signing documents, the president should indicate the capacity in which he is signing to avoid any personal liability since his signature, under most circumstances, will bind the association under a doctrine of inherent powers.

The president also assumes general charge of the day-to-day administration of the association and has the authority to authorize specific actions in furtherance of the board's policies. As chief executive officer, the president serves as spokesman for the board of administration in most matters relating to general association business.[10] Like all officers of the association, the president has an affirmative duty to carry out the responsibilities of the office in the best interests of the association.[11] The president serves at the will of the board of administration and can be removed with or without cause at any time by majority vote of the full board.

The president cannot, without specific board approval, borrow funds in the name of the association or otherwise act beyond the scope of the authority established by the condominium documents and board. The president does have the inherent authority to appoint committees to advise him and to advise the board. (See 5.14). The president also has the authority to appoint certain officers to assist him with his duties such as vote tellers, inspectors of elections, sergeants at arms, and a temporary secretary or

---

[7] § 718.111 (1)(b), F.S.

[8] § 718.112 (2)(a) 1., and § 617.0840 (1), F.S.

[9] *Robert's Rules of Order Newly Revised*, § 46.

[10] § 718.112 (2)(a), F.S.

[11] § 718.111 (1)(d), F.S

recorder unless the bylaws otherwise make some provision for selection of these positions.[12]

5.4   Secretary. The secretary is customarily responsible for keeping and maintaining a record of all meetings of the board and the membership and is the custodian for most of the official records of the association.[13] The position of secretary is not simply a clerical position, however. In many cases, the secretary will not actually keep the minutes of the meetings, but will be responsible for obtaining someone who will do so as a recorder or assistant secretary. As the custodian of the minutes and the other official records of the association, the secretary is responsible for insuring access to those records by the owners and their authorized representatives.[14]

Unless the community documents otherwise provide, the secretary will be in charge of giving all of the required notices to both the board and association members in accordance with the documents of the community and Florida's Condominium Act. As the custodian of the records, the association secretary may also be responsible for filing the annual reports with the Division of Florida Condominiums, Timeshares, and Mobile Homes and with Florida's Division of Corporations.

The secretary of the association is the designated custodian of the "corporate seal." The seal must contain the words "corporation not for profit," but there is no other required content for the seal. The board should adopt a format for it and when executing an instrument on behalf of the association, the seal must be used.[15] Under most circumstances, the signature of the president will bind the corporation, and the secretary, as custodian of the seal, traditionally verifies the president's authority by also signing or attesting to the president's signature and placing the corporate seal on the appropriate document.

5.5   Treasurer. The treasurer is the custodian of the funds, securities and financial records of the association. When the association has a manager or other employee that actually handles the funds, then the treasurer's duties will include overseeing the appropriate employees to insure that the financial records and reports are properly kept and maintained. Unless the bylaws otherwise specify, the treasurer is responsible for coordinating the

---

[12] § 617.0840 (2), F.S.
[13] § 617.0840 (3) and § 617.0841, F.S.
[14] § 718.111 (12), F.S.
[15] § 617.0302 (3), F.S.

development of the proposed annual budget and for preparing and giving the annual financial report. (See 7.14). The annual financial report must be provided at the end of each fiscal or calendar year and will cover the preceding twelve (12) months of the association's activities. Copies of the report must be maintained by the association and be available to both unit owners and prospective purchasers.[16]

The treasurer does not have the authority to bind the association or the board when dealing with third parties unless the board has provided express authority for the treasurer to do so.[17] As with the association's secretary, the treasurer does not have to actually perform the day to day record keeping functions of the association, but the treasurer will ultimately be responsible to make sure that the financial records of the association have been maintained properly in accordance with good accounting practices.

5.6   Vice President. The vice president of the association is vested with all of the powers which are required to perform the duties of the association president in the absence of the president. The vice president does not automatically possess inherent powers to act in the capacity of chief executive, and may act for the president only when the president is actually absent or otherwise unable to act. The vice president may assume such additional duties as are defined by the board of administration.[18]

In many communities the vice president will be assigned specific areas of responsibility which may include the grounds and buildings, the recreational properties, or other association activities. The vice president may also be designated to serve as the executive director or the employee manager for the association. Each of these duties must be specifically conveyed by the board of administration upon the vice president, and the scope of this authority and responsibility should be defined in writing and placed in the minutes or in the bylaws of the association.

5.7   Registered Agent and Office. The registered agent is a ministerial officer of the association and it is an officer that is required of all corporations in Florida. In addition to naming a registered agent, each corporation must also maintain a registered office for the association, although it does not need to be the same as the corporation's place of business.[19] The registered

---

[16] § 718.111 (13), F.S.
[17] *Ideal Foods, Inc. v. Action Leasing Corp.,* 413 So.2d 416, 417 (Fla. 5th DCA 1982).
[18] § 718.112 (2)(a) and § 617.0841, F.S.
[19] § 617.0501, F.S.

agent receives all formal service of legal papers on behalf of the association, including all lawsuits.

The registered agent is an important link for the association since many formal and important communications will be received by this association officer.[20] When these communications or documents are received, they must be brought immediately to the attention of the board of administration. The registered agent must be aware of the responsibilities of the office, and the board of administration may desire to assign this responsibility to a member of the current board or to the association's legal counsel.

The name of the registered agent and the street address of the registered office can be changed by the board of administration at any time by simply filing written notice with the Division of Corporations. The address for the registered office of the association must be a street address. A post office box is not acceptable. The new registered agent must sign the change in designation, acknowledging and accepting the responsibilities of the position.[21]

5.8   Other Officers. Unless prohibited in the bylaws, the board of administration may appoint other officers and grant to them duties and responsibilities that the board feels are appropriate.[22] Other officers may include an assistant secretary, additional vice presidents or other positions which will serve merely as agents to carry out specific association responsibilities. These other officers will help divide the responsibilities of the association into manageable categories, and each office can be assigned specific authority by the board of administration to carry out the assigned duties and responsibilities.

The responsibilities of supplemental association officers may include the authority to sign liens, demand letters, and checks for the association. They may include the authority to manage the day-to-day maintenance responsibilities for the condominium or other specific activities sanctioned by the board. Custom allows third parties to rely on agents and officers of the association. A commitment made in the normal course of business by agents and officers may bind the corporation.[23] When creating additional officers, the board should specify, in writing, the scope of authority for the

---

[20] § 617.0503 and § 617.0504, F.S.
[21] § 617.0502, F.S.
[22] § 718.112 (2)(a) and § 617.0841, F.S.
[23] *Edward J. Gerrits, Inc. v. McKinney,* 410 So.2d 542, 545 (Fla. 1st DCA 1982).

office and the specific duties and responsibilities of the officer. The limits imposed upon the officer's authority should also be expressed.

5.9   Eligibility and Removal. Unless the bylaws of the association mandate otherwise, an officer of the association is not required to be a member of the association, a member of the board, a unit owner or an employee of the association. Traditionally, the president, vice president, secretary and treasurer are members of both the association and the board, but their association membership is not required by law. An individual is also eligible to hold more than one office in the association at one time.[24]

Officers of the association serve at the pleasure of the board of administration unless the bylaws provide for specific terms of office or conditions for removal from the office.[25] If the officer serves at the pleasure of the board, removal of the officer can be done with or without cause when the board feels it is in the best interest of the association.[26] Once the vacancy occurs, the board of administration may fill the vacant office immediately.[27] When an officer or an agent is elected by the members, however, the officer cannot be removed by the board of administration and must be removed by the membership.

Removal of an officer may also result for other reasons. An officer who is more than ninety (90) days delinquent in the payment of any monetary obligation due to the association is deemed to have abandoned the office, creating a vacancy in the position.[28] The Division of Florida Condominiums, Timeshares, and Mobile Homes may remove an individual as an officer of the association for violation of the Condominium Act,[29] and an officer charged with a felony theft or embezzlement offense involving funds of the association is automatically removed, creating a vacancy in the office.[30]

5.10 Fiduciary Relationship, Indemnification and Insurance. Officers and directors of the association must devote enough time and effort to the performance of their duties to ensure that they are reasonably and faithfully carried out on behalf of the association. Officers are presumed

---

[24] § 617.0840 (4), F.S.
[25] § 718.112 (2)(a), F.S.
[26] § 617.0840 (2), F.S.
[27] § 617.0842 (1), F.S.
[28] § 718.112 (2)(n), F.S.
[29] § 718.501 (1)(d) 4., F.S.
[30] § 718.112 (2)(o), F.S

to know the duties and responsibilities of the office they are assuming, and they have an affirmative fiduciary responsibility to the members of the association in the same manner as the members of the board.[31] Directors and Officers who control and disburse funds are also required to be bonded. (See 4.13).

Officers and directors must avoid conduct which will result in private or personal gain from their position and they must restrict themselves to the scope of the duties assigned to them.[32] An officer may be liable to the association members for breaches in trust, fraud or negligence,[33] and he or she may be subject to removal from office and other civil penalties imposed by the Division of Florida Condominiums, Timeshares, and Mobile Homes for a willful and knowing violation of the Act or a rule of the Division.[34] In determining whether an officer or board member has willfully and knowingly violated a portion of the Act or a rule or order of the Division, the Division considers: (1) whether the individual sought and followed professional advice;[35] (2) whether a previous order has been entered against the association concerning the subject matter; (3) whether the individual failed to follow a written statement of the Division; and (4) the relative complexity of the facts and law involved in the matter.[36]

It is unlawful for any officer, board member, or manager employed by the association to solicit or accept any thing or service of value from any person or company providing or seeking to provide goods or services to the association. Any officer who accepts a prohibited gift or gratuity is subject to a civil penalty imposed by the Division.[37] Services and items received in connection with trade fairs or education programs by an officer, board member or manager, however, are permissible.[38]

When officers and directors are properly carrying out their duties within the scope of responsibility assigned to them, they may be indemnified by the association and its members when claims or suits are brought against

---

[31] § 718.111 (1)(a), F.S.; *B & J Holding Corp. v. Weiss, supra* note 3.
[32] *Sonny Boy, L.L.C. v. Bhagwan Asnani, et, al.,* 879 So.2d 25, 27 (Fla. 5th DCA 2004).
[33] § 718.111 (1)(d), F.S
[34] § 718.501 (1)(d), F.S.
[35] *Farrington v. Casa Solana Condominium Ass'n, Inc.,* 517 So2d 70,71 (Fla. 3rd DCA 1987).
[36] § 61B-23.0025, F.A.C.
[37] § 718.501 (1)(d), F.S.
[38] § 718.111 (1)(a), F.S.

them for their actions.[39] To protect the officers and the membership which they serve, the board should maintain "errors and omissions" insurance coverage on each officer and director. The board must also maintain the required insurance or fidelity bonding for all persons who control and disburse the funds of the association.[40] (See 4.13).

5.11   Compensation. The directors and officers of the association are not entitled to compensation for their services unless the bylaws of the association specifically permit the compensation to be paid.[41] If compensation is allowed by the bylaws, the conditions for compensation should be strictly followed. Directors and officers should not be allowed to fix or increase their salaries unless expressly authorized to do so by the articles of incorporation or the bylaws of the association.

Since the condominium manager or other agent may be considered an officer of the association, it is important to review the bylaws and the articles of incorporation for authority to employ and compensate a manager and other individuals who serve as agents on the association's behalf. Although compensation may not be allowed to most officers, they are entitled to reimbursement for reasonable expenses incurred in the performance of their duties. The board of administration should require a specific accounting for such expenses before any reimbursement is made.

5.12   Committees. The use of committees is an effective way to conduct portions of the association's business. Whether a committee is a permanent standing committee, or a temporary advisory group, committees have the ability to provide additional assistance, recommendations and information for the association's use and benefit.[42] The committees of the association can be placed in one of two categories. The first category is one where the committees are purely advisory and do not make budget recommendations or have no authority to actually carry out specific functions. These advisory committees help analyze problems, review facts, gather information and alternatives, and submit their conclusions as recommendations to the board or the president of the association.

---

[39] § 617.0831, F.S.
[40] § 718.111 (11)(d), F.S.
[41] § 718.112 (2)(a), F.S.
[42] § 718.103 (7), F.S.

The second category of committees is one in which the committee is vested with authority to carry out, or to exercise a portion of the board of administration's responsibility. An executive committee is the most common example of this second type of committee. There are limits on the type of power which may be conferred upon such a committee of the board. For a committee to have the authority to act and carry out duties, the committee must be created by the articles of incorporation, the bylaws of the association or by a resolution which is adopted by a majority of the full board of administration.[43]

Committees created under the articles of incorporation or the bylaws of the association will have specified duties and functions. When a committee is created by resolution of the board of administration, the board must also identify in the resolution the amount of authority being given to the committee and the limits on the duties and functions which can actually be performed by it. The well-planned use of committees by the board, whether they are created by the documents or by the board itself, can contribute significantly to the entire community.

5.13 Nominating Committee. The board of administration is not permitted to create or appoint a committee for the purpose of nominating candidates to the board of administration.[44] The board may, however, appoint a search committee to identify potential candidates even though the committee cannot nominate individuals and the candidates must qualify themselves.

The documents in many communities create a nominating committee to screen and recommend candidates for election to the board, but 1991 revisions to the Condominium Act made the role of the nominating committee of limited value. Each interested member must give written notice of his or her candidacy to the association secretary not less than forty (40) days prior to election.[45] (See 4.4). The law makes no provision for a committee or another unit owner to nominate a candidate for the board unless the candidate further complies with the written notice requirement.[46] Accordingly, a nominating committee established by the bylaws serves

---

[43] § 617.0825 (1), F.S.
[44] § 61B-23.0021 (3), F.A.C.
[45] § 718.112 (2)(d) 3., F.S.
[46] § 718.112 (2)(d) 1., F.S.

only to recruit candidates and encourage them to file their written notice of candidacy, or to endorse candidates from among those who do file their written notices with the secretary.

5.14   Committee Appointments. When a committee is granted the authority to exercise a portion of the duties normally exercised by the board of administration, the committee must be appointed by a majority of the full board. The appointed members of the committee must come from the board itself. Individuals not serving on the board may not serve as a member of a committee where substantive authority is being exercised as an extension of the board of administration.[47] The appointments for such committees must be made at a duly called meeting of the board and recorded in the written minutes of the meeting.

Advisory and fact finding committees may be appointed either by an officer of the association, traditionally the president, or by the board of administration. In some circumstances, the bylaws of the association impose additional restrictions and they should be consulted. Advisory committees have no power to act for the board or to bind the association. They are not necessarily created by formal provisions in the community's documents or by resolution of the board. Although formal written authority is not required for the advisory committee appointments, the better practice is to do so by written resolution of the board or by letter of authority by the appointing officer.

5.15   Committee Authority. The board has the power to appoint committees and to give them authority. The authority of the board to delegate powers to committees is not unlimited, however. The authority of a committee is restricted by the limits placed upon it by the articles of incorporation, the bylaws and the resolution adopted by the board of administration creating the committee.[48] When a committee is created by resolution of the board, the resolution should specifically express the powers being delegated and the limits on that power. The resolution should be in writing, although the lack of a written resolution will not destroy the effectiveness of the committee under most circumstances.

Advisory committees do not have the authority to act for or to bind the association in any way. Advisory committees are limited to fact

[47] § 617.0825, F.S.
[48] *Id.*

finding, information gathering and to making recommendations to the appointing authority. The function and tenor of advisory committees should be documented in writing but the failure to do so does not jeopardize their creation. These committees help to ease the responsibilities of the board of administration but they cannot replace it.

The fact that the board creates a committee and conveys to it powers and duties, does not relieve the board of administration and the individual members of the board of their ultimate fiduciary responsibility. They must ensure that the operations of the association are carried out in the best interest of the unit owners,[49] and ultimately they are responsible for all of the acts of the committees that they create.

5.16 Committee Meetings and Minutes. All committees of the association, whether advisory or exercising substantive authority, are open to the members of the association. The only exception to this open meeting requirement is when the meeting has the association's attorney present to provide advice concerning proposed or pending litigation. (See 4.17). As a matter of good practice, all rights and privileges extended to unit owners at meetings of the board should also be extended to owners at all committee meetings.

Meetings of a committee to take final action on behalf of the board or to make recommendations to the board regarding the association's budget must comply fully with the notice requirements established for meetings of the board of administration. (See 4.16 and 4.17). This will include notice or waiver of notice by members of the committee, and the posting of notice at least forty-eight (48) hours in advance of committee meetings for the benefit of association members. Meetings of committees that do not take final action on behalf of the board or make budget recommendations to the board may be exempted from these formal notice requirements when the bylaws of the association permit such exemptions.[50]

When the committee is advisory in nature, a formal record of the proceedings does not need to be maintained. A summary of the findings of fact or the recommendations will be sufficient and the summary will be submitted as the committee's report to the appointing authority. If the committee has substantive authority and is carrying out a portion of the

---

[49] § 617.0825 (4), F.S.
[50] § 718.112 (2)(c), F.S.

responsibilities of the board, a formal record of each meeting must be kept in the same way as the board itself maintains a record of its proceedings. As a general rule, any committee exercising authority of the board should be guided by all of the same procedural requirements that govern the board, including the right of unit owners to speak with reference to all items of business.[51]

5.17   Committee Reports. A summary of a committee's findings, conclusions and recommendations may be brought to the board or the membership either orally or in written form. It is preferable that the committee's report be in writing and that it be addressed to the secretary of the association. A synopsis of an oral report should be included in the minutes of the meeting at which the report is presented.

Upon receipt of a committee report, the meeting may accept and implement the recommendations, it may modify and change the recommendations, or, finally, it may simply accept them and place them in the records of the association for future action and reference.

When the report of a committee has been received at a meeting of the board of administration or of the membership, it becomes a part of the permanent association records. Like other official records of the association, committee reports are open for inspection by unit owners or their representatives at all reasonable times and the owners may obtain copies of the reports.[52]

5.18   Special Councils. Many communities have special purpose bodies which serve a unique or special function tailored to the individual community. A "council of presidents" or a "commons council" is an example of a special purpose committee. These councils are established when a community has many associations and needs a coordinated scheme of management for the entire community. A special management council may balance representation among buildings or among various geographical parts of a community to ensure participation by the entire community.

Special councils may also be established for other purposes, such

---

[51] § 617.0825 (2) and § 718.112 (2)(c), F.S.
[52] § 718.111 (12), F.S.

as providing security for the community, or establishing a communications network in the condominium. A network of floor or building representatives establishes a loose network, or committee, where members may rarely, if ever, actually meet as a group. These special councils or committees are, in many cases, carrying out limited special functions on behalf of the board of administration and it is appropriate to recognize these functions and duties by formal written resolution by the governing board.

5.19   Social Clubs. Recreation committees, bridge clubs, and other types of social organizations are normally not thought of as a committee, nor as a formal part of the association's structure. If these clubs are exercising authority over a specific recreational function, if they are raising and spending funds, or if they are using common facilities with the approval of the board, their acts may be considered a part of the association activities. Social clubs or recreational committees serve a valid function for an association and should not be discouraged, but they must be handled properly within the association's framework.

The fact that social clubs may take on certain powers allowing them to make limited financial commitments on behalf of the community, or to perform certain functions which may make them liable for negligence or injury occurring in the course of their events, necessitates that the board deal with them as part of the association structure. When a social club or committee assumes a permanent and regular presence in the community, the board should be prepared to confirm the presence in resolution form. Proper financial accountability and adequate insurance coverage for club activities are responsibilities of the association.

ACCEPTANCE OF APPOINTMENT OF REGISTERED AGENT AND DESIGNATION OF REGISTERED OFFICE

Pursuant to the provisions of Section 617.0501 and 617.0502, Florida Statutes, Waterfront XX Condominium Association, Inc., organized under the laws of the State of Florida, submits this statement for the purpose of changing its registered office and registered agent in the State of Florida as authorized by a resolution duly adopted by the Board of Administration on the 10th day of January, 2011, to the following:

JOSEPH JONES
101 Waterfront Drive
Waterfront, Florida 33444

Date: _____   _____
                                               Secretary

ACKNOWLEDGMENT

Having been named to accept service of process for the above stated corporation, at the place designated in this certificate, I hereby accept to act in this capacity, and agree to comply with the provisions of the law relative to keeping open said office.

Date: _____   _____
                                               Registered Agent

WATERFRONT XX CONDOMINIUM ASSOCIATION, INC.
A Corporation Not-for-Profit

A RESOLUTION OF THE BOARD OF ADMINISTRATION CREATING A COMMITTEE OF THE BOARD TO SELECT AND RECOMMEND A MANAGER FOR THE CONDOMINIUM.

BE IT HEREBY RESOLVED by the Board of Administration of Waterfront XX Condominium Association, Inc., as follows:

Section 1.   THAT a committee for the selection of a manager of the condominium is hereby created, and Joseph A. Jones, Nancy Thomas and David Smith are appointed to serve as members of the committee. Nancy Thomas shall serve as the chairman of the committee.

Section 2.   THAT the committee shall have the authority to expend up to $500.00 in costs for advertisements and other related expenses in recruiting potential candidates for the position of manager.

Section 3.   THAT the committee shall have the authority to investigate and interview candidates on behalf of the board of administration, and shall select from the candidates the three individuals which the committee feels are best qualified to fill the position of manager, and shall recommend them, in order of preference, to the full board of administration prior to the next regular quarterly meeting.

Section 4.   THAT the committee shall not be authorized to hire any individual for the position of manager or otherwise expend, or commit to expend, any funds of the Association except as specifically authorized by this resolution.

ADOPTED by the Board of Administration this 10th day of January, 2011.

(CORPORATE SEAL)   WATERFRONT XX CONDOMINIUM
                          ASSOCIATION, INC.

ATTEST:

_____   By: _____
Secretary   President

WATERFRONT XX CONDOMINIUM ASSOCIATION, INC.
A Corporation Not-for-Profit

DECLARATION OF THE PRESIDENT

COMES NOW, Peter Johnson, President of Waterfront XX Condominium Association, Inc., and does hereby exercise the authority granted in the bylaws of the association and does state and declare as follows:

1.   THAT, there is created a bylaw committee to study and evaluate the recent amendments to the Condominium Act, and to make a review of the bylaws of the Condominium Association.

2.   THAT, the membership for the committee shall consist of Matthew Marshall, Marc Wesley and Sara Harris. Sara Harris is hereby designated to serve as chairman of the committee.

3.   THAT, the committee shall make recommendations for proposed amendments to the bylaws which govern the condominium community, and shall advise the President on any amendments to the law which may require changes to the policies and procedures of the Condominium Association.

4.   THAT, the committee shall not have the authority to act for, or to bind the Association, nor shall it have the authority to expend any funds of the Association. The existence of the committee shall terminate upon submitting its final report to the President.

DONE this 10th day of January, 2011.

By:_____
    President

Executive Declaration Creating Committee Form 5.03

WATERFRONT XX CONDOMINIUM ASSOCIATION, INC.
A Corporation Not-for-Profit

REPORT OF THE SPECIAL BYLAW COMMITTEE

TO: President And Members Of The Board Of Administration, Waterfront XX Condominium Association, Inc.

FROM: Special Bylaw Committee, By Appointment Of The President, January 10, 2011

The special bylaw committee met on three (3) occasions, after posting notice forty-eight (48) hours in advance of each meeting, to evaluate the amendments to the Condominium Act and to consider amendments to the Association's bylaws. As a result of the committee's study, the following changes are recommended:

1.   The Association establish a standing committee for budget and finance.

2.   The Association revise its fining policy to limit the amount to no more than $100.00.

3.   The Association establish a uniform procedure for reviewing new owners and providing them copies of the condominium documents.

The committee additionally recommends the following changes and additions be made to the bylaws of the association:

1.   Addition of a section to provide for the voluntary binding arbitration of disputes between owners and the Association.

2.   Deletion of the section allowing members of the board of administration to abstain from voting.

Committee Report FORM 5.04

3.   Amendment to the section of the bylaws relating to the term of office for board members to permit members to serve for staggered terms of two (2) years.

Respectfully submitted this 30th day of March, 2011.

_____

Chairman

_____

Member

_____

Member

6

Rules of Procedure— A Short-Hand Guide

RULES OF PROCEDURE FORMS

6.1   General. Basic parliamentary procedure is nothing more than a set of rules to govern the conduct of meetings in a way that will allow all interested individuals to participate and be heard, and will permit decisions to be made orderly and without confusion. The Condominium Act specifically authorizes the association to adopt reasonable rules of procedure to govern the participation of unit owners at both meetings of the board and the membership.[1]

When the proper rules of procedure are followed, a meeting will be fair, it will protect the rights of individual members, there will be enough flexibility to deal with the full panorama of issues, and it will allow for a democratic result to be reached on each decision which comes before the meeting.[2] *Robert's Rules of Order* (latest edition) is the basic manual used by most organizations and it is frequently incorporated by specific reference into the bylaws of the association.

The uniform parliamentary procedures enumerated in *Robert's Rules of Order* will yield to the bylaws when provisions are inconsistent. The meeting chairman must be familiar both with the general rules of procedure and the specific variations of procedures contained in the condominium documents and the Condominium Act. While individual documents and individual community customs may dictate some variations in meeting practices, the overriding principles of parliamentary procedure are to insure that fair and open meetings are used to carry out the business of the condominium association.[3]

6.2   Meeting Organization. Meeting preparation is an important partner with parliamentary procedure. For a well run community meeting, organization will consist of a pre-meeting checklist to insure that notice has been properly given to all members, that a chairman has been or will be selected to preside over the meeting, and that a secretary or recorder has been chosen to keep a record of the proceedings. The presiding officer of the meeting should have an organizational outline, or guide, prepared prior to the meeting.

The chairman's guide will anticipate the business of the meeting,

---

[1] § 718.112 (2)(c) and (d) 6., F.S.

[2] "Corporations must be allowed to function under majority control, so long as the majority does no actual wrong to the minority or to others." *Coleman v. Plantation Golf Club, Inc.,* 212 So.2d 806, 808 (Fla. 4th DCA 1968).

[3] *Abbey Properties Co., Inc. v. Prudential Insurance Co.,* 119 So.2d 74 (Fla. 2nd DCA 1960).

the motions which will be made, and the individuals who will desire to be recognized to speak, make motions and submit nominations. A properly organized meeting will also anticipate the special needs which may arise from items of business on the agenda, such as properly prepared ballots to insure full membership participation in voting.

The presiding officer or the secretary should have a copy of the association's bylaws, the rules of procedure which govern the association's meeting and other community documents available for easy reference to deal with questions of proper meeting conduct when they arise. In addition to having these documents available, the presiding officer must also have a general working familiarity of them to insure that they are properly applied during the course of the meeting.

6.3   Order of Business. It is customary for each association to have a permanent order of business or agenda, and the agenda must accompany or be incorporated into the notice of the meeting.[4] The fixed order of business must be followed unless the rules are waived or suspended by a two-thirds vote of those participating in the meeting. The two-thirds vote to waive the procedural rules governing the meeting is different from the two-thirds vote required for certain business by the Condominium Act. The Act requires the vote to be based on the entire membership, whether present or not, while a waiver of the rules requires a two-thirds vote of only those voting interests that are actually present.[5]

The order of business will serve as a guide not only for the presiding officer, but also for each of the members participating. The agenda allows a meeting to proceed in order and for the presentation of business to be organized effectively under the control of the presiding officer. When the order of business or the agenda is not being followed, it is the right of any member to request that the proper order of business be addressed.[6] A member wishing to exercise this right may do so by calling a "point of order" and requesting that the chairman require the rules of procedure to be followed. (See 6.9).

It is also the right of the presiding officer not to recognize any subject which is out of its order on the agenda or to terminate a presentation which

---

[4] § 718.112 (2)(c) and (d) 2., F.S.
[5] *Robert's Rules of Order Newly Revised,* § 40.
[6] *Robert's Rules of Order Newly Revised,* § 41.

is not part of the order of business under current consideration. All agenda items or "questions" are disposed of in their proper order of business unless a subsequent motion of higher priority is made under the rules of procedure or unless there is a waiver of the rules.

6.4   Motions and Seconds. Subjects which are introduced for consideration and vote before a meeting are presented by motions.[7] Main motions introduce subjects for meeting consideration while subsidiary motions, privileged motions and incidental motions seek to modify consideration of a main motion or modify the normal course of the meeting business.

As a general rule, all motions must have a second by another member at the meeting. The purpose of a second to the motion is to avoid wasting time when only one person has an interest in the subject of the motion and others do not wish to discuss it. When a motion does not receive a second, the presiding officer will declare that the motion fails for lack of a second and proceed to the next order of business.

The meeting may consider only one main motion at a time. In order to make a motion, the member must first obtain the recognition of the presiding officer for the purpose of making a motion. The motion is then stated to the meeting by the member who has been recognized. If the motion receives a second, then the presiding officer will state the motion before the meeting and declare that it has a second. Once made, seconded and stated, the motion is then in the possession of the meeting and it cannot be withdrawn by the maker without the consent or approval of the meeting membership.

As a general rule, all main motions are debatable unless a motion to eliminate or limit debate has been adopted by a two-thirds vote of the membership present. Under the provisions of the Condominium Act, however, the ability to eliminate or limit debate is restricted. Unit owners have the right to participate at meetings of the membership with regard to all designated agenda items.[8] An owner desiring to speak on designated items is entitled to do so, and restrictions on the time allowed for his or her debate must be reasonable.[9]

---

[7] *Robert's Rules of Order Newly Revised,* § 3 and § 4.
[8] § 718.112 (2)(d) 6., F.S.
[9] § 61B-23.002 (7), F.A.C.

After debate, the question is "put" to the membership for a vote. Once the results have been determined, the chairman declares the results of the motion, and it is then disposed of. It is then in order to make another main motion. Continued discussion of the motion disposed of is out of order unless a motion to reconsider is made.

6.5 Subsidiary and Incidental Motions. Subsidiary motions are those which are applied to other motions for purposes of modifying, amending, postponing or otherwise disposing of the other motion. Subsidiary motions are of higher priority and they will supersede the main motion and must be disposed of before voting on the main motion.[10] Examples include subsidiary motions to limit debate, amend the main motion or to move the "previous question" on the main motion.

A motion for the previous question is made to halt further debate and is often misunderstood. It is a subsidiary motion, and it must be adopted by a two-thirds vote of those present before debate can be eliminated and a vote on the main motion taken. Unless a motion for the previous question or a motion to limit debate is adopted by a two-thirds vote, debate will continue until no one else wishes to be recognized. The ability to make the motion for the previous question is restricted under the Condominium Act, and it may not be used to prevent a unit owner from speaking at least once for a minimum of three (3) minutes on designated agenda items.[11] When no one else seeks recognition, a motion for the previous question is unnecessary.

Incidental motions may or may not arise out of another pending motion or question before the meeting. The incidental motions do not seek to modify or amend another motion, but address how or when another motion or question will be dealt with by the meeting. Under most circumstances, an incidental motion must be disposed of first before consideration of a main motion can continue. Examples of incidental motions include motions to suspend the rules, motions to divide a question before the meeting or motions to waive the rules. As a general rule, incidental motions are not debatable and cannot be amended by the meeting.

6.6 Privileged and Unclassified Motions. Matters of privilege and privileged motions do not relate directly to pending questions before the meeting. Matters of privilege are considered of the highest importance

---

[10] *Robert's Rules of Order Newly Revised,* § 6.
[11] § 718.112 (2)(d) 6., F.S.

to the meeting and the conduct of the meeting itself. Motions of privilege take precedent over all other questions before a meeting and they must be disposed of before further business can be conducted. As a general rule, motions and matters of privilege are not debatable once they have been made and seconded.[12]

Examples of privileged motions and matters of privilege include motions for adjournment, motions to recess, demands that the meeting conform to the proper order of business and questions of privilege claimed by an individual member for himself or on behalf of the meeting. When seeking the floor for a motion of privilege, a member follows the same procedure for making any other motion. When seeking the floor on a matter of privilege, a member will state that he wishes to take the floor on a point of personal privilege or to state a point of order.

There are some motions which are not classified in the other groupings due to their unique nature, or because they may be applied to a motion in any of the other categories. Unclassified motions include dilatory and frivolous motions. The presiding officer may choose not to recognize, or may rule out of order, these type of motions because they abuse the rules of parliamentary procedure and delay the proper course of the meeting business.

A motion to ratify an act previously done by an officer, the board, or committees of the board is also an unclassified motion, and the motion is used to cure procedural defects in a previously taken action.[13] A motion to ratify can be approved only if the act could be properly done if authorized in advance by the meeting membership. A motion to ratify a previous action is generally used after emergency action has been taken by the board to cure a potential procedural defect in the act,[14] or when there is a question concerning the limits of authority when the act was originally taken by the board. As a general grouping, most privileged and unclassified motions are not needed during most meetings and they are used only on infrequent occasions.

6.7   Reconsideration. The most common of the unclassified motions

---

[12] *Robert's Rules of Order Newly Revised,* § 6.

[13] *Wimbledon Townhouse Condominium I, Ass'n, Inc. v. Wolfson,* 510 So.2d 1106, 1108 (Fla. 4th DCA 1987).

[14] § 718.112 (2)(c), F.S

is the motion to reconsider. It is also the most frequently used unclassified motion and it can be made relating to any motion previously adopted in the meeting. A motion to reconsider the vote on a motion is debatable if the motion it seeks to reconsider is also debatable.[15] The motion to reconsider must be made by a member who is on the prevailing side of the previous vote. Once the motion to reconsider has been disposed of it cannot be reconsidered a second time without the unanimous approval of the membership.[16]

Reconsideration is in order and available for use at anytime during the meeting at which the main motion was voted upon. The most common use for the motion is to revisit an issue previously adopted for purposes of clarifying or modifying when the original motion was incomplete or incorrect. On some occasions, the purpose of the motion will be to reverse the substance of the original motion by changing it significantly or defeating it outright.

Because consideration of a motion may be made only once, caution must be used by both the maker of the motion and the presiding officer to ensure that the meeting does not foreclose its consideration of an issue by prematurely disposing of a motion to reconsider. Once it has been voted upon, both the motion to reconsider and the main motion cannot be brought up again during the meeting without the unanimous approval of all members present.

6.8   Priority of Motions. While only one main motion may properly be considered by the meeting at one time, subsidiary, incidental and privileged motions may be made during the consideration of a main motion. These motions may be made to modify the main motion or to modify how the meeting will consider the main motion.[17] *Robert's Rules of Order* lists over forty-four (44) different motions and variations of motions, and each has its priority in relation to the others. A motion having higher dignity than the one currently before the meeting can be made and must be disposed of before continuing with the regular meeting business.

A motion of lesser dignity than the one being considered by the meeting cannot be made, and is out of order until the higher ranking motion is disposed of. The following commonly used motions are listed in their

---

[15] *Robert's Rules of Order Newly Revised,* § 36.
[16] *Id.*
[17] *Robert's Rules of Order Newly Revised,* § 5.

priority ranking with the motion of highest dignity listed first:[18]

1.   Adjourn at a fixed time.

2.   Adjourn.

3.   Recess.

4.   Reconsideration.

5.   Question of privilege.

6.   Call for orders of the day.

7.   Lay on the table.

8.   Previous question.

9.   Limit debate.

10. Postpone to a certain time.

11. Amend the motion.

12. Postpone indefinitely.

13. Main motion.

By disposing of motions in their proper priority, the business of the meeting can be completed as intended under the rules of procedure and without confusion. It is particularly important for the presiding officer to understand the basic priority of motions in order to maintain the proper order of business during the meeting.

6.9   Matters Out of Order. The rules of parliamentary procedure establish an order for business of the meeting and the manner in which business is presented and disposed of by those in attendance at the meeting. A matter can be out of order when it is presented at the wrong time,[19] or when it is presented in the wrong way.[20] Under either of these circumstances it is the prerogative and the duty of the presiding officer to rule the matter out of order.

A main motion is out of order when another main motion is already pending, or when the main motion is on a subject which should arise under a different order of business on the agenda. A motion will also be out of order when a motion of higher dignity is already being considered by the meeting.

---

[18] *Robert's Rules of Order Newly Revised,* Charts, Tables and Lists, § 1.

[19] *Robert's Rules of Order Newly Revised,* § 40.

[20] *Robert's Rules of Order Newly Revised,* § 5.

A member may be out of order if not properly recognized by the chairman or if the member seeks to make a dilatory or frivolous motion.

To call a point of order, or to demand that the proper order of business be followed is a privileged matter, or motion, for any member. When claiming a point of order, it is proper for the member to rise and state the point. It does not require a second to be considered by the chairman. A question, or point or order, cannot be amended by another member and must be decided by the presiding officer without debate.[21]

The presiding officer may seek consultation with the meeting's legal advisor or parliamentarian before ruling on the point of order, but it is the presiding officer's duty to enforce the rules and the order of business of the meeting without debate or unnecessary delay. It is the right of every member who notices a departure from the rules or from the order of business to insist upon proper enforcement.

6.10   Waiving the Rules. It is permissible to depart from the normal order of meeting business, or to return to a previous point of the meeting agenda, if a motion to waive the rules of parliamentary procedure is adopted first. When a motion to waive the rules is adopted, the subject matter may be brought before the meeting out of the regular order of business, and it is not subject to a point of order by a member of the meeting. A motion to waive the rules is an incidental motion and it must be decided by the meeting without debate. It requires a favorable vote of two-thirds of the voting interests present at the meeting for adoption, and the motion itself cannot be amended.[22]

Waiver of the rules is an extraordinary procedure, but it has its proper place and uses in the parliamentary rules. Excessive use of the motion can be avoided when the agenda for the meeting is clear and detailed, and when the presiding officer of the meeting is deliberate and well prepared. When it does become necessary to waive the rules, the motion should be clearly stated, and the part, or parts of the rules being waived should be specifically identified. Since the motion is not debatable and because it requires an extraordinary vote for adoption, it must be carefully and completely presented to the membership before the question is put to a vote.

---

[21] *Robert's Rules of Order Newly Revised,* § 23.
[22] *Robert's Rules of Order Newly Revised,* § 25.

6.11 Debate. Every unit owner has the right to speak and debate on the designated agenda items at all meetings of the membership, subject, however, to reasonable parliamentary rules governing the frequency, duration and manner of unit owner participation.[23] Any rules governing debate must be in writing and must be a part of, or incorporated by reference, into the articles of incorporation, bylaws or rules of the condominium association.[24] In many communities *Robert's Rules of Order* are adopted by the condominium documents, and they control participation at membership meetings so long as they are not inconsistent with the Condominium Act.

Debate begins after a motion has been made, seconded and stated by the presiding officer to the participants at the meeting. Each individual desiring to debate a motion must first be recognized by the chairman of the meeting.[25] If *Robert's Rules of Order* is being used, no member may speak more than a total of ten minutes on any single issue. A member is not permitted to speak a second time on the issue until all persons desiring to be heard the first time have had an opportunity to speak.

Members' debate must be confined to the specific issue before the meeting. Debate must be presented in a respectful manner so as to avoid personality conflicts and personal attacks. The maker of the motion, or the person presenting the subject, is the member allowed to speak last, unless a motion for the previous question is adopted to close or eliminate all debate. Any motion to limit or to close debate must be adopted by two-thirds of the voting interests present. No debate is permitted after the vote to close debate has been adopted. Under the Condominium Act and the rules of the Division, the opportunity to debate designated agenda items must be afforded to all unit owners at least once, although each owner's time may be reasonably restricted.[26]

No debate on a motion is in order after the vote has been taken and announced by the presiding officer. During debate it is permissible for a member to ask questions when another person is debating the issue, but all questions must be asked through the chairman. If the speaker is willing to yield to the question, then the member desiring to ask the question may do so.

---

[23] § 718.112 (2)(d) 6., F.S.
[24] § 61B-23.002 (7), F.A.C.
[25] *Robert's Rules of Order Newly Revised,* § 42.
[26] § 718.112 (2)(d) 6., F.S and § 61B-23.002 (7), F.A.C.

All main motions are debatable, as are motions to postpone a matter indefinitely and motions to rescind an action or to ratify an action. A motion to reconsider is debatable if the motion which is being reconsidered was debatable at the time it was made. Motions and matters of privilege, motions to waive the rules, motions to adjourn and to recess, and certain other incidental and subsidiary motions are not debatable.

6.12 Speaking at Meetings of the Board.

All unit owners have the right to speak at meetings of the board of administration and meetings of committees of the board or the association.[27] This is a variation to the parliamentary concept of debate which is carried on among those individuals who take part in the decision-making deliberations and vote on the outcome of individual issues. Unit owners, however, have no vote at the meetings of the board or committees, and their participation is limited to remarks on issues before the meeting, subject to reasonable rules adopted by the association governing the frequency, duration, and manner of such statements.[28]

Rules governing unit owner participation may limit each owner to a maximum of three (3) minutes or more, and may require an owner desiring to speak to file a request in writing in advance of the meeting. The rules, however, may not limit the number of owners entitled to speak, and any unit owner wishing to address a meeting may do so provided that the owner complies with the rules concerning participation.[29] Rules concerning unit owner participation must be adopted in written form, and must be a part of the rules of the board, the association bylaws or the articles of incorporation.[30] (See Form 11.01)

Establishing uniform guidelines for unit owners to follow when addressing the board is important, and it will help to avoid unnecessary disruption, while assuring that the right of each owner to speak is preserved. The forum and format of the presentation may vary. All unit owner remarks on all agenda items may be scheduled at the beginning of each meeting, or unit owners may be recognized on each separate agenda item as it arises. When adopting rules, consider that each owner must be afforded an opportunity to address each agenda item. Board members also have the right to debate each matter before voting on an item. Separation of the remarks of unit owners

---

[27] § 61B-23.002 (7), F.A.C.
[28] § 718.112 (2)(c), F.S.
[29] § 61B-23.002 (7), F.A.C.
[30] *Id.*

from the debate by members of the board, in most circumstances, is the preferred protocol to follow.

Unit owners also have the ability to add items to the agenda of a meeting of the board of administration by petition and to speak before the board on the item. This occurs when twenty percent (20%) of the total voting interests in the association petition the board to address an item of business. When the petition is received, the item must be scheduled for consideration by the board at a regular or special meeting within sixty (60) days of the receipt of the petition.[31]

6.13   Voting. When it is time to vote, or "put the question," the chairman should restate the issue clearly for the membership. The vote may be taken in one of five (5) ways:[32]

1. It may be done on a voice vote, where the chairman calls for "ayes" in favor of the motion, and "nays" opposed to the motion.

2. The vote may be taken by a show of hands or by requesting the voting members to stand when the "yes" and "no" votes are called for.

3. The vote may be by individual roll call, where a member stands and states his vote for or against the proposition.

4. The vote may be by a ballot which is marked in secret and delivered to the chairman or other official for tabulation.

5. Finally, voting may be by general consent, which occurs most frequently on procedural or non-controversial matters. When general consent is requested by the presiding officer, and no objections are raised, the chairman will declare that the issue was adopted without objection and the secretary will reflect that the vote was unanimous.

Depending on the matters being voted upon, some types of voting may be inappropriate. If a large number of proxies are voting at a particular meeting, a show of hands or a voice vote may be unacceptable since there is no way to determine how the proxies are to be counted. When an extraordinary vote is required, a count may be needed to determine whether or not the motion has carried. When secrecy is required, as in an election for

---

[31] § 718.112 (2)(c), F.S
[32] *Robert's Rules of Order Newly Revised,* § 44.

the board, only the ballot form of voting is authorized by the Condominium Act.[33]

The results, when voting is by voice, by show of hands or by general consent, are determined by the call of the presiding officer who has the responsibility to announce, or declare, the results of the vote. A member may change his vote at any time until the vote is announced by the chairman. Once a vote has been announced, then no change may be made without the unanimous approval of all members at the meeting.

In most cases, an issue before the meeting can be decided by a majority of the votes cast. When there is a tie vote, the motion is not carried and the issue is lost. Under some circumstances, the rules of parliamentary procedure require a two-thirds vote by those present and voting to adopt a motion. On some issues the condominium documents or the Condominium Act will require an extraordinary vote of the full membership, whether present or not, to adopt the issue, document amendment or other proposition before the meeting. Determining the proper vote necessary to adopt the motion or issue before the meeting is the responsibility of the presiding officer.

In all voting, it is also important to remember that the voting interests of units owned by the association may not be counted or considered for any purpose, whether for determining a quorum, an election outcome, or deciding any other matter that comes before a meeting of the membership.[34]

6.14 Decorum. Decorum for a successful meeting is built on mutual respect between the membership and the presiding officer of the meeting. All issues and requests to speak should be presented through the chairman of the meeting. Members wishing to obtain the floor for any purpose should do so properly and seek the recognition of the presiding officer. Once a member assumes the floor, the rules of debate should be obeyed and all comments should be confined to the question before the meeting. Comments and statements relating to personal motives and to personalities should not be made and may be ruled out of order by the presiding officer.[35]

---

[33] § 718.112 (2)(d) 3., F.S.
[34] § 718.112 (2)(b) 2., F.S
[35] *Robert's Rules of Order Newly Revised,* § 42.

Proper decorum at a meeting is no more than the exercise of common courtesy and maintaining respect for the rights of others. To assure that decorum is maintained, the presiding officer of the meeting should guide members through the proper order of business. The presiding officer must require that the rules be followed at all times. At the same time, the chairman must be both flexible and patient with members who are unfamiliar with the formal rules of parliamentary procedure. The chairman should not permit conduct which is disruptive, tedious or dilatory.

PRE-MEETING CHECKLIST

1. Confirmation of First Notice of Election
    and Date of Mailing   _____
2. Confirmation of Second Notice of Election
    and Date of Mailing (Includes Candidate
    Information Sheets and Ballots)   _____
3. Notice Confirmation and Date of Mailing and Posting   _____
4. Affidavit of Notice by Secretary   _____
5. Selection of Presiding Officer   _____
6. Selection of Secretary or Recorder for Meeting   _____
7. Identification of Reports to be presented   _____
8. List of owners wishing to videotape or record meeting _____
9. List of members making procedural motions   _____
10. Receptacle for ballots   _____
11. Selection of vote tellers (inspectors of election)   _____
12. Ballot preparation and production   _____
13. Roster of Owners (for verification of ballots)   _____
14. Organization for check-in stations   _____
15. Organization for meeting room (seating, podium, etc.) _____
16. Designation of Smoking and Non-smoking areas   _____
17. Copy of Rules of Procedure   _____
18. Copy of Condominium Documents and Condominium Act _____

Pre-Meeting Checklist FORM 6.01

CHAIRMAN'S MEETING GUIDE

I.   CALL TO ORDER:

"The 2010 annual membership meeting of Waterfront XX Condominium Association, Inc., will now come to order. The first order of business is determination of a quorum."

II.   CALLING THE ROLL AND CERTIFYING THE PROXIES:

"The secretary will please call the roll"

(or)

"The number of members present in person and by proxy has been determined during the check-in procedure. There are 50 members present in person and 30 members are represented by proxy. A quorum of the association is present."

III.   PROOF OF NOTICE:

"The affidavit of the Secretary of the Association, stating that notice has been given in accordance with the Condominium Act and the bylaws of the Association, has been presented to the chairman. The proof of notice shall be filed with the permanent records and is available for inspection by the members."

IV.   READING OF MINUTES:

"The next order of business is the reading of minutes from the last meeting."

(Mr. Jones will move to waive reading; Mr. Marshall will second.)

V. ELECTIONS:

"Tabulation of ballots for members to serve on the board will now begin. The chairman appoints Mr. Davis, Mr. Wesley and Mr. Marshall as inspectors of election."

(The meeting will stand in informal recess until ballots are counted. Results to be announced when meeting is reconvened.)

VI. UNFINISHED BUSINESS:

"Is there unfinished business to come before the meeting?"

(Mr. Wesley will move that statutory budget reserves be waived.)

VII. NEW BUSINESS:

"New business is now in order and the first item to be considered is the schedule of amendments to the bylaws. Without objection, chairmanship of the meeting will be assumed by the association's attorney to handle the presentation, explanation and voting on the amendments."

(If there are no objections, the attorney will assume the chairmanship of the meeting until consideration of the amendments is complete. Mr. Davis will move adoption of the amendments; Mr. Marshall will second.)

VIII. ADJOURN:

"Is there any further business to come before the meeting?"

(If there is no further business, Mr. Wesley will move to adjourn the meeting; Mr. Marshall will second.)

SAMPLE MOTIONS

To make a motion, a member must rise and address the presiding officer of the meeting by title and state the motion that member wishes to make. Each motion will be preceded by a preface in substantially the following form:

"Mr. Chairman, I move that . . ."

The motion is then stated and must be seconded before it can be considered further by the meeting.

I.   MAIN MOTIONS

A.   **Waiver of Minutes:** " . . . the reading of the minutes from the previous meeting be waived and that the minutes be accepted as presented by the secretary."

B.   **Waiver of Treasurer's Report:** " . . . the reading of the Treasurer's report be waived and that the report be filed with the financial records of the association for audit."

C.   **Waiver of Reserves:** " . . . the statutory reserves be waived for the 2011 fiscal year of the association."

D.   **Waiver of Reserves, Partial:** " . . . the statutory reserves be waived for the 2011 fiscal year of the association, and that reserves be set in an amount equal to one-half of those shown in the proposed budget."

E.   **Recall of Board Member:** " . . . Joseph Jones be recalled as a member of the board of administration to be effective immediately upon conclusion of the tabulation of the voting."

F.   **Approval of Material Modification:** " . . . material modifications to the common elements be allowed for installation of exterior storm shutters in accordance with the uniform architectural standards adopted by the board of administration."

G.   **Adopting Document Amendments:** " . . . the schedule of amendments to the declaration of condominium and the bylaws be approved as presented to the membership meeting."

H.   **Terminating Management Contract:** " . . . the management agreement between the association and the XYZ Management Company, dated January 1, 2010, be canceled effective January 1, 2011."

Sample Motions   FORM 6.03

II.   SUBSIDIARY MOTIONS

A.   **To Amend:** " . . . the motion to allow for material modifications to the common elements be amended to allow for the enclosure of balconies and patios."

B.   **Previous Question:** " . . . the previous question now be put," or "I move the previous question." (Debate ceases and the meeting proceeds to vote—requires a two-thirds vote for adoption.)

C.   **Postpone to a Time Certain:** " . . . the consideration of the alteration of the common elements be postponed until the annual meeting of the association in 2011."

D.   **Limit Debate:** " . . . the debate be limited to three (3) minutes per person." (Requires a two-thirds vote for adoption.)

E.   **Postpone Indefinitely:** " . . . consideration of the motion be indefinitely postponed."

III.   INCIDENTAL MOTIONS

A.   **Closing Nominations:** " . . . the nominations for the chairmanship of the meeting now be closed."

B.   **Divide the Question:** " . . . the main motion be divided to allow for a separate vote on the schedule of amendments to the bylaws and the schedule of amendments to the declaration of condominium."

C.   **Waiver of the Rules:** " . . . the rules be waived and the meeting return to the unfinished business portion of the agenda." (Requires a two-thirds vote for adoption.)

Sample Motions   FORM 6.03

IV.   PRIVILEGED AND UNCLASSIFIED MOTIONS

A.   **Adjourn at a Fixed Time:** " . . . the meeting of the membership adjourn at the hour of 10:30 p.m."

B.   **Adjourn and Reconvene:** " . . . upon tabulation of the votes on the amendments to the declaration of condominium, if it is determined that the extraordinary majority necessary to adopt the amendments is not present, that the meeting be adjourned until October 23 at the hour of 7:30 p.m. for purposes of obtaining the extraordinary majority. I further move that the votes present be recorded and counted at the reconvened portion of the meeting on October 23."

C.   **Recess:** " . . . the meeting stand in recess until the tabulation of votes has been completed."

D.   **Reconsideration:** " . . . the motion approving the material modifications to the common elements be reconsidered." (Mover must have voted on the prevailing side of the original motion.)

E.   **Ratify Act of Board:** " . . . the expenditures for the repair of the storm drainage to the roof be ratified and approved."

Sample Motions   FORM 6.03

7

The Budget and Financial Reports

BUDGET AND FINANCIAL REPORT FORMS

7.1   General. Each association must have a financial plan that sets forth the proposed expenditure of funds for the maintenance, management, and operation of the condominium association and the condominium. The first financial plan, or budget, is established by the developer at the time that the condominium is created.[1] Thereafter, the association must annually prepare a budget governing the community's financial affairs.

The budget is the initial step in implementing the association's assessment authority. When it is adopted, it imposes upon each unit owner the responsibility to contribute to the operation of the association and the condominium of which the unit is a part. The budget of the association is adopted for a twelve- (12) month period,[2] and it must provide a detailed listing of the estimated revenues and expenses that the community reasonably projects for the coming fiscal year.[3]

The budget is the foundation document for the condominium community's financial operation and stability. It provides a preview of the coming year's expenditures, and provides a benchmark by which the year's expenditures can be judged and evaluated. The budget and its adoption are regulated by the provisions of the Condominium Act.[4] Care must be taken to assure that the budget is properly proposed and adopted in accordance with the Act.

7.2   Budget for General Operations. There are many potential parts to the budget for the condominium community, but its main components govern regular operations. These operations deal with the every day recurring expenditures for the condominium and the condominium association. The operations portion of the budget will identify each proposed item of expense, from administration to management, and from taxes to insurance. The expenses for general operations must be listed by account and classification, and should project the total proposed annual expenditure in each classification.[5] If the association maintains limited common elements with the cost to be shared by those entitled to use them, separate classifications must be established in the budget for these items as well.

Detail by specific category is required for all common expenses. It is

---

[1] § 718.504 (21)(c), F.S.
[2] § 718.504 (21)(d), F.S.
[3] § 718.112 (2)(f) 1., F.S.
[4] § 718.112 (2)(e) and (f), F.S.
[5] § 718.112 (2)(f), F.S.

also required for all expenses incurred for association property not included within categories of common expense, and for all expenses of individual unit owners for items that are administered by the association. An analysis of the categories of expense will enable a classification to be made for each by either (1) common expenses, (2) expenses for association properties, (3) expenses for limited common elements, or (4) expenses for unit owners. Collectively, the recurring regular expenses for all of these areas make up the general operations portion of the budget. These operating funds, once collected from unit owners, must be maintained in the association's name, and cannot be commingled with the reserve funds of the association unless combined for investment purposes.[6]

If the funds are commingled for investment purposes, the law requires that the operating and reserve monies be accounted for separately, and at no time must the account balance in the commingled account be less than the identifiable balance of the reserve funds in the combined account.[7]

7.3   Budget for Capital Expenses and Deferred Maintenance.

A separate portion of the budget for every condominium must be set aside for capital expenses and deferred maintenance. More frequently referred to as "reserves," this part of the budget must also be set out by account and expense classification. The Condominium Act requires, at minimum, three (3) categories of reserves in each proposed budget—roof replacement, building painting and pavement resurfacing. The Act further requires a reserve account for any item for which deferred maintenance expense or replacement cost is greater than $10,000.[8] It is appropriate for the community to consider these additional categories of required expenditures. Such items of deferred maintenance may include other major property components such as the swimming pool, seawall or similar improvement. Each new budget must state the balance existing in each reserve account at the time the budget is adopted.

Some communities include a budget category for general reserves or "contingency reserves" that are not restricted to a specified use or component of the condominium property. These contingency reserves and other categories of expense not restricted to a specific use are not considered

---

[6] § 718.111 (14), F.S.
[7] *Id.*
[8] § 718.112 (2)(f) 2., F.S.

reserves under the Condominium Act, and are appropriately stated in the operating portion of the budget rather than the reserve portion of the budget.[9]

The required reserve categories of the budget are for specified items of expense that do not occur on a regular or recurring basis.[10] These accounts provide funds for the major capital repairs or replacements that are needed intermittently throughout the life of the condominium. Replacement of a roof may occur once every twenty years, while repainting of the exterior of the buildings may occur once every five years. The reserve items in the budget are designed to ensure that funds will be available for these repairs when they are needed without the necessity of large special assessments against individual unit owners.[11] The reserve funds of the association must be maintained in separate accounts and may only be commingled with the operating funds of the association when the reserve funds are separately accounted for in the combined account.[12]

Traditionally, the amount of reserves for each budget category is computed by means of a formula. It is based upon the estimated life and estimated replacement cost for the capital component of the condominium property involved. The formula will vary with each condominium because it is based upon the specific factual situation surrounding the improvement for which the reserve is being established. The formula may be adjusted annually to take into account any extension of the useful life of a property component as a result of deferred maintenance.[13]

As an alternative to the traditional method of calculating individual reserve accounts, the association is permitted to maintain a pooled account for two or more of the required reserve assets. The formula to fund the pooled reserve account must provide for an annual contribution that will ensure that the balance on hand in the pooled account is equal to or greater than the annual projected outflows from the account.[14] An association electing to use the alternative pooled account for reserve funding should do so with the assistance of the community's accountant.

---

[9] § 61B-22.003 (2), F.A.C.
[10] § 61B-22.005, F.A.C.
[11] § 61B-22.005 (1), F.A.C.
[12] § 718.111 (14), F.S.
[13] § 718.112 (2)(f) 2., F.S.
[14] § 61B-22.005 (3)(b), F.A.C.

No matter which alternative for reserving is selected, the board of administration has the latitude to evaluate the estimated useful life of the budget item, the approximate cost of its repair or replacement, and the amount that should be properly allocated to the current year's budget. Although no specific basis for the formula is set out in the Condominium Act, the building inspection report provided by the developer at the time of transition will provide the essential information for calculating the reserves.[15] The formula must be a part of the association's financial records and stated or shown in the proposed budget.[16]

To the extent permitted by the Condominium Act,[17] or by vote of the members, the association may choose to reserve based upon a percentage of the overall operating budget. (See 7.9). In such circumstances, the basis or formula for calculating the actual reserve amounts should be stated as part of the budget. Account balances and expenditures during the previous fiscal year should also be set out in the budget for the benefit of members.

7.4　Budgets　for　Multicondominiums. For condominium communities created prior to January 1, 1977, it is permissible for a condominium association to provide for the consolidated financial operation of two or more condominiums when either the declarations of condominium or the bylaws of the association permit.[18] Otherwise, each condominium association is required to maintain separate accounting records, including separate budgets, for each condominium that it manages.[19] The financial planning of an association governing multiple condominiums should include a separate budget for each condominium operated by the association, a separate budget for the property serving more than one condominium and a separate budget for the operation of the condominium association itself.[20]

Expenses should be appropriately allocated to specific condominiums, although expenses shared by multiple condominiums may be divided proportionately among them. Expenses for the administration of the multicondominium association itself may also be proportionately allocated among the condominiums that it operates. The requirement for

---

[15] § 718.301 (4)(p), F.S.
[16] § 61B-22.003 (1)(e), F.A.C.
[17] § 718.112 (2)(f) 2., F.S.
[18] § 718.111 (6), F.S.
[19] § 718.112 (2)(f) 4., F.S.
[20] § 61B-22.003 (4), F.A.C.

separate budgets extends to both general operations and to the reserves for capital expenses and deferred maintenance.

Provided that operating and reserve monies are separately accounted for, operating and reserve funds of separate condominiums may be commingled for investment purposes.[21] When waiver of the required reserves is sought within an association managing multicondominiums, the waiver must be by individual condominium and not by the association at large. For the waiver to be effective, a majority of the voting interests from each condominium must be present, and a majority from each must vote to approve the waiver.[22]

7.5   Developing the Proposed Budget. The "proposed budget" is the preliminary draft of the community's financial plan that is offered by the board for formal adoption as the budget. The development of the proposed budget may be by the association treasurer, a finance committee, the community's management company, or by the board of administration itself. The board should bring as much expertise as possible to the development of the proposed budget. This helps to assure accuracy and compliance with statutory guidelines once the actual budget is adopted.

The development of accounts and expense classifications for the proposed budget are based upon the community's financial history and the experience of previous years' expenditures. New anticipated expenses can be estimated from comparisons in the marketplace or from the experience of other condominium communities. Accounts are to be separated into categories of general operations and into at least three (3) mandatory reserve categories. Consideration should also be given to the amount of percentage increase over the previous year's budget.

Categories and classifications within the proposed budget must deal separately with the common expenses of the condominium, expenses for the maintenance and operation of association-owned property, expenses for limited common elements maintained by the association, and for expenses directly attributable to individual unit owners. Each classification should be based upon realistic estimates, and should be set forth in sufficient detail so that each category can be understood and evaluated by the members of the association.[23]

---

[21] § 718.111 (14), F.S.
[22] § 718.112 (2)(f) 2., F.S.
[23] § 718.112 (2)(f) 1., F.S. and § 718.504 (20), F.S.

7.6   Proposed Budget and Mandatory Reserves. There is an important and clear distinction between the "proposed budget" of the association and the actual budget which takes effect after formal adoption and which governs the financial affairs of the condominium. The proposed budget is a draft of the financial plan as it exists prior to formal adoption in the manner specified in the bylaws. It must be forwarded to each unit owner with the notice of the meeting where the budget will be adopted to allow each owner the opportunity to analyze the complete financial needs of the community.[24]

The proposed budget must contain all of the reserve expense classifications required by the Condominium Act, with the projections for full funding of the capital expenditures and deferred maintenance shown. The proposed budget cannot anticipate that reserves will be waived by the membership or that they will provide for reserves in an amount less than is adequate.[25] During the formal adoption procedures the proposed budget becomes the actual budget, but only a majority of the membership present may remove or modify the reserve provisions. (See 7.9).

7.7   Notice and Adoption of the Budget. Whether the budget is to be adopted by a vote of the membership or by a vote of the board of administration, written notice and copies of the proposed annual budget must be mailed, hand delivered or electronically transmitted to the unit owners.[26] This notice must be given to each owner at least fourteen (14) days before the meeting is actually held. If the budget is to be adopted by the unit owners, then the notice will be for a membership meeting. If the budget is to be adopted by the board of administration, then the notice shall be for the board meeting and shall invite owners to attend, speak and observe.

The written notice for either budget meeting must provide the time and place for the meeting and must state that the purpose is for the consideration and adoption of the budget. Evidence that notice for the budget meeting has been properly given must be by an affidavit of an officer of the association, or the manager or other person providing notice of the meeting. The affidavit must be maintained as part of the official records of the association.[27]

When the bylaws or the declaration of condominium permit, the

---

[24] § 718.112 (2)(e), F.S.
[25] § 61B-22.003 (1)(d), F.A.C.
[26] § 718.112 (2)(e), F.S.
[27] *Id.*

budget may be adopted by the board of administration.[28] For proper adoption, a quorum of the board must be present at the meeting and a majority of the quorum must approve the budget. If the bylaws or the declaration do not permit the board to adopt the budget, then the budget must be adopted by the membership. The budget may be considered at a membership meeting where a quorum is present and approved upon a majority vote of the quorum.

The minutes of the meeting where the budget is approved should reflect the motion of adoption, and the budget thereafter becomes a permanent part of the association's financial records. A copy of the proposed and adopted budgets must be maintained as part of the financial records of the association.

7.8   Reconsideration by the Membership. A budget adopted by the board of administration may be reconsidered by the unit owners if the assessments required to fund it exceed 115% of the previous year's assessments. The request for reconsideration must be a written application to the board and at least 10% of the voting interests of the association must join in the written petition. The petition must be received by the board within twenty-one (21) days of the adoption of the budget. After receiving the petition, the board must call a special meeting of the unit owners within sixty (60) days after adoption of the budget, and must give at least fourteen (14) days written notice of the meeting stating that its purpose is to reconsider the previously adopted budget.[29]

At the special meeting, all members may consider and enact a budget if a majority of all the voting interests in the community approve the budget. If the bylaws of the association provide for a different majority, the bylaws should be followed in adopting the budget. When the meeting is called and a quorum is not obtained or if a substitute budget is not adopted by a majority of all the voting interests in the community, the budget originally adopted by the board of administration will remain in effect.

When calculating the 115% threshold for comparison to the previous year's budget, not all expense categories are included. Reserves for capital expenditures and deferred maintenance, expenses which are not anticipated on a regular or annual basis, and assessments for betterments and improvements are excluded from the computations.[30]

---

[28] *Id.*
[29] *Id.*
[30] *Id.*

The Condominium Act does not prohibit budgets that exceed 115% of the previous year's budget and reconsideration is not automatic when the 115% threshold is achieved. Reconsideration must be initiated by the membership and formal application from 10% of the voting interests must be obtained before a special meeting can be called.

7.9   Waiver of Mandatory Reserves. Reserves for capital expenditures and deferred maintenance can be waived from the annual budget, but only by a vote of the membership. The vote must take place at a properly called membership meeting, and the motion must be approved by a majority of the voting interests present at a meeting where a quorum was established. In a multicondominium community, the only interests that are eligible to vote on the waiver or reduction of reserves are those voting interests of the units subject to assessment to fund the reserves in question.[31]

If proxies are used in the voting to waive reserves, they must be limited proxies substantially conforming to the form adopted by the Division of Florida Condominiums, Timeshares, and Mobile Homes.[32] The limited proxies must also contain the following statement in capitalized bold letters:

WAIVING RESERVES, IN WHOLE OR IN PART, OR ALLOWING ALTERNATIVE USES OF EXISTING RESERVES MAY RESULT IN UNIT OWNER LIABILITY FOR PAYMENT OF UNANTICIPATED SPECIAL ASSESSMENTS REGARDING THOSE ITEMS.[33]

The waiver of reserves by the membership affects the current budget only and a separate vote must be taken each year that a waiver of the reserves is desired. Any attempt to vary the statutory formula for mandatory reserves or to provide for reserves less adequate than the formula requires also requires a membership vote. The waiver vote and proxy disclosure statement required are the same as for a complete waiver of the reserves.[34]

The proposed budget submitted by the board of administration must include the mandatory reserves when it is distributed to the membership. It is permissible, however, for the board to include supplemental information

---

[31] § 718.112 (2)(f) 2. and 4., F.S.

[32] § 718.112 (2)(b) 2., F.S.

[33] § 718.112 (2)(f) 4., F.S.

[34] § 718.112 (2)(f) 2., F.S. and § 61B-22.005 (8), F.A.C.

that compares the proposed budget and assessment levels with reserves to an alternative which shows a financial plan and assessment levels if the reserves are waived by a proper membership vote. Unless properly waived or reduced, reserves must be fully funded in at least the same frequency that assessments are due from unit owners.[35]

7.10 Use of Reserve Funds. Reserve funds must be segregated from the general operating funds of the association and specifically identified as reserves. By doing so, the association will avoid adverse income tax consequences on funds which are collected and held for a period longer than the association's fiscal year. Reserve funds may be commingled in an account with operating funds for investment purposes, provided that the reserve funds are accounted for separately by the association and the balance in the account is never less than the identified balance of the reserve funds in the account.[36]

The funds on deposit in the association reserve accounts and interest earned and allocated to individual reserve accounts may be used by the board of administration from time to time so long as they are spent for the same purposes for which they were collected. Reserve funds in the roofing account must be used for roof repairs. Those in the building painting account are for building painting purposes. Funds and accrued interest from one category of reserves may not be used for another category or for other general operation purposes without a specific vote of the community membership.[37]

The vote of the membership to use reserve funds for purposes other than that for which they were collected must take place at a properly called members' meeting. The alternative use of reserve funds must be approved by a majority of the eligible voting interests present at a membership meeting of the association at which a quorum is present. The restriction on the use of reserve funds for capital expenditures and deferred maintenance applies to monies which are collected through the normal budgetary process and to any interest which is earned on the collected funds.[38] Such funds may not be diverted to other uses without first obtaining a majority vote of the eligible

---

[35] § 61B-22.005 (1) and (3), F.A.C

[36] § 718.111 (14), F.S.

[37] § 718.112 (2)(f) 3., F.S. and § 61B-22.005 (3) and (8), F.A.C. Pursuant to § 61B-22.005 (7), F.A.C., interest that is not actually allocated to an individual account may be used for any capital expenditure.

[38] § 718.112 (2)(f) 3., F.S.

voting interests in the community.[39]

7.11 Amending the Budget. It is permissible to amend the budgets of the association and the condominium. Some budget amendments require specific membership approval, such as those that authorize the use of designated reserves for other purposes. General budget amendments not requiring a special vote or the adoption of an amended budget, require the board of administration to follow the same procedures that are used for adopting the original budget.[40] The amended budget, or budget amendment, together with a notice of the meeting at which it is to be considered, must be mailed to all the unit owners prior to adoption.[41]

If a fully amended budget is to be considered, then the proposal must include the mandatory reserves. If only a part of the association budget is being amended and no change is proposed to the policy previously established on reserves, then reserves or a waiver of the reserves does not have to be considered at the time that the budget amendment is considered. Any budget amendment will apply only for the remaining balance of the twelve (12) month period of the originally adopted budget.

7.12 Unbudgeted Expenses. Unbudgeted expenses are also the unexpected expenses that the community is not prepared to meet from its current operating revenues or reserve funds. Unexpected expenses will occur infrequently for all associations as a result of the association's affirmative duty to keep the common elements and the condominium property in a state of good repair.[42] Unbudgeted expenses may result from judgments against the association, accidental occurrences or from normal items of deferred maintenance in a condominium community where reserves have been waived from the annual budgets.

The board of administration has three (3) basic options to pursue when meeting an unbudgeted expense item. First, the board may implement special assessment procedures to raise the necessary funds.[43] Second, the board may seek approval of the membership to borrow the necessary monies from another portion of the community's reserve accounts, or third, the board may seek to borrow the funds from a full service bank or other

---

[39] § 61B-22.005 (7), F.A.C.
[40] § 61B-22.003 (7), F.A.C.
[41] § 718.112 (2)(e), F.S.
[42] § 718.111 (4) and (5), F.S.
[43] § 718.103 (24) and § 718.116 (10), F.S.

traditional lending source.[44]

The borrowed funds allow the board to meet the immediate need of the unbudgeted expense item, while amortizing the total expense over a future period with payments to be included as an account item in future budgets. Unless the bylaws or articles of incorporation provide to the contrary, the board of administration has the authority to borrow funds from a bank or other lending institution, and to levy a special assessment to repay the loan without the vote of the membership. The board must seek membership approval, however, when it seeks to borrow from one of the community's already existing reserve accounts.[45]

7.13 Funds in Excess of Budget. The unexpended portions of the budget become part of the common surplus of the condominium. This surplus includes all excess monies retained by the association after deduction of all the expenses incurred in carrying out the affairs of the association.[46] The excess funds result from unexpected income and from expenses less than those actually anticipated. The board should accurately determine the amount of excess funds in the possession of the association at the end of the fiscal year so an appropriate disposition of these monies can be made.

If the association has been organized as a corporation not-for-profit and the common surplus does not result from excess funds from a special assessment, it cannot be returned directly to the unit owners and an alternative disposition must be used.[47] The excess funds can be credited towards the next year's budget for the benefit of unit owners in the same percentage as their ownership in the common elements,[48] or the surplus can be allocated to the reserve accounts of the association.

When a special assessment has raised funds for a specific purpose or purposes and there are funds remaining once the work is complete, these excess funds are also considered common surplus. (See 8.7). This surplus may, at the discretion of the board of administration, either be returned to the unit owners or applied as a credit toward future assessments.[49] The disposition of all surplus funds is a decision within the discretion of the

---

[44] § 617.0302 (7), F.S.

[45] § 718.112 (2)(f) 3., F.S. and § 61B-22.005 (3) and (8), F.A.C.

[46] § 718.103 (10), F.S.

[47] § 617.01401 (5) and § 617.0505 (1). F.S.

[48] § 718.115 (3), F.S.; *Century 21 Commodore Plaza, Inc. v. Commodore Plaza at Century 21 Condominium Ass'n, Inc.,* 340 So.2d 945 (Fla. 3rd DCA 1976).

[49] § 718.116 (10), F.S.

board and no membership vote or approval is required to implement the decision of the board.

7.14 Annual Financial Report. Each year the board of administration must prepare and complete a financial report of the previous year's financial activities within ninety (90) days following the end of the association's fiscal year, or on such other date as the bylaws of the association require. Within twenty-one (21) days after the financial report is completed, but not later than one hundred twenty (120) days after the end of the fiscal year or other date specified in the bylaws, the association must mail or hand deliver a copy of the report to each unit owner. In the alternative, the association may provide notice that a copy of the financial report will be mailed or hand delivered to the unit owner, without charge, upon receipt of a written request from the unit owner.[50]

The report must consist of a complete set of financial statements for the preceding year. Based upon the size of the condominium community, the financial statement must be compiled, reviewed or audited in accordance with generally accepted accounting principles, consistent with uniform accounting rules adopted by the Division of Florida Condominiums, Timeshares, and Mobile Homes.[51] (See 7.15).

If approved by a majority of the voting interests present at a properly called meeting of the association, the association may waive the statutory reporting requirements and prepare a report of cash receipts and expenditures in lieu of a compiled, reviewed or audited financial statement. The membership meeting must occur prior to the end of the fiscal year and the waiver is effective only for the fiscal year in which the vote is taken. The report must be prepared using a cash method of accounting; show the expenditures by account and classification, including a summary for all transactions in the reserve accounts of the condominium; and disclose the amount of annual funding needed to fully fund each reserve account.[52] If the association elects to waive the statutory reporting requirements, the option is limited and the association is not permitted to waive the requirements for more than three (3) consecutive years.[53]

---

[50] § 718.111 (13), F.S.
[51] § 718.111 (13)(a), (b) and (c), F.S.
[52] § 61B-22.006 (3) and (6), F.A.C.
[53] § 718.111 (13)(d), F.S.

Copies of the annual financial report must be maintained by the association, and additional copies are available to both unit owners and prospective purchasers at a reasonable cost.[54] A copy of the report must be provided to each purchaser of a condominium unit in the community at the expense of the seller at the time that a unit is resold, and each purchaser is required to acknowledge receipt of the information prior to acquiring the property.[55] Similarly, the developer is obligated to provide a copy of the report, together with the required prospectus, to all new unit owners purchasing in the community.[56]

7.15 Financial Statements and Audit. For condominium associations that operate and manage less than seventy-five (75) condominium units, regardless of annual income, the annual financial report may consist of a report of cash receipts and expenditures in lieu of compiled, reviewed or audited statements. For condominium associations of seventy-five (75) or more units, unless the requirement is waived by a majority of the voting interests of the association present at a duly called meeting, the report must be a complete set of financial statements formally compiled, reviewed, or audited by a certified public accountant in accordance with good accounting principles.[57]

Associations having annual receipts in excess of $100,000.00, but less than $200,000.00 must deliver "compiled" financial statements to the owners. This standard is a basic gathering of the association's financial information in the generally accepted format for financial statements. The statements must be prepared on the accrual basis using fund accounting and they must include a statement of revenues and expenses, a statement of charges in fund balances, a statement of sources and uses of cash, and a balance sheet and notes.[58]

Condominium associations having annual receipts of at least $200,000.00, but less than $400,000.00, must deliver "reviewed" financial statements to owners. The review is a basic critique and analysis of the financial policies, practices and trends of the association with appropriate analysis by the accounting professional. For associations having annual

---

[54] § 718.111 (12)(c), F.S.
[55] § 718.503 (2)(a) and (c), F.S.
[56] § 718.504, F.S.
[57] § 718.111 (13)(b), F.S.
[58] § 718.111 (13)(a), F.S.

receipts of $400,000.00 or more, audited financial statements are required.[59] The audited financial statements are an independent confirmation of the association's financial activities by the professional accountant. The accountant will be required to make actual inspection of the association's receipts and expenditures and other financial source documents, and must then provide the appropriate formal audit analysis.

The requirement to have the financial statements of the association compiled, reviewed, or audited may be waived for any fiscal year by the unit owners. The waiver must be approved at a membership meeting of the association held prior to the end of the fiscal year by a majority of the voting interests of the association present at the meeting, and the waiver is effective for only one (1) fiscal year. In an association in which turnover of control by the developer has not occurred, the developer may vote to waive the audit requirement for the first two (2) years of the operation of the association. After the initial two-year period, the waiver must be approved by a majority of the voting interests other than the developer for no more than three (3) consecutive years.[60] (See 7.14).

7.16 Governmental Financial Filings. Each incorporated condominium association has at least three (3) governmental filings that must be made in each calendar year. The first filing is with the Division of Condominiums, Timeshares, and Mobile Homes for the purpose of remitting the annual fee required by the Condominium Act. The amount of the annual fee is based on the number of residential units that the association operates and it has varied in recent years. Beginning January 1, 1992, the annual fee is $4.00 per residential unit. The fee must be paid on or before January 1st of each year. If the fee is not paid by June 1st of that year, the Division has the right to assess a 10% penalty against the association and the association is prohibited from maintaining or defending any action in the Florida courts.[61]

Each association must additionally file an annual report with the Division of Corporations between January 1st and July 1st of each year. The report is filed on Division forms and must set forth the corporate name, the

---

[59] *Id.*

[60] Any audit or review prepared prior to turnover must be paid by the developer. § 718.111 (13)(b), F.S.

[61] § 718.501 (2)(a), F.S.

address of the principal office, the corporation's federal tax identification number, and the name and the mailing address for each officer and director effective as of December 31st of the year immediately preceding the due date of the report. Failure of the board of administration to file this report with the Division of Corporations results in the dissolution of the corporation.[62] The annual report must be accompanied by a filing fee payable to the Division.[63]

Finally, each condominium association, whether organized for profit or not-for-profit, is required to file an annual income tax return with the Internal Revenue Service. A corporation not-for-profit organized under Chapter 617, F.S., is neither tax-exempt, nor exempt from the filing of an annual tax return. The Internal Revenue Service Code allows condominium associations special treatment for some of their activities, including the retention of reserve accounts, but proper accounting for these funds and the filing of an income tax return are annual requirements for each condominium community.

---

[62] § 617.1622 (8), F.S.
[63] § 617.0122 (19), F.S.

WATERFRONT XX CONDOMINIUM ASSOCIATION, INC.
A Corporation Not-for-Profit

2011 BUDGET

I. **Expenses for the Association and Condominium**

	Monthly	Annually
A. Administration of Association	$100.00	$1,200.00
B. Management Fees	702.00	8,424.00
C. Building Cleaning and Maintenance	100.00	1,200.00
D. Lawn and Property Maintenance	500.00	6,000.00
E. Rent for Recreation and Other Commonly Used Facilities	100.00	1,200.00
F. Expenses on Association Property		
1) Taxes	21.00	252.00
2) Cleaning & Maintenance	10.00	120.00
G. Taxes on Leased Property	10.00	120.00
H. Electricity (Common Elements)	320.00	3,840.00
I. Water, Sewer and Garbage Service	900.00	10,800.00
J. Insurance	625.00	7,500.00
K. Miscellaneous:		
1) Annual Filing Fee with the Division	2.00	24.00
2) Professional Services (legal and accounting)	100.00	1,200.00

L. Security Provisions	.00	.00
M. Pest Control	<u>100.00</u>	<u>1,200.00</u>
TOTAL	$3,590.00	$43,080.00

II. **Reserves**

A. Building Painting	$384.00	$4,608.00
B. Pavement Resurfacing	75.00	900.00
C. Roof Replacement	250.00	3,000.00
D. Swimming Pool Reserves	<u>50.00</u>	<u>600.00</u>
TOTAL	$759.00	$9,108.00

III. **Expenses for a Unit Owner**

A. Rent Payable for recreation lease or commonly used facilities	$10.00	$120.00
B. Expenses for limited common elements:		
1) Parking Garage maintenance	5.00	60.00
2) Storage locker maintenance	<u>5.00</u>	<u>60.00</u>
TOTAL	$20.00	$240.00

BUDGET NOTES

1.   The expense for individual units is as follows:
      a. A-Type units (.0188 per unit) $ 81.76
      b. B-Type units (.0194 per unit) $84.37
      c. C-Type units (.0393 per unit) $170.92

2.   The balance in the reserve accounts of the Association at the beginning of the current budget year is as follows:
      a. Building Painting $23,040.00
      b. Pavement Resurfacing   7,200.00
      c. Roof Replacement 24,000.00
      d. Swimming Pool Reserves 3,000.00

3.   The formula for each reserve category is based on the following estimates:

      a. Building painting to occur every 8 years and one-eighth of the total estimated cost is allocated to each fiscal year. Six of the eight years are currently on deposit.

      b. Pavement resurfacing to occur every 15 years and one-fifteenth of the total estimated cost is allocated to each fiscal year. Nine of the fifteen years are currently on deposit.

      c. Roof replacement to occur every 20 years and one-twentieth of the total estimated cost is allocated to each fiscal year. Eight of the twenty years are currently on deposit.

      d. Swimming pool deferred maintenance to occur every 6 years and one-sixth of the total estimated cost is allocated to each fiscal year. Five of the six years are currently on deposit.

WATERFRONT XX CONDOMINIUM ASSOCIATION, INC.
A Corporation Not-for-Profit

NOTICE OF BUDGET MEETING

NOTICE IS HEREBY GIVEN, in accordance with the bylaws of the Association and Florida's Condominium Act, that the Board of Administration of the Association will consider the adoption of the budget for the coming fiscal year of the Condominium and the Condominium Association at the following date, time and place:

Date: December 15, 2010

Time: 7:00 p.m.

Place: Clubhouse
Waterfront XX Condominium
100 Waterfront Drive
Waterfront, Florida 33444

Agenda: The order of business for the regular meeting of the Board of Administration shall be as follows:
1.   Reading of minutes of the previous meeting.
2.   Comment and discussion by unit owners.
3.   Consideration of budget.
4.   Adjournment.

This notice shall be posted upon the condominium property at least forty-eight (48) hours in advance of the scheduled meeting.

WATERFRONT XX CONDOMINIUM

ASSOCIATION, INC.

By: _____
Secretary

Dated: This 1st day of December, 2010

WATERFRONT XX CONDOMINIUM ASSOCIATION, INC.
A Corporation Not-for-Profit

BUDGET MEETING
PROOF OF NOTICE AFFIDAVIT

STATE OF FLORIDA)
COUNTY OF PINELLAS   )

The undersigned Secretary of the Association, being first duly sworn, deposes and says that the notice of the budget meeting for 2011 calendar year was mailed or hand delivered to each unit owner at the address last furnished to the Association in accordance with the requirements of Section 718.112(2)(e), F.S., not less than 14 days prior to the meeting at which the budget was to be considered.

Dated this 15th day of December, 2010.

By:_____
Secretary

The foregoing Affidavit was acknowledged before me this 15th day of December, 2010, by Sara Harris, the Secretary of Waterfront XX Condominium Associations, Inc.

_____
Notary Public

My Commission Expires:

WATERFRONT XX CONDOMINIUM ASSOCIATION, INC.
A Corporation Not-for-Profit

2010 ANNUAL FINANCIAL REPORT

I. Expenses for the Condominium Association Expenditures

	Budgeted	Actual
A. Administration of Association	$1,200.00	$1,200.00
B. Management Fees	8,424.00	8,424.00
C. Building Cleaning & Maintenance	1,200.00	1,200.00
D. Lawn and Property Maintenance	6,000.00	5,750.00
E. Rent for Recreation and Other Commonly Used Facilities	1,200.00	1,200.00
F. Expenses on Association Property		
1) Taxes	252.00	252.00
2) Cleaning & Maintenance	120.00	250.00
G. Taxes on Leased Property	120.00	120.00
H. Electricity (common elements)	3,840.00	2,910.00
I. Water, Sewer and Garbage Service	10,800.00	11,300.00
J. Insurance	7,500.00	7,489.00
K. Miscellaneous		
1) Annual Filing Fee	24.00	24.00
2) Professional Services (legal and accounting)	1,200.00	1,300.00
L. Security Provisions	0.00	300.00
M. Pest Control	1,200.00	1,000.00
TOTAL	$43,080.00	$42,719.00

II. Income

A. Assessment Collections from Unit Owners	$52,188.00
B. Interest Income from Operation Account	186.16
C. 2009 Surplus	<u>210.12</u>
	$52,584.28

III. Summary

A.	TOTAL INCOME	$52,584.28
B.	TOTAL EXPENSES FOR OPERATIONS	-42,719.00
	SUB-TOTAL	$9,865.28
C.	TOTAL RESERVE COLLECTIONS (2010)	<u>- 9,108.00</u>
	COMMON SURPLUS	$757.28

IV. Reserves

	Building Painting	Paving Resurfacing	Roof Replacement	Pool Reserves
Beginning Balance	$16,996	$5,835	$25,200	$2,220
2010 Collections	4,608	900	3,000	600
Interest Earned	<u>1,436</u>	<u>465</u>	<u>1,800</u>	<u>180</u>
SUBTOTAL	$23,040	$7,200	$30,000	$3,000
2010 Expenditures	<u>0</u>	<u>0</u>	<u>6,000</u>	<u>0</u>
TOTAL RESERVES AT 2010 YEAR END	$ 23,040	$ 7,200	$ 24,000	$3,000

8

Assessments—Levy and Collection

ASSESSMENT FORMS

8.1   General. The condominium is sometimes referred to as a quasi-government and a democratic sub-society.[1] To the extent that a condominium association can be compared to the governing body of a quasi-government or mini-democracy, the power to tax is equally analogous to the condominium association's power to levy and collect assessments from its members. The power and authority to exercise this responsibility is mandated by the Condominium Act, and the power to assess is an inherent tool that allows the association to carry out its ultimate responsibility for the management, operation and maintenance of the condominium.[2]

The ability of the association to levy and collect assessments is part of the plan to maintain the properties for the benefit of all who own and reside in the condominium. To be ultimately successful, each owner must pay the share for which he or she is responsible. The power of the board of administration and the association to require these payments is tempered so that assessment authority is not abused or made punitive.

The Condominium Act strikes a balance between the requirements that impose upon each unit owner an obligation to pay his or her fair share and the protections that prevent a unit owner or a small group of owners from being unfairly treated in the assessment process. The board of administration must follow these statutory provisions closely to assure that both the levy and the collection of assessments is properly accomplished and that the standards and protections of the Act are preserved.[3]

8.2   Funding the Budget. The most common assessments are those required to fund the annual budget of the condominium association.[4] The funding requirements for the budget and the assessments that are required from each owner to meet those requirements are determined simultaneously when the community's budget is adopted.

Once the budget has been adopted, the total amount of revenue required for the fiscal year of the association has also been determined.[5] The board of administration must next identify each source of revenue that will help to fund the annual budget, including the unit owners' assessments. Some associations may have rental fees or other sources of revenue to

---

[1] *Hidden Harbour Estates, Inc. v. Norman,* 309 So.2d 180, 181 (Fla. 4th DCA 1975).
[2] § 718.111 (4), F.S.
[3] § 718.116, F.S.
[4] § 718.103 (1), F.S.
[5] § 718.112 (2)(f), F.S.

help defer the costs of the annual budget, but the substantial share of the funds required for the payment of the common expenses and funding of the budget will be levied as assessments against the individual unit owners of the condominium.[6]

When the amount of the assessments has been determined, the board of administration is required to establish a payment schedule for the owners in the manner required by the association bylaws. In making such a determination, the board must require that the payments be made in advance and that they be made at least quarterly. The payments must be sufficient to provide the funds necessary to pay for all of the anticipated operating expenses and all unpaid expenses previously incurred.[7] The most traditional payment schedule for assessments is monthly, in advance, although the board is allowed the flexibility to tailor payment schedules to fit the particular accounting practices of the community to the extent that the association bylaws permit.

8.3 Allocation of Common Expenses. The allocation of common expenses and, in turn, the assessment amounts which are attributed to each unit in a residential condominium are determined by the formula established in the Condominium Act. The formula requires that each unit owner's share of the common expenses be based on the same percentage as the unit's ownership interest in the common elements.[8] There are some rare exceptions to this mandated formula where unit owners have been guaranteed a different common expense allocation by a contract entered into prior to 1976.

The selection of the percentage of ownership in the common elements that is to be assigned to each unit is initially made by the developer at the time that the declaration of condominium is recorded.[9] Once the assignment has been made, it becomes a vested property right with the unit to which it is assigned, and it cannot be later changed or modified without the owner's consent.[10]

Prior to January 1, 1992, there was no standard or formula which the developer was required to follow when selecting the common element percentages. In any declaration of condominium recorded after January 1,

---

[6] § 718.103 (1), F.S.
[7] § 718.112 (2)(g), F.S.
[8] § 718.115 (2), F.S.
[9] § 718.104 (4)(g), F.S.
[10] § 718.110 (4), F.S.

1992, however, the share of common elements assigned to each unit must be based upon the square footage of the unit or upon equal shares for each unit.[11] The formula for allocation of common expenses, once selected by the developer, must be followed by the board of administration without variation.[12] There is no flexibility within the community to modify the formula until each affected unit owner agrees to the change. (See 9.15).

It is not uncommon to find differences of opinion on what is a fair allocation of common expenses. Some owners will advocate that expenses should be shared equally, regardless of unit size, while others will feel that the value of the unit or its overall square footage should be the basis for the allocation. These debates, which arise occasionally within a community, have little value since the percentages originally selected, for whatever reason, must be followed in the allocation of expenses.[13]

8.4   Allocation of Expenses for Association Property. The condominium association has the authority to acquire and hold property for the use and benefit of its members. It may include additional real property adjacent to the existing condominium community or personal property which is used within the condominium.[14]

The expense that is incurred by the association for the maintenance, use and upkeep of association-owned property is properly categorized as a common expense.[15] Common expenses are, in turn, allocated and assessed among the owners of units based upon the percentage of ownership which each unit has in the common elements.[16] Accordingly, the expenses for the association property and the assessments incidental to them are dealt with in the same manner as expenses for the common elements of the condominium.

8.5   Allocation of Expenses for Communication Services and Cable Television. The cost of communication services, including Internet and cable television, may be considered a common expense under one of two circumstances specified in the Condominium Act. First, the cost of the service will be a common expense if the provisions of the declaration of

---

[11] § 718.104 (4)(f), F.S.
[12] *Clearwater Key Ass'n-South Beach, Inc. v. Thacker,* 431 So.2d 641 (Fla. 2nd DCA 1983).
[13] § 718.104 (4)(g) and § 718.115 (2), F.S.
[14] § 718.111 (7) and § 718.103 (3), F.S.
[15] § 718.103 (9), F.S and § 718.115 (1)(a), F.S.
[16] § 718.115 (2) and (4)(a), F.S.

condominium so provide. If the declaration does not make provision for communication services, the costs may still be deemed a common expense if the service is provided by a bulk contract approved by the board of administration. The bulk contract must be in writing and be for a minimum period of two (2) years. The charges for the service may be allocated on an equal, per unit basis even if the other common expenses of the condominium are not equally shared by the unit owners.[17]

Any bulk communication service contract may be canceled by the unit owners at the next regular or special meeting of the association following the contract's approval by the board. Any association member may make a motion to cancel the contract, but if the motion is not made or if the motion fails to win by a majority of those in attendance at the meeting, then the contract becomes effective for the balance of its designated term.[18]

Ordinarily, liability for assessments may not be avoided by a unit owner who waives the use of the common elements or common services in a condominium.[19] Under limited circumstances, cable television or video service is an exception to this requirement. If a unit owner is legally blind or hearing impaired and does not occupy the unit with a sighted or hearing person, the unit owner may discontinue the cable television or video service without penalty or charge. Similarly, a unit owner receiving supplemental security income under Title XVI of the Social Security Act or food stamps may discontinue the service. The expenses for the bulk service contract are then to be shared by the remaining unit owners in the condominium.[20]

8.6   Allocation of Expenses for Unit Owner. The allocations of some expenses for upkeep of the condominium property are not classified as common expenses to be shared by all owners. Many declarations of condominium require that the association actually maintain a portion of the unit which is the exclusive property of a particular owner. The responsibility for payment of such maintenance expenses is attributable to the individual owner benefiting from the maintenance.[21]

The condominium documents may also provide an owner with the exclusive use of certain limited common elements or other appurtenances

---

[17] § 718.115 (1)(d), F.S.
[18] § 718.115 (1)(d) 1., F.S.
[19] § 718.116 (2), F.S.
[20] § 718.115 (1)(d) 2., F.S.
[21] § 718.113 (1), F.S. and § 718.504 (21)(c), F.S.

to the exclusion of others and will require that the expenses for the maintenance of these limited common elements be assumed by the owner receiving the exclusive benefit.[22] The operating budget must separately reflect the estimated expenses attributable to a unit owner for the limited common elements serving his unit, the maintenance of the owner's property performed by the association, and other expenses that are personal to the individual owner.[23]

The association may not collect a fee from a unit owner for the use of the common elements or the association property unless it is pursuant to a written lease or unless the documents of the community specifically provide for such a fee.[24] If such fees are permitted, they should be allocated to the unit directly responsible for payment and assessed to the owner in the manner provided by the association bylaws.

8.7   Special Assessments. Funding of the budget is accompanied by assessments against each unit owner that ensure that funds are available to meet the anticipated expenditures. A special assessment is one that is levied against unit owners for expenses over and above those anticipated by the annual budget.[25] The need for special assessments may arise from unanticipated expenses, the need to fund insurance deductibles, or from expenses to meet deferred maintenance not otherwise provided for in the reserve accounts of the association budget.

Unless the declaration of condominium or other governing documents in the community require a membership vote, special assessments are adopted by the board of administration. Prior to adoption, the board must identify the estimated costs and specific purposes of the special assessment and must mail, electronically transmit or deliver written notice of the meeting where the special assessment will be considered to each unit owner at least fourteen (14) days prior to the meeting. The notice must also be posted conspicuously on the condominium property not less than fourteen (14) days prior to the meeting. After adoption, a second notice must be mailed, hand-delivered or electronically transmitted to each unit owner stating that the special assessment has been adopted and further stating the purpose or

---

[22] § 718.106 (2)(b) and § 718.113 (1), F.S.; see also *Rosso v. Golden Surf Towers Condominium Ass'n,* 651 So.2d 787, 788 (Fla. 1995).

[23] § 718.504 (20)(b), F.S.

[24] § 718.111 (4), F.S.

[25] § 718.103 (24), F.S.

purposes for which it was adopted.[26]

All of the proceeds collected from special assessments must be used for the specific purpose or purposes set forth in the notice to unit owners. Once the purpose or purposes of the special assessment have been completed, the excess funds are considered common surplus, and may, at the discretion of the board, either be returned to the unit owners or applied as a credit towards future assessments.[27]

8.8   Time for Payment and Delinquency. The timely remittance of assessments and assessment installments from each unit owner is essential to the smooth functioning of the condominium association and the proper maintenance of the condominium property. The association, through its board of administration, has the power to make and collect the assessments and establish the time when each assessment or assessment installment is due.[28] The payment schedule to fund the annual budget must require each owner to pay installments in advance and not less frequently than quarterly.[29]

When exercising its authority to set assessments and to provide for their manner of payment, the board of administration must be specific. In addition to establishing the time and method of payment, the board should expressly state the due date of the assessment or the assessment installment, as well as the date when the payment becomes delinquent.[30] Each element becomes important when it is necessary to enforce the payment of delinquent assessments. The board of administration has wider latitude to provide for the payment terms of a special assessment. Payments may spread over a longer period and the unpaid portion of the assessment may be secured by recording a declaration of assessment setting out the payment terms.[31]

To insure that the enactment of the assessment, the terms of its payment, its due date and its date of delinquency are completely and specifically identified, each of these details should be set forth in an assessment resolution by the board of administration. The resolution should then be incorporated into the minutes of the meeting at which the assessment is formally adopted.

---

[26] § 718.112 (2)(c) and § 718.116 (10), F.S.

[27] § 718.116 (10), F.S.

[28] § 718.111 (4) and § 718.116 (3), F.S.

[29] § 718.112 (2)(g), F.S.

[30] "Before a unit owner is liable for an assessment, that assessment must be due against him." *Palm Bay Towers Corp. v. Brooks,* 466 So.2d 1071, 1073 (Fla. 3rd DCA 1984).

[31] § 617.0302 (7) and 15), F.S.

8.9   Assessment Records and Estoppel Certificate. The board of administration is required to keep an account for the assessments levied against each unit owner and paid on behalf of each unit.[32] These accounts are part of the permanent records of the association and they must state the name and current mailing address of the unit owner, the amount of each assessment which has been levied, the date and amount of each installment that comes due, the amount that has been paid, and the balance which remains unpaid.[33]

Assessment records must be maintained for each unit managed by the condominium association and they must be available for inspection by the unit owner or the owner's representative at any reasonable time.[34] In addition to making the assessment records available for inspection, the board must also be prepared to deliver an estoppel certificate stating the status of all assessments affecting the unit within fifteen (15) days after a request by an owner or by a mortgage holder.[35] The association or its authorized agent may charge a reasonable fee for the preparation of the certificate, and the unit owner is responsible for ensuring that the fee is paid.[36]

The assessment certificate is a statement of all the assessments and other monies owed to the association by the unit owner. Any person, including a mortgage lender or a purchaser of the unit, other than the current owner, who relies upon the assessment certificate is protected by its content and may presume it to be accurate.[37] Keeping assessment records current will insure that the certificate can be accurately supplied within the fifteen (15) day time period as required by the Condominium Act.

8.10   Assessment Declaration and Satisfaction. On occasion, the association may find it necessary to levy a special assessment, the amount of which may be unmanageable to some owners if the payment is required within a short period of time. Under such circumstances, the board of administration has the discretion to allow the special assessment to be

---

[32] § 718.111 (12)(a) 11. b., F.S; *Hobbs v. Weinkauf,* 940 So2d 1151 (Fla. 2nd DCA 2006).

[33] § 718.111 (12)(a) 11., F.S.

[34] § 718.111 (12)(c), F.S.

[35] § 718.116 (8), F.S.

[36] The fee must be paid in conjunction with a closing on the unit or collected in the same manner as an assessment. § 718.116 (8)(d), F.S.

[37] *Id.*

paid over a period of time in manageable installments. Unit owners may then elect to make time payments in lieu of payment of the entire special assessment.[38]

The board of administration may borrow funds from traditional lending sources and secure their repayment with a pledge of the special assessments being paid by installment.[39] The implementation of such a proposal requires that the board of administration evidence the unpaid balance of the assessments on the public records of the county where the condominium is located. When the special assessment is paid in full, a "satisfaction of assessment" will be recorded in the public records showing that the obligation is satisfied.

The "declaration of assessment" should state the nature of the special assessment, the date that it was levied, and the number of the unit and the name of the owner responsible for payment of the assessment. The declaration of assessment must be executed by the officers of the association and be recorded with the Clerk of the Circuit Court. For each owner who pays the special assessment in full or who has completed the installment payment process, a satisfaction of the assessment must also be prepared for execution by the officers of the association and recorded with the Clerk to discharge the obligation.

8.11 Liability for Assessments. The condominium unit serves as security for the payment of all assessments that are properly levied by the association. The owner of the condominium unit is liable for all assessments coming due while he or she is the owner of the unit. When a unit is sold, the buyer becomes jointly and severally liable for all unpaid assessments for common expenses prior to the time of the sale.[40] The buyer may attempt to recover the unpaid assessments from the seller, but the condominium association may look to both individuals for payment of the unpaid assessment.[41]

Liability for assessments by a unit owner cannot be avoided by waiver of the use or the enjoyment of either the unit or the common elements by the owner.[42] No unit owner may be relieved of liability for all or any

---

[38] § 718.111 (4), F.S. and § 718.116 (3), F.S.
[39] § 617.0302 (7), F.S.
[40] *Karpay v. Las Brisas Condominium Ass'n, Inc.*, 517 So.2d 756, 757 (Fla. 2nd DCA 1987).
[41] § 718.116 (1)(a), F.S.
[42] § 718.116 (2), F.S.

part of an assessment unless all other owners in the condominium are also proportionately excused from the liability for payment.[43]

No special deal or arrangement may be made separately with the developer to relieve an owner of the assessment obligation imposed by the Condominium Act. A separately negotiated deal or modification with the developer for the payment of assessments does not bind the condominium association. When such an arrangement exists, the association is entitled to receive the full payment from the owner and the unit owner must seek to recover any supplemental funds from the developer once the assessment has been paid.

Similarly, dissatisfaction with the association or the board, or the maintenance being performed by them, is not a basis for withholding payment of assessment sums due to the association.[44] The assessments must be paid and the dissatisfaction pursued separately as permitted in the condominium documents and the Condominium Act.

8.12　Interest, Late Charges, Costs and Penalties. Assessments and assessment installments that are not paid when due bear interest at the rate provided in the declaration or, if no rate is provided, then at a rate of 18% per year.[45] When examining the declaration of condominium, the board should be aware that there is a distinction between the "legal rate," which is 12% per year, and the "highest rate allowed by law," which is 18% per year.[46] Interest accrues from the date when the assessment becomes delinquent until it is paid. Interest charges for nonpayment of assessments are not considered a late fee, fine or other penalty where such charges are calculated over the actual period of deficiency. It is important, therefore, to state the due date for each assessment or installment at the time the board makes the assessment levy.

In addition to interest on delinquent assessments, the association may levy an administrative late fee if permitted either by the declaration of condominium or the bylaws of the association. The amount of the charge may not exceed the greater of $25 or 5% of each assessment or assessment installment that is delinquent.[47] The association may also accelerate the

---

[43] § 718.116 (9)(a), F.S.
[44] *Id.*
[45] § 718.116 (3), F.S.
[46] § 687.01 and § 687.02, F.S.
[47] § 718.116 (3), F.S.

assessments of a delinquent unit owner. By accelerating the assessments, the sum due the association includes the amounts due for the remainder of the budget year in which the claim of lien is filed. (See 8.14). The accelerated assessments are deemed due and payable on the date the claim of lien is filed.[48]

The condominium association is also entitled to recover any attorney's fees and costs that it incurs in the collection of a delinquent assessment or assessment installment. The "claim of lien" recorded to secure the association's interests in a delinquent assessment includes all of the unpaid assessment, accrued interest, costs and attorney's fees, and all additional assessments that may come due during the enforcement proceedings.[49]

Under the Condominium Act, a delinquent unit owner is subject to other sanctions in addition to the fees and costs associated with the collection of the delinquent funds. The association may suspend the voting rights of a unit owner who is more than ninety (90) days delinquent in any monetary obligation due to the association.[50] The association may also suspend the rights of the owner and occupants of the unit to use the common elements, recreational facilities, and other association property until the delinquent obligation is satisfied.[51] (See 13.7).

Finally, when a unit is being rented by an owner who is delinquent in any obligation due to the association, the association may collect the delinquent sums from the tenant pursuant to procedures in the Act.[52] The association must make a written demand on the tenant for payment and provide written notice to the unit owner that the demand has been made. The payments by the tenant to the association must be limited to the amount that would otherwise be paid to the unit owner.[53]

8.13 Application of Partial Payment of Delinquent Assessment.

Any payment of a delinquent assessment received by the association shall be applied first to any interest accrued by the association; then to any administrative late fee; then to any costs or attorney's fees incurred in

---

[48] § 718.112 (2)(g), F.S.
[49] § 718.116 (5)(a), F.S.
[50] § 718.303 (5), F.S.
[51] § 718.303 (3), F.S. The suspension cannot deny the owner or unit occupants access to the unit, the unit's utility services, parking, or elevators.
[52] § 718.116 (11), F.S.
[53] *Id.*

collection; and finally to the principle balance of the delinquent assessment or assessment installment. This priority for crediting a delinquent payment to each category of charges applies even if a unit owner attempts to place a restrictive endorsement on his or her check or other payment instrument. The Condominium Act establishes the priority notwithstanding any restrictive endorsement, designation, or instruction placed on or accompanying the delinquent payment.[54]

8.14   Claim of Lien. The association has a lien for all unpaid assessments and evidences its claim for a delinquent assessment or assessment installment by filing a "claim of lien" with the Clerk of the Circuit Court in the county where the condominium is located. Prior to filing the claim of lien, however, the association must give the delinquent unit owner thirty (30) days' written notice by certified mail of its intent to make the filing.[55] The claim of lien is effective from the time of its recording for a period of one (1) year. It secures all unpaid assessments, interest, costs and attorney's fees that are due, and all those that come due during enforcement proceedings until the entry of a final judgment in foreclosure.[56]

The board of administration must be sensitive to the one (1) year period of the lien, which begins on the date that the claim of lien is recorded with the Clerk. If an enforcement action is not started by the board within the one (1) year period, the lien will be void.[57] The Division of Florida Condominiums, Timeshares, and Mobile Homes further feels that when the claim of lien becomes void, the association is not able to ever re-file the lien for the same claim.

A claim of lien must state the legal description of the condominium unit, the owner of the unit, and the amount and date when the assessment or installment became due. The lien must be signed by an officer or agent of the association with the formality of a deed prior to recording. The association attorney or manager may serve as an authorized agent for executing the claim of lien of the association if the board of administration approves such authority.[58]

[54] § 718.116 (3), F.S.; *Ocean Two Condominium Ass'n, Inc. v. Kliger*, 983 So.2d 739, 741 (Fla. 3rd DCA 2008).
[55] § 718.121 (4), F.S.
[56] § 718.116 (5)(a), F.S.
[57] *Id.*
[58] *Id.*

When the recorded claim of lien is returned from the Clerk, a copy should be forwarded to the unit owner with a notice of the association's claim. The notice must be given personally to the unit owner or provided by certified or registered mail with a return receipt requested. The notice should include a copy of the lien and a statement of the interest and costs secured by the lien. The notice should additionally contain a statement advising the owner that the association intends to foreclose the lien if the owner has not satisfied the obligation within thirty (30) days from the date of receiving the notice.[59]

8.15 Withholding Payment and Contesting the Lien. The time to challenge the legality of an assessment is when the assessment or an installment of the assessment is sought to be collected by the board.[60] An owner withholding payment is challenging the validity of the assessment or its enactment. Withholding payment will create a delinquency and a subsequent lien by the board of administration.

An owner wishing to object to a claim of lien may do so by the filing of a "notice of contest of lien" with the Clerk of the Circuit Court. The notice of contest will state that the owner objects to the lien by referring to the official record book and page where it is recorded and stating that the association must commence enforcement within ninety (90) days from the date that the notice of contest is received by the board. The notice may be signed by the owner or the attorney for the owner objecting to the assessment and the lien.[61]

The grounds for withholding payment of an assessment by a unit owner are limited. Assessments which are discriminatory or which have been improperly levied by the board of administration may be successfully challenged. Objections to inferior workmanship by the board of administration or by the developer, or to incomplete work by either the board or the developer, do not provide sufficient legal basis for successfully withholding the assessments.[62]

---

[59] § 718.116 (6)(b), F.S.

[60] *Margate Village Condominium Ass'n, Inc. v. Wilfred, Inc.,* 350 So.2d 16, 18 (Fla. 4th DCA 1977).

[61] § 718.116 (5)(a), F.S.

[62] " . . . (I)f the officers or directors act in an unauthorized manner, the unit owners should seek a remedy through election, or if factually supported, in an action for breach of fiduciary duty. The owners' remedies do not include failing to pay an assessment. . . ." *Ocean Trail Unit Owners Ass'n, Inc. v. Mead,* 650 So.2d 4, 7 (Fla. 1994).

At any time when an owner withholds payment of an assessment and files a notice of contest of the lien, the board must commence enforcement action within ninety (90) days or the claim of lien is voided and the objection of the unit owner is presumed to be valid.[63]

8.16   Foreclosing the Lien. The board of administration may bring an action to foreclose a claim of lien for unpaid assessments in the Circuit Court in the same way that a mortgage on real estate is foreclosed. The homestead protections provided by Florida's Constitution do not prevent the foreclosure and sale of the condominium unit.[64] To preserve its rights to recover the fees and costs secured by the claim of lien, the association must give the delinquent owner written notice of its intention to foreclose thirty (30) days before the action is commenced. If the notice is not given, the fees and costs cannot be recovered.[65]

The foreclosure notice requirements are considered satisfied when the owner records a notice of contest of lien. They may also be dispensed with when a mortgage foreclosure suit is already pending against the unit and the position of the association may be prejudiced by waiting the thirty (30) day period.[66] In addition to an action of foreclosure, the board of administration may also seek to recover a separate money judgment for the unpaid assessments without waiving the claim of lien.[67]

8.17   Rights of First Mortgage Holder. The Condominium Act extends a special protection to the holder of a first mortgage on a condominium unit. When it becomes necessary for the mortgage to be foreclosed or for the holder of the mortgage to accept a deed in lieu of foreclosure, the liability of the mortgage holder is limited to the share of assessments coming due during the twelve (12) months immediately preceding acquisition of title to the unit by the mortgage holder or one (1) percent of the original mortgage debt, whichever is less.[68] After the title has been acquired, the new owner must pay the amount of any other assessments due the association within thirty (30) days.[69]

---

[63] § 718.116 (5)(c), F.S.
[64] *Bessemer v. Gersten,* 381 So.2d 1344, 1347 (Fla. 1980)
[65] § 718.116 (6)(a), F.S.
[66] § 718.116 (6)(b), F.S.
[67] § 718.116 (6)(a), F.S.
[68] § 718.116 (1)(b), F.S.; *Bay Holdings, Inc. v. 2000 Island Boulevard Condominium Ass'n, Inc.,* 895 So.2d 1197 (Fla. 3rd DCA 2005).
[69] § 718.116 (1)(c), F.S.

The unpaid portion of the assessments of the prior owner become uncollectible at the time a final judgment of foreclosure is entered or a deed in lieu of foreclosure is delivered to the first mortgage holder. The uncollectible assessments thereupon become a common expense to be shared by all owners including the former first mortgagee. The new owner of the foreclosed unit is responsible for a proportionate share of the total uncollected assessments in the same proportion as the common ownership percentage that is attributable to the unit that has been foreclosed.[70]

Once the first mortgage holder has acquired title to the condominium unit, the mortgage holder becomes liable for the payment of all assessments for common expenses coming due during the mortgage holder's ownership, whether the unit is occupied or not. Responsibility for the assessments begins when a deed in lieu of foreclosure is given by the unit owner or when a final order in the foreclosure proceedings vests title to the unit in a new owner.

8.18 Developer Obligation for Assessments. The condominium developer is entitled to a special exemption from the payment of assessments for so long as the developer guarantees to each purchaser that assessments for common expenses will not be increased. The developer must pay the excess common expenses incurred but not covered by unit owner payments during the period of guarantee.[71] During this period of developer guarantee, reserve funds and funds collected for start-up costs and other non-assessment revenue cannot be used by the developer-controlled association for the payment of operating expenses.[72]

The developer's assessment guarantee does not extend to uninsured losses resulting from a natural disaster or an act of God, provided that the developer-controlled association has obtained and maintained the required insurance for the condominium. Should a casualty loss occur to the condominium property that is not covered by the required insurance, each unit owner, including the developer for units owned by the developer, assumes a proportional share of the uninsured loss.[73]

---

[70] *Id*

[71] § 718.116 (9)(a) 1. and 2., F.S.

[72] § 718.116 (9)(b) and § 61B-22.004 (4), F.S.

[73] § 718.116 (9)(a), F.S.

While the developer holds units for sale in the ordinary course of business, the association cannot pass assessments for capital improvements chargeable to the developer without the developer's consent.[74] The association may increase the assessments for operating expenses and apply them to the developer's units so long as there is no discrimination in the assessment levy.[75] As long as the developer controls the board of administration, the board may not impose assessment increases in any year which are greater than 115% of the previous year without the approval of a majority of the voting interests in the condominium.[76]

To insure that the developer has complied with the terms of the assessment guarantee, the developer must support his actions with financial statements provided at the time of transition. The statements must show that the developer was charged and paid the proper amounts of assessments.[77]

8.19 Rights of Association to Acquire Unit. The association has the power to acquire a condominium unit at foreclosure sale for unpaid assessments or to accept a deed in lieu of foreclosure.[78] This authority allows the board of administration to acquire a unit to protect its right to recover the unpaid assessments. Towards that end, the association may hold, lease, mortgage, and convey a unit that it owns for the benefit of the association membership, but the voting interests attributed to a unit owned by the association may not be exercised or considered for any purpose.[79]

During the time that the association owns title to a condominium unit, it must pay the assessments which come due in the same manner as all other unit owners.[80] The assessments due from the association-owned unit are common expenses and are shared by all the owners. Also, while a unit is owned by the association, the voting rights appurtenant to it may not be used for any purpose.[81] (See 6.13).

The ability of the association to acquire a unit and to rent and resell it provides flexibility to the board of administration when it attempts to recover unpaid funds due the association. The ability to mortgage a condominium

---

[74] § 718.301 (3)(a), F.S.
[75] § 718.301 (3)(b), F.S.
[76] § 718.112 (2)(e), F.S.
[77] § 718.301 (4)(c), F.S.
[78] § 718.111 (9) and § 718.116 (6)(d), F.S.
[79] § 718.112 (2)(b) 2., F.S.
[80] § 718.116 (1)(a) and (9)(b), F.S.
[81] § 718.112 (2)(b) 2., F.S.

unit enhances the flexibility of the board under such circumstances. It permits a prudent board of administration to protect its lien on a unit so the delinquent assessments are not lost by the foreclosure of a first mortgage.

8.20 Uncollectible Assessments. On occasion, the bankruptcy of a unit owner or the foreclosure of a first mortgage will eliminate the ability of the board of administration to collect assessments against a unit owner. These unpaid assessments become legally uncollectible and a common expense of the association at the time the mortgage holder takes ownership of the unit.[82] At that time, the uncollectible assessments are allocated among all of the unit owners, including the new owner of the unit where the assessments were determined to be uncollectible.[83]

The fact that the unpaid assessments become a burden upon the remaining unit owners is ample reason for the board of administration to pursue all of its available collection alternatives when an owner withholds payment of an assessment or an assessment installment. Additionally, the board should not overlook the responsibility of the new owner of a unit where assessments were determined to be uncollectible to ensure that the new owner assumes a proportionate share of the uncollectible expenses.[84]

---

[82] § 718.115 (1)(c), F.S.
[83] § 718.116 (7), F.S.
[84] § 718.116 (1)(c) 2., F.S.

A RESOLUTION OF THE BOARD OF ADMINISTRATION ADOPTING A SPECIAL ASSESSMENT FOR BUILDING AND GROUND MAINTENANCE; ESTABLISHING A DUE DATE FOR PAYMENT; ESTABLISHING METHOD FOR PAYMENT

THAT WHEREAS, the Board has determined that the buildings of the condominium are in need of painting and repair, and that the plants and shrubs on the condominium property have been damaged by the winter freezes, and

WHEREAS, the reserve funds of the Association are insufficient to provide for the needed maintenance, repair and replacement.

NOW, THEREFORE, BE IT RESOLVED by the Board of Administration of Waterfront XX Condominium Association, Inc., as follows:

Section 1. THAT there is hereby levied a special assessment in the total sum of $11,000.00 for the purposes of painting and repairing the condominium building and for the replacement of plants and damaged shrubbery on the common elements of the condominium. All funds not expended for such purposes shall be deposited in the reserve account for building painting.

Section 2. THAT the assessment shall be allocated among the condominium units in the same percentage that each unit shares ownership of the common elements.

Section 3. THAT the assessment shall be due on March 1, 2011, and shall be delinquent thereafter. The assessment may be paid in full on or before the due date without penalty, or may be satisfied by paying $200.00 on or before March 1, 2011, and $100.00 on the lst day of each month thereafter, together with interest at the rate of 18% per annum, until the special assessment is fully paid.

ADOPTED by the Board of Administration this 10th day of January, 2011.

(CORPORATE SEAL)   WATERFRONT XX CONDOMINIUM
ASSOCIATION, INC.

ATTEST:

_____   By:_____
Secretary   President

Assessment Reoslution FORM 8.01

WATERFRONT XX CONDOMINIUM ASSOCIATION, INC.
A Corporation Not-for-Profit

ASSESSMENT RECORDS

2011

Unit No.	Owner Assessment	Date Payment	Received		
			Jan	Feb	Mar
#101 (.125)	Joseph A. Jones	$1,875/yr $156.33/mn	1/3	2/1	3/2
#102 (.250)	Matthew Marshall	$3,750/yr $312.50/mn	1/4	2/20	
#103 (.125)	Peter Johnson Susan Johnson	$1,875/yr $156.33/mn	1/4	2/2	3/1
#104 (.250)	David R. Smith Nancy H. Smith	$3,750/yr $312.50/mn	1/10	2/10	3/9
#105 (.125)	Marc Wesley	$1,875/yr $156.33/mn	1/3	2/4	3/3
#106 (.125)	ABP Corporation	$1,875/yr $156.33/mn	1/5	2/2	3/2

WATERFRONT XX CONDOMINIUM ASSOCIATION, INC.
A Corporation Not-for-Profit

SPECIAL ASSESSMENT NOTICE

NOTICE IS HEREBY GIVEN that the Board of Administration has adopted a special assessment to be used for the painting and exterior repair of the building and the replacement of freeze-damaged shrubbery. The assessment has been allocated among the unit owners based upon each unit's allocated share of the common elements as follows:

Unit	Assessment Amount
#101	$1,100.00
#102	$1,100.00
#103	$1,100.00
#104	$1,100.00
#105	$1,100.00
#106	$1,100.00

DUE DATE for the special assessment is March 1, 2011, and the Board has authorized alternative methods for payment as follows:

1.   The owner may pay the full assessment on or before March 1, 2011, or;

2.   The owner may pay $200.00 on or before March 1, 2011, and $100.00 on or before the first of each month thereafter, together with interest at the rate of 18% per annum, until the special assessment is paid in full.

DONE AND ORDERED by the Board of Administration on January 10, 2011.

WATERFRONT XX CONDOMINIUM
ASSOCIATION, INC.

By: _____
Secretary

WATERFRONT XX CONDOMINIUM ASSOCIATION, INC.
A Corporation Not-for-Profit

CERTIFICATE OF ASSESSMENT

TO: FIRST SAVINGS AND LOAN ASSOCIATION

      POST OFFICE DRAWER 101

      WATERFRONT, FLORIDA   33444

RE: UNIT 105; MARC WESLEY, OWNER

In response to your request, the undersigned, on behalf of the Board of Administration, does hereby provide the Association's certificate on the status of assessments with respect to the above condominium parcel, as follows:

1.   Total Annual Assessment $1,875.00

2.   Monthly Assessment Installment $156.33

3.   Special Assessments Due $0.00

4.   Other Monies Due Association $0.00

All assessment installments through February 1, 2011, have been paid in full by the owner. The next assessment installment is due March 1, 2011.

CERTIFIED this 10th day of February, 2011.

WATERFRONT XX CONDOMINIUM
ASSOCIATION, INC.

By: _____
     Treasurer

DECLARATION OF ASSESSMENT
OF
WATERFRONT XX CONDOMINIUM ASSOCIATION, INC.
A Corporation Not-for-Profit

WATERFRONT XX CONDOMINIUM ASSOCIATION, INC., hereby gives notice that, by action of the Board of Administration on January 10, 2011, after notice of its intention to consider an assessment at a meeting on said date, a special assessment was levied against each unit in the condominium. At the option of the unit owner, the assessment was payable in full on or before March 1, 2011, or by paying $200.00 on or before March 1, 2011, and $100.00 the first of each month thereafter, together with interest at the rate of 18% per annum, until the assessment is paid in full. The owners of units electing to pay by installment are set forth below and the Association does hereby declare that the assessments are outstanding and payable as described above.

> Unit Number, Waterfront XX
>
> Condominium, pursuant to the
>
> Declaration of Condominium

Owner	Recorded in O.R. Book 800, Page 100, Public Records of Pinellas County, Florida	Principal Amount of Assessment
Joseph A. Jones & Ann Marie Jones	Unit #101	$1,100.00
Matthew Marshall	Unit #102	$1,100.00
ABP Corporation	Unit #106	$1,100.00

DONE AND EXECUTED this 30th day of January, 2011.

(CORPORATE SEAL)   WATERFRONT XX CONDOMINIUM
                        ASSOCIATION, INC.

ATTEST

_____   By: _____

Secretary   President

STATE OF FLORIDA   )
COUNTY OF PINELLAS   )

On this 30th day of January, 2011, personally appeared Joseph A. Jones, President, and acknowledged before me that he executed this instrument for the purposes herein expressed.

_____

Notary Public

My commission expires:

WATERFRONT XX CONDOMINIUM ASSOCIATION, INC.

A Corporation Not-for-Profit

SATISFACTION OF ASSESSMENT

THIS SATISFACTION OF ASSESSMENT made this 30th day of September, 2011, by Waterfront XX Condominium Association, Inc. is hereby given as evidence that the Declaration of Assessment levied against the units described hereinbelow on January 30, 2011, and recorded in O.R. Book 1001 at Page 101, Public Records of Pinellas County, Florida, has been paid in full and is duly satisfied as to said units, to wit:

Owner	Unit Number, Waterfront XX Condominium, pursuant to the Declaration of Condominium Recorded in O.R. Book 800, Page 100, Public Records of Pinellas County, Florida	Principal Amount of Assessment
Joseph A. Jones & Ann Marie Jones	Unit #101	$1,100.00
Matthew Marshall	Unit #102	$1,100.00

DONE AND EXECUTED this 30th day of September, 2011.

(CORPORATE SEAL)   WATERFRONT XX CONDOMINIUM
ASSOCIATION, INC.

ATTEST:

_____   By: _____
Secretary   President

STATE OF FLORIDA   )

COUNTY OF PINELLAS   )

On this 30th day of September, 2011, personally appeared Joseph A. Jones, President, and acknowledged before me that he executed this instrument for the purposes herein expressed.

_____

Notary Public

My commission expires:

CLAIM OF LIEN

BY

WATERFRONT XX CONDOMINIUM ASSOCIATION, INC.

A Corporation Not-for-Profit

STATE OF FLORIDA   )
COUNTY OF PINELLAS   )

In accordance with the authority of the Declaration of Condominium and Chapter 718, Florida Statutes, WATERFRONT XX CONDOMINIUM ASSOCIATION, INC., hereby claims a lien for all unpaid assessments now delinquent and hereafter accrued against the condominium unit and owner described below, in the initial amount and from the date stated, together with interest and reasonable attorney's fees and costs incident to the collection hereof, as follows:

Owner: Marc Wesley

Due Date: June 15, 2011

Assessment: $100.00

PROPERTY DESCRIPTION

Unit 105, WATERFRONT XX, A CONDOMINIUM, according to the Declaration of Condominium recorded in O.R. Book 800, Page 100, and Condominium Plat Book 8, Page 10, Public Records of Pinellas County, Florida, together with an undivided 2.537% of the common elements appurtenant thereto.

EXECUTED this 15th day of July, 2011.

(CORPORATE SEAL)　　　　WATERFRONT XX CONDOMINIUM
　　　　　　　　　　　　　ASSOCIATION, INC.

ATTEST:

_____　By: _____
Secretary　　　　　　　　　　　President

　　　SWORN TO and subscribed before me this 15th day of July, 2011,
by JOSEPH A. JONES, President, for the purpose therein expressed.

　　　　　　　　　　　_____
　　　　　　　　　　　Notary Public

　　　　　　　　　　　My commission expires:

Claim of Lien FORM 8.07

SATISFACTION OF LIEN
BY
WATERFRONT XX CONDOMINIUM ASSOCIATION, INC.
A Corporation Not-for-Profit

STATE OF FLORIDA   )
COUNTY OF PINELLAS)

FOR AND IN CONSIDERATION of a valuable sum in dollars, receipt of which is hereby acknowledged, the undersigned releases the lien recorded in Official Records Book 1000, Page 100, Public Records of Pinellas County, Florida, from the property owned by Marc Wesley and described as follows:

Unit 105, WATERFRONT XX, A CONDOMINIUM, according to the Declaration of Condominium recorded in O.R. Book 800, Page 100, and Condominium Plat Book 8, Page 10, Public Records of Pinellas County, Florida, together with an undivided 2.537% of the common elements appurtenant thereto.

DONE AND EXECUTED this 23rd day of October, 2011.

(CORPORATE SEAL)   WATERFRONT XX CONDOMINIUM
ASSOCIATION, INC.

ATTEST

_____ By: _____
Secretary   Joseph A. Jones, President

On this 23rd day of October, 2011, personally appeared, JOSEPH A. JONES, President, and acknowledged that he executed this Satisfaction of Lien for the purpose therein expressed.

_____
Notary Public

My commission expires:

Satisfaction of Lien FORM 8.08

WATERFRONT XX CONDOMINIUM ASSOCIATION, INC.
100 Waterfront Drive
Waterfront, Florida 33444

July 20, 2011

Mr. Marc Wesley
105 Waterfront Drive
Waterfront, Florida 33444

Re: Claim of Lien, Unit 105, Waterfront XX Condominium

Dear Mr. Wesley:

This is to advise you that Waterfront XX Condominium Association, Inc., filed its Claim of Lien on July 15, 2011, a copy of which is enclosed, against the unit owned by you. You are further notified that the Association intends to foreclose the Claim of Lien pursuant to Section 718.116, Florida Statutes.

To satisfy the Claim of Lien and avoid foreclosure, the following must be remitted:

Delinquent Assessment(s)	$100.00
Interest through August 1, 2011	2.25
Clerk of Court—Recording	9.00
Certified Postage	1.55
Attorney's Fee	100.00
TOTAL (August 1, 2011)	$212.80

Please be further advised that the delinquent assessment is accruing interest at the rate of 4.9 cents per day subsequent to August 1, 2011.

WATERFRONT XX CONDOMINIUM
ASSOCIATION, INC.

By: _____
President

Enclosure: Certified Copy of Claim of Lien

Notice of Lien and Intent to Foreclose FORM 8.09

NOTICE OF CONTEST OF LIEN

TO: JOSEPH JONES, President
Waterfront XX Condominium Association, Inc.
100 Waterfront Drive
Waterfront, Florida 33444

YOU ARE NOTIFIED that the undersigned contests the claim of lien filed by you on July 15, 2011, and recorded in Official Records Book 1000, at Page 100, of the Public Records of Pinellas County, Florida, and that the time within which you may file suit to enforce your lien is limited to ninety (90) days from the date of service of this notice.

EXECUTED this 5th day of August, 2011.

/s/ Marc Wesley

_____

Owner, Unit 105

STATE OF FLORIDA   )
COUNTY OF PINELLAS)

On this 5th day of August, 2011, personally appeared Marc Wesley and acknowledged before me that he executed this Notice of Contest of Lien for the purposes herein expressed.

_____

Notary Public

My commission expires:

9

Promulgating Rules, Amending the Documents, and Modifying the Condominium Property

AMENDMENT FORMS

9.1   General. As covenants running with the land, the condominium documents create both the restrictions and the responsibilities that set the tenor and character for the community and its residents.[1] The condominium documents and the Condominium Act are designed to allow a community to promulgate supplemental rules to refine its restrictive covenants.[2] The declaration of condominium and other source documents may also be amended to fit the needs and the desires of the residents of the community.[3]

The authority to make rules and amend the documents allows the association significant flexibility. Members may add provisions that were overlooked when the documents were originally prepared, and may change unwanted restrictions initially imposed by the developer. Each new rule or document amendment must be correctly enacted and must not infringe improperly on the vested rights of existing owners. By following proper procedural guidelines, these pitfalls can be avoided and the community can set its own standards and restrictive covenants.

9.2   Authority and Scope of Rules. Condominium rules falling under the general heading of use restrictions emanate from two sources. The first source is the declaration of condominium and the use restrictions and rules that are actually set forth and expressed in that document. The second source is the rules promulgated by the board of administration to carry out the community's policies and the expressed restrictions in the declaration of condominium.[4]

By specific provision in most declarations of condominium, articles of incorporation or the bylaws, the board of administration is granted authority to promulgate rules governing the use of the condominium property.[5] The rule-making authority granted by the Condominium Act to boards is discretionary, and to be exercised, the authority must be specifically expressed somewhere in the condominium documents.[6] This authority may

---

[1] § 718.104 (5), F.S.; *Woodside Village Condominium Ass'n, Inc. v. Jahren*, 806 So.2d 452, 456 (Fla. 2002); *Pepe v. Whispering Sands Condominium Ass'n, Inc.*, 351 So.2d 755, 757 (Fla. 2nd DCA 1977).

[2] § 718.112 (3)(a), F.S.

[3] § 718.110, F.S.

[4] *Hidden Harbour Estates, Inc. v. Basso*, 393 So.2d 637 (Fla. 4th DCA 1981.

[5] § 718.112 (3)(a), F.S.

[6] Rules enacted by the board cannot contravene an express provision of the declaration or a right reasonably inferable therefrom. *Beachwood Villas Condominium v. Poor*, 448 So2d 1143 (Fla. 4th DCA 1984).

exist at the time that the declaration of condominium is originally recorded, or it may be incorporated into the condominium documents by subsequent amendment by the membership.[7]

The restrictions specifically contained in the declaration are clothed with a very strong presumption of validity. The law requires their full disclosure prior to the time of sale and the owner receives complete notice of their content prior to the purchase.[8] Rules and regulations adopted by the board of administration, on the other hand, are treated differently and have a different test for determining their validity. They come into existence after the condominium's creation and may affect the rights of unit owners originally granted by the declaration of condominium.

To be valid and enforceable, a rule or regulation of the board of administration must meet a two-tier test. First, it must be within the scope of authority of the board of administration. Second, the rule or regulation must be reasonable and not arbitrary or capricious.[9] The board may not adopt rules modifying provisions of the declaration of condominium without following the proper amendment procedures to amend the declaration.[10]

To be within the scope of authority of the board, the right to promulgate rules must be expressed in the documents and the rules must not contravene an express provision of the declaration of condominium or a right reasonably inferred from the declaration.[11] If the rules and regulations apply equally to all members of the association and if they are uniform in their application and enforcement, they will meet the second requirement of reasonableness.[12]

9.3   Review and Analysis of Documents. An analytical review of the declaration of condominium and its exhibits is advisable following the transition from developer control and prior to the promulgation of rules and regulations or the making of amendments to the documents themselves. The board of administration may wish to consider the appointment of a special committee to make such a review or to consider a standing committee which

---

[7] § 718.110 (1), F.S.

[8] § 718.503, F.S.

[9] *Hidden Harbour Estates, Inc. v. Norman*, 309 So.2d 180 (Fla. 4th DCA 1975).

[10] *Gordon v. Palm Air Country Club Condominium Ass'n No. 9, Inc.*, 407 So.2d 1284 (Fla. 4th DCA 1986).

[11] *Koplowitz v. Imperial Towers Condominium, Inc.*, 478 So.2d 504, 505–506 (Fla. 4th DCA 1985).

[12] *White Egret Condominium, Inc. v. Franklin*, 379 So.2d 346, 352 (Fla. 1979).

will monitor the application of the rules and restrictions on a continuous basis. (See 5.12).

The document review and analysis is designed to accomplish three goals. The review will identify the authority and the scope that the board has to make rules and to propose amendments to the documents. It will identify unwanted provisions placed in the documents by the developer and ambiguous provisions needing further definition or clarity to insure that the intent is correctly expressed.

The review and analysis of documents helps to insure that there will be consistency among the declaration of condominium and the other documents on the same subject matter. Often, use restrictions, such as rental restrictions and pet restrictions, are referred to in several parts of the condominium documents. Consistency between each of these parts is essential to effective enforcement of the restrictive covenants.

9.4   Adopting and Amending the Rules. The Condominium Act does not set out a specific procedure for the board or the association to follow when adopting or amending its rules and regulations. The board must rely upon the procedures that are contained in the condominium documents governing the community. If authority to promulgate rules is conferred directly on the board of administration, or upon the association without specifying the requirement of a membership vote, then the board may adopt and amend the rules and regulations.[13] The board may do so in the normal course of its duties in the same manner as it undertakes other actions on the association's behalf. When the board intends to consider rules regarding the use of units, notice of the board meeting must be mailed or delivered to unit owners and conspicuously posted on the condominium property not less than fourteen (14) days prior to the meeting.[14]

When the documents require a specific vote of the membership, then board action alone is not enough to pass or amend the rules. If the rules and regulations are attached to the declaration of condominium at the time it is originally recorded, amendments to the recorded rules and regulations must be presented to the membership for a vote. Recorded rules and regulations are part of the original disclosure at the time of purchase and all owners are

---

[13] § 617.0801, F.S.
[14] § 718.112 (2)(c), F.S.

on notice of their content. Accordingly, the membership is entitled to vote on changes to the recorded rules unless an express provision to the contrary is contained in the rules. A majority vote of the members present at a valid meeting will be sufficient to adopt amendments to the recorded rules unless a greater majority is set out in the rules themselves.

All rules or amendments, whether adopted by the board or by a membership vote, should be set forth in full at the meeting considering them. Their full content and the vote of approval should be recorded in the meeting minutes or annexed to them as an exhibit. The rule or amendment should express a clear effective date and a copy of the rule or amendment should be provided to each owner prior to the time when it becomes effective.

9.5   Proposing Amendments to the Documents. Amendments to the declaration of condominium, articles of incorporation and bylaws for the condominium can be successfully adopted only after they have been proposed to the membership by specific procedures. The special requirements of the Condominium Act and the condominium documents must be carefully considered and correctly followed.[15]

The Condominium Act does not permit amendments to the declaration of condominium, articles of incorporation or bylaws to be proposed by simple reference to the title or number of the section being amended. All proposed amendments must contain the full text of the amendment being offered for consideration to the membership.[16]

The documents in most communities require additional formal action by the board of administration prior to the submission of a proposed amendment for vote by the membership. When no specific requirement for proposing amendments is expressed in the documents, the board of administration may do so at one of its meetings by majority vote, or any owner may do so as long as the format of the amendment and the proper notice requirements are met prior to the amendment's consideration.

9.6   Format of Proposed Amendments. The Condominium Act requires that a specific format be used when presenting proposed amendments to the condominium documents. The format for amendment to an existing section must contain the full text of the provision being amended with new words inserted in the text and underlined. Words and phrases being

---

[15] *Biancardi v. Providence Square Ass'n, Inc.,* 481 So.2d 1272, 1274 (Fla. 4th DCA 1986).
[16] § 718.110 (1)(b), F.S. and § 718.112 (2)(h) 2., F.S.

eliminated from the existing text must be shown and lined through with hyphens.[17]

When the proposed amendment or change is so extensive that these procedures would be confusing and would hinder rather than assist in understanding the amendments, an alternative format can be used. The alternative format permits the proposed amendment to be set out in its full text with a notation inserted immediately prior to the amendment in the following form: "Substantial rewording of section. See Article X, Section 1, for present text." If a completely new section is being added by the proposed amendment, the same procedure should be followed, but the notation inserted should state: "New provision. Amendment does not change present text."[18]

9.7 Notice of Proposed Amendments. In many condominium documents specific meeting notice is required prior to the adoption of proposed amendments. If the documents do not provide specific requirements, the board of administration should follow the general notice requirements for membership meetings when presenting amendments to the members. (See 3.4–3.9).

Notice must be given at least fourteen (14) days prior to the scheduled meeting. The notice must state that proposed amendments to the condominium documents will be discussed[19] and copies of the actual text of the proposed amendments should be distributed with the notice. The board may find it helpful to enclose an explanation with the notice explaining the proposed amendments and the voting procedures that will be used when the amendments are considered.

9.8 Adopting the Amendments. After proper preparation and notice, amendments must be adopted by an extraordinary vote of the entire membership.[20] The required extraordinary vote is generally set out in the document being amended and the requirement may vary from community to community. Declarations of condominium recorded after January 1, 1992 cannot require a vote of more than four-fifths of the membership for an amendment unless the amendment is considered a material modification to the condominium property or an owner's unit. (See 9.13 and 9.15). In

---

[17] *Id.*

[18] *Id.*

[19] § 718.112 (2)(d) 2., F.S.

[20] See *Pepe v. Whispering Sands Condominium Ass'n, Inc., supra* note 1, holding that a "straw vote" was insufficient to amend the declaration of condominium.

the event that no vote requirement is specified in the documents, then the required favorable majority is not less than two-thirds of all the eligible voting interests for adoption of the amendment.[21] If proxies are used in the voting process, they must be limited proxies conforming substantially to the form adopted by the Division.[22]

Reaching the extraordinary vote to adopt amendments to the condominium documents is difficult to obtain even when the proposed changes are not controversial. If the community is scheduled to vote a series of amendments to the documents and some of them may be controversial, the board may want to consider implementing voting procedures that will allow each proposal to be voted on separately. Passage of non-controversial amendments will then not be jeopardized by controversial amendments in a single vote.

Adopting amendments in communities where a single association operates more than one condominium may require a special determination of voter eligibility on individual propositions. If the proposed amendment is to a declaration of condominium, only those owners in the affected condominium are eligible to vote and to be counted toward the extraordinary majority. If the proposed amendment is to the articles of incorporation or the bylaws, then all of the members of the association are eligible to vote on the proposition.[23]

Special provision is made in the Condominium Act for the creation, enlargement, merger, consolidation and change of name of a multi-condominium association and for modifying the percentage used to determine the liability for common expenses and ownership of the common surplus in a multi-condominium. Unless a greater percentage of the voting interests is expressly required in the declarations of condominium, such amendments may be approved by a majority of the total voting interests of each condominium operated by the multi-condominium association.[24]

9.9 Recording the Amendments and Notice to Members.
No amendment to the declaration of condominium or an exhibit to the declaration becomes effective until it has been recorded with the Clerk of

---

[21] § 718.110 (1)(a), F.S.
[22] § 718.112 (2)(b) 2., F.S.
[23] § 718.110 (1), F.S.; § 617.1002, F.S.
[24] § 718.110 (12)(b), F.S.

the Circuit Court in the county where the condominium is located.[25] The completed certificate for recording the adopted amendments should state the name of the condominium, the official record book and page numbers where the declaration was initially recorded in the public records, and the date that the amendment was adopted. The certificate of amendment must be executed by the officers of the association with the formality of a deed. It may then be delivered to the Clerk and will take effect upon recording.[26]

The document amendment process is completed when the board of administration provides the association membership with notice of the amendment's adoption and a complete copy of the amendment's text. The notice should be distributed to each owner personally or by United States mail. It should advise each member of the effective date of the change, as well as providing the owner a permanent copy of the amendment. Non-material errors or omissions in the amendment process will not invalidate an otherwise properly adopted amendment.[27]

When a developer is still holding a unit or units for sale in the condominium, the developer is required to file any amendment to the condominium documents with the Division of Florida Condominiums, Timeshares, and Mobile Homes together with a fee of up to $100.00 as established by the Division. The developer must also deliver copies of the amendment to all purchasers prior to closing, but in no event, later than ten (10) days after the amendment is effective.[28]

9.10 Amendments to the Articles of Incorporation. The procedures for proposing and adopting amendments to the articles of incorporation for the condominium association are, in all respects, similar to those for amending the declaration of condominium and other condominium documents.[29] One additional step is required to complete the process, however. Upon adoption, amendments to the articles of incorporation must be set out in articles of amendment and filed with Florida's Division of Corporations.[30]

The articles of amendment to the articles of incorporation must state the name condominium association, the authority for the amendment's

---

[25] § 718.110 (3), F.S.
[26] § 718.110 (2) and (3), F.S.
[27] § 718.110 (1)(c), F.S.
[28] § 718.502 (3), F.S.
[29] § 718.110 (1), F.S.; § 617.1002, F.S.
[30] § 617.1006, F.S.; § 617.0122, F.S.

adoption, and the full text of the amendment. The articles of amendment take effect after they have been properly recorded with the Clerk of the Circuit Court[31] and filed with the Division of Corporations.[32]

9.11 Priority of Documents. Consistency among the documents and the rules and regulations is a desired goal of each condominium. When inconsistencies arise among the documents, however, the document of highest priority will prevail.[33] In a similar fashion, a rule which is of lesser dignity than the other condominium documents cannot be used to amend provisions of the other documents or to carry out a purpose inconsistent with them. Because of the established priority among the condominium documents, there are potential pitfalls to be avoided when amending the documents. The adoption of an amendment or a rule which is inconsistent with a provision in a document of higher priority is simply ineffective.

When the subject of the rule or amendment is dealt with in more than one of the condominium documents, care should be taken to insure that both provisions are amended and that they remain consistent with one another. By example, if provisions relating to rental restrictions are found in both the bylaws and in the declaration of condominium but only the bylaw provision is amended, the amendment is not effective if it is inconsistent with the declaration.

9.12 "Grandfather Provisions." Declarations of condominium and their exhibits contain broad statements of general policy and use restrictions regulating the condominium property. They are clothed with a strong presumption of validity, and each owner acquiring a unit is entitled to benefit from the rights and the protections conferred by the declaration of condominium and its exhibits.[34] Proposed amendments to the condominium documents will, in many cases, modify, change or eliminate rights initially granted. Such amendments or changes cannot be implemented if they result in significant harm or prejudice to owners who have relied on the document restrictions as they existed at the time of initial purchase.

The procedure which allows for the implementation of an amendment changing the rights and restrictions, while preserving an

---

[31] § 718.110 (3), F.S.

[32] § 617.0123, F.S.

[33] *San Souci v. Division of Florida Land Sales and Condominiums,* 421 So.2d 623 (Fla. 1st DCA 1982).

[34] *Hidden Harbour Estates, Inc. v. Basso, supra* note 4.

individual owner's rights who relied on the original documents, is known as "grandfathering." The concept of grandfathering existing situations and permitting them to continue is not based upon a specific provision in the Condominium Act. Instead, it rests upon principles of basic fairness and due process.[35] Application of the grandfathering principle will vary in individual circumstances, depending upon the restriction being changed and the existing rights which are being affected.[36]

An example of a grandfather clause or provision would include an amendment that prohibits pets, but allows current owners to retain their pets until the pet dies or until the owner moves from the community. In such cases, the grandfathering provision preserves the owner's rights to rely on the documents when their pet was acquired and does not attempt to seek a retroactive application of the new amendment. If the grandfather provision is not expressly stated, the concept will most likely be applied by a court if enforcement proceedings seek to remove an existing pet.

There is a distinct difference between a provision that prohibits retroactive application of a restriction and a provision which attempts to create separate categories of ownership based upon the date of ownership or classes of occupants (i.e., owners and renters). (See 13.5.) The latter would, in most cases, be considered discriminatory,[37] while the former prevents the impairment of an individual contract right which has been exercised prior to the change in the restriction.

The Condominium Act recognizes that rental restrictions set out in the declaration of condominium create special privileges, and the privileges are "grandfathered" for existing owners who do not consent to amendments that change the provisions relating to the duration of the rental period. A properly adopted amendment relating to the rental period for units applies only to the unit owners who consent to the amendment and unit owners who purchase their units after the effective date of the amendment.[38]

9.13 Material Modifications and Alterations. No material modifications, alterations or additions to the condominium units or the appurtenances to the units are permitted without specific unit owner

---

[35] *Chattel Shipping and Investment, Inc. v. Brickell Place Condominium Ass'n,* 481 So.2d 29 (Fla. 3rd DCA 1985).

[36] *Everglades Plaza Condominium Ass'n, Inc. v. Buckner,* 462 So.2d 835 (Fla. 4th DCA 1984).

[37] *Woodside Village Condominium Ass'n, Inc. v. Jahren, supra* note 1.

[38] § 718.110 (13), F.S.

approval. The required unit owner approval will be 100% of all of the owners and all of the owners of liens upon the units, unless the declaration of condominium, as originally recorded, provides another method for making such modifications, alterations or additions.[39]

Material alterations or substantial additions to the common elements or to real property which is association property also requires unit owner approval in most circumstances. The required unit owner approval will be that which is provided in the declaration of condominium, and if none is specified in the declaration, the approval must be by not less than 75% of the total voting interests of the association.[40]

A material alteration or substantial addition to the condominium property may be made by the board of administration, without unit owner approval, in some limited circumstances.[41] If the documents permit such modifications by the board, then they may be made under the conditions that the documents allow. The board may also make such changes without express permission from the documents if the material modifications or alterations are incidental to the repair, preservation or replacement of existing improvements in the condominium.

Special provision is made in the law for the installation of solar panels and other energy-saving devices on the condominium property, and the addition of such devices are not considered a material modification or alteration.[42] The installation of solar panels and other energy-saving devices on the common elements of the condominium may be made by the board of administration without unit owner approval,[43] and the devices may be installed within the boundaries of a condominium unit at the discretion of the unit owner.[44]

---

[39] § 718.110 (4), F.S.; see also *Island Manor Apartments of Marco Island, Inc. v. Division of Florida Land Sales, Condominiums, and Mobile Homes*, 515 So.2d 1327, 1329–1330 (Fla. 2nd DCA 1987); *Tower House Condominium, Inc. v. Millman*, 410 So.2d 926 (Fla. 3rd DCA 1981); and *Beau Monde, Inc. v. Bramson*, 446 So.2d 164 (Fla. 2nd DCA 1984).

[40] § 718.113 (2), F.S. No vote is required for a special assessment where the work to be done is not a material alteration or addition to the common elements. See *Farrington v. Casa Solana Condominium Ass'n, Inc.*, 517 So.2d 70, 72 (Fla. 3rd DCA 1987).

[41] *Sockolof v. Eden Point North Condominium Ass'n, Inc.*, 487 So.2d 1114, 1115 (Fla. 3rd DCA 1986).

[42] § 163.04, F.S. and s. 718.113 (6), F.S.

[43] § 718.113 (6), F.S.

[44] § 718.113 (6), F.S.; *Sorrentino v. River Run Condominium Ass'n*, 925 So.2d 1060 (Fla. 5th DCA 2006).

Sometimes the subtle distinction between a repair or replacement and a material alteration or substantial addition presents the board with a difficult dilemma.[45] Changes in maintenance responsibilities,[46] installation of a new seawall, changes in color scheme,[47] or other modifications to preserve existing improvements,[48] or replacement of a community television antenna with commercial cable television service may fall into either classification. When faced with such a dilemma requiring the board to reach a legal conclusion between the two categories, the board should seek the advice of the association's attorney.

The declaration of condominium describes in detail the full extent of the condominium property and its improvements.[49] The improvements are described in both the text and on the plot plan and survey attached to the declaration. Any attempt to materially alter or modify any of these improvements or to make additions to them may also require a document amendment. If a document or plot plan amendment is required, it must be adopted by the same membership vote required for approval of the material alterations.

9.14 Installation of Hurricane Shutters. The installation, replacement, and maintenance of hurricane shutters or other hurricane protections in accordance with specifications approved by the board of administration are not considered to be a material alteration or substantial addition to the property under the Condominium Act. The Act specifically authorizes the installation and upkeep of hurricane shutters and other hurricane protection by a unit owner without a vote by the association membership, and any provisions requiring a vote of the members are preempted by the law.[50]

The board of administration is required to adopt specifications to govern the installation of hurricane shutters by a unit owner, including their color, style and other factors which the board deems relevant. All specifications must comply with applicable building codes, and the board

---

[45] *George v. Beach Club Villas Condominium Ass'n,* 833 So.2d 816 (Fla. 3rd DCA 2002); *Reuter v. Courtyards of the Grove Condominium Ass'n,* 785 So.2d 687 (Fla. 3rd DCA 2001).

[46] *Hillsboro Light Towers, Inc. v. Sherrill,* 474 So.2d 1219 (Fla. 4th DCA 1985).

[47] *Islandia Condominium Ass'n, Inc. v. Vermut,* 501 So.2d 741, 742 (Fla. 4th DCA 1987).

[48] *Ralph v. Envoy Point Condominium Ass'n, Inc.,* 455 So.2d 454, 455 (Fla. 2nd DCA 1984); *Cottrell v. Thornton,* 449 So.2d 1291 (Fla. 2nd DCA 1984); and *Tiffany Plaza Condominium Ass'n, Inc. v. Spencer,* 416 So.2d 823 (Fla. 2nd DCA 1982).

[49] § 718.104 (4), F.S.

[50] § 718.113 (5)(d), F.S.

may not refuse to approve the installation or replacement of any shutters conforming to the specifications.

Upon the approval of a majority of the voting interests in the condominium, the board may install and maintain hurricane shutters and other hurricane protection for the entire condominium. Once installed, the board may operate the shutters and other protection without the permission of the unit owners when it is necessary to preserve and protect the condominium property.[51] The expenses for the installation and maintenance of hurricane shutters installed by the board of administration are considered a common expense of the condominium, but if the maintenance and repair of the shutters and other protections are assigned to the unit owners pursuant to the declaration of condominium, the expenses are the responsibility of the unit owner.[52]

9.15 Amendments to the Unit and the Common Elements.
Ownership of property and rights inherent with property ownership are among our most important constitutional rights. These property rights cannot be taken forcibly from an owner who is unwilling to relinquish them. Ownership of an undivided share of the common elements is vested with a condominium unit at the time the declaration of condominium is recorded. Ownership of that percentage cannot be taken away or reduced unless the owner of the unit consents.[53]

Any amendment attempting to change the configuration or size of a unit or the proportional percentage by which the owner shares the common expenses or owns the common elements requires not only the approval of the affected owner, but also the approval of all owners of liens on the unit and all other unit owners in the condominium.[54] When attempting to amend portions of the documents requiring unanimous approval of owners and lienholders, the approval must be by written joinder and not simply by vote.[55] The written joinder requires each owner and lienholder to sign before two (2) witnesses and a notary public to be properly completed.

---

[51] § 718.113 (5)(c), F.S

[52] § 718.115 (1)(e), F.S.

[53] § 718.110 (4), F.S.

[54] § 718.110 (4) and § 718.113 (2), F.S. See also *Wellington Property Management v. Parc Corniche Condominium Ass'n Inc.,* 755 So2d 824, 826 (Fla. 5th DCA 2000) and *Schmeck v. Sea Oats Condominium Ass'n, Inc.,* 441 So.2d 1092, 1095 (Fla. 5th DCA 1983).

[55] § 718.110 (4), F.S.

The common elements may be enlarged without unanimous membership approval if the ownership percentages assigned to each unit do not change. Association-owned property may be made part of the common elements by amendment to the declaration of condominium in the same manner that other amendments to the declaration are adopted. If no percentage is specified in the declaration, the approval is by three-fourths of the entire voting interests of the community.[56]

The amendment submitting interest in property to the terms of the declaration of condominium as common elements must state that the association ownership is being transferred or divested. Upon recording, the amendment will place the title to a share of the property in each owner as a part of the common elements, without naming the owners, in the same percentage as they own the existing common elements in the community.[57]

When a portion of the common elements serves only one unit or a group of units, the common elements may be reclassified as limited common elements by an amendment to the declaration of condominium. The amendment must be adopted by an extraordinary vote of the unit owners in the same manner as other amendments to the declaration are approved.[58] (See 9.5–9.9).

9.16 Merger and Consolidation.
Merger or consolidation within a condominium community can be approached in one of two ways. In the first case, the merger can be a consolidation of several condominiums into a single, new condominium combining common elements, common expenses and condominium associations. Under the second option, the consolidation may be of the condominium associations only and, upon merger or consolidation of the associations, the single corporate entity will continue to operate the affairs of several separate condominiums.

The effort to merge two or more independent condominiums into a single condominium is a difficult task since property rights and ownership in the common elements are involved. The Condominium Act permits the merger if the declarations of condominium expressly permit it and the vote required by the original documents is obtained within the community. If no specific right to merge condominiums is contained in the respective declarations of condominium, merger of two or more condominiums will

---

[56] § 718.110 (2) and § 718.113 (2), F.S.
[57] § 718.110 (6), F.S.
[58] § 718.110 (1)(a), F.S.

require the unanimous approval of all unit owners and all lien holders.[59] Once the required approvals are obtained, a new or amended declaration should be recorded for the condominium.

If merger or consolidation is only between condominium associations, the merger is accomplished by obtaining approval of the required voting interests necessary to amend the articles of incorporation and the declaration of condominium. If no requirement is specified, it will be upon a favorable vote of two-thirds of all the voting interests in each of the merging corporations.[60]

The merger of condominium associations takes place after a plan of merger has been presented and approved by the required voting interests. The articles of merger must be filed with the Division of Corporations and the Clerk of the Circuit Court in the county where the condominium is located.[61] Merger of the associations allows a single corporation to manage several condominiums, but the corporation must still maintain separate books and records for each condominium.[62]

A limited, third consolidation option exists for condominium communities created prior to January 1, 1977. Under this third option, two or more condominiums operated by a single condominium association may provide for the consolidated financial operations of the condominiums. To implement consolidated financial operations, the authority for the association to do so must be contained in the declarations of condominium, or the members of the condominium association must approve an amendment to the bylaws of the association authorizing the consolidated operations by a vote of not less than two-thirds of the total voting membership of the association.[63]

9.17 Correcting a Scrivener's Error. Occasionally, clerical or "scrivener's" errors are discovered in the condominium documents. When it is determined that such a scrivener's error results in a unit not receiving its appropriate undivided share of the common elements or of the common expenses, or if the total undivided shares does not equal 100%, the error may be corrected by an amendment approved by either the board of

---

[59] § 718.110 (7), F.S.
[60] § 718.110 (1)(a); § 617.1103 and § 617.1101, F.S.
[61] § 718.110 (3) and § 617.1105 (4), F.S.
[62] § 718.111 (12), F.S.
[63] § 718.111 (6), F.S.

administration or a majority of the voting interests in the community.[64] Like all other amendments, the amendment correcting a scrivener's error must be recorded with the Clerk of the Circuit Court and the certificate of amendment should specifically state that it is recorded to correct a clerical or "scrivener's" error.

Other errors in the declaration of condominium that do not relate to the undivided shares in the common elements may also be corrected by a majority of the voting interests in the association, provided that the amendment does not materially or adversely alter or affect the property rights of a unit owner or owners. If there is a material or adverse effect to a particular owner, in addition to the approval by a majority of the voting interests, the affected owner must also consent in writing.[65]

The simplified process for correcting errors or omissions in the condominium documents is intended to assist communities in curing defects and oversights, but it must be used cautiously. Before relying on this amendment process, and the lesser required vote, the nature of the error or omission must be clear and the amendment which corrects it must not materially or adversely affect the rights of any unit owner.

9.18 Corrective Amendments by the Circuit Court. The Condominium Act establishes a format and certain required elements for a condominium to be validly created.[66] When an omission or error in the declaration of condominium or other documents affects the valid existence of the condominium and it cannot be corrected by the other amendment procedures in the Act, the Circuit Court has jurisdiction to entertain a petition by one or more unit owners or the association for purposes of correcting the error. When the petition has been filed with the Court, the Court may order the correction to the declaration of condominium, or it may submit options to the community allowing the owners to choose the method by which the omission or error is to be corrected.[67]

If a petition has not been filed with the Circuit Court within three (3) years from the time that the declaration of condominium is recorded, the declaration is considered valid for purposes of creating the condominium,

---

[64] § 718.110 (5), F.S.
[65] § 718.110 (9), F.S.
[66] § 718.104, F.S.
[67] § 718.110 (10), F.S.

whether the error is material or not. Even though the condominium will be considered valid after the three (3) year period, a petition may still be filed with the Court to correct the error or omission in the condominium documents.

SCHEDULE OF AMENDMENTS

TO

DECLARATION OF CONDOMINIUM

FOR

WATERFRONT XX CONDOMINIUM

1.   Section 3, Article 21 of the Declaration of Condominium is amended to read as follows:

> "Section 3. No unit shall be leased or rented for a period of less than ~~thirty (30)~~ ninety (90) days. <u>All leases shall be in writing.</u>"

2.   Article 21 of the Declaration of Condominium is amended by adding a new Section 8 to read as follows (New provision. Amendment does not change present text):

> "<u>Section 8. No guest shall be permitted to occupy a unit overnight unless the owner of the unit shall also be present in the unit.</u>"

3.   Section 4, Article 22 of the Declaration of Condominium is amended to read as follows (Substantial rewording. See Section 4, Article 22, for present text.):

> "<u>Section 4. No lease or rental of a condominium unit shall be made without the prior approval of the board of administration. The board of administration may promulgate rules to implement such approval process and charge a preset fee of $50.00 for each such requested approval.</u>"

CERTIFICATE OF AMENDMENT
TO
DECLARATION OF CONDOMINIUM
OF
WATERFRONT XX CONDOMINIUM

NOTICE IS HEREBY GIVEN that at a duly called meeting of the members on September 30, 2011, by a vote of not less than two-thirds of the voting interests of the Association and after the unanimous adoption of a Resolution proposing said amendments by the Board of Administration, the Declaration of Condominium for WATERFRONT XX CONDOMINIUM, as originally recorded in O.R. Book 800, Page 100, et seq., in the Public Records of Pinellas County, be and the same is hereby amended as follows:

1.   The Declaration of Condominium of WATERFRONT XX CONDOMINIUM is hereby amended in accordance with Exhibit A attached hereto and entitled "Schedule of Amendments to Declaration of Condominium."

2.   The Bylaws of WATERFRONT XX CONDOMINIUM ASSOCIATION, INC., being Exhibit B to said Declaration of Condominium, are hereby amended in accordance with Exhibit B attached hereto and entitled "Schedule of Amendments to Bylaws."

IN WITNESS WHEREOF, WATERFRONT XX CONDO-MINIUM ASSOCIATION, INC., has caused this Certificate of Amendment to be executed in accordance with the authority hereinabove expressed this 15th day of October, 2011.

(CORPORATE SEAL)   WATERFRONT XX CONDOMINIUM
                          ASSOCIATION, INC.

ATTEST:

_____   By: _____
Secretary   President

STATE OF FLORIDA   )
COUNTY OF PINELLAS   )

On this 15th day of October, 2011, personally appeared Joseph A. Jones, President, and acknowledged before me that he executed this instrument for the purposes herein expressed.

                            _____

                            Notary Public

                            My commission expires:

ARTICLES OF AMENDMENT
TO
ARTICLES OF INCORPORATION
OF
WATERFRONT XX CONDOMINIUM ASSOCIATION, INC.
A Corporation Not-for-Profit

The undersigned do hereby make, subscribe, acknowledge and file with the Secretary of State these Articles of Amendment in accordance with the vote of not less than two-thirds of the entire voting interests of the association at a duly called meeting of the members on September 30, 2011, after unanimous adoption of a Resolution proposing said amendments by the Board of Administration.

The Articles of Incorporation of WATERFRONT XX CONDOMINIUM ASSOCIATION, INC., are, and shall hereby be, amended in accordance with the Schedule of Amendments to the Articles of Incorporation attached hereto as Exhibit A and by reference made a part hereof.

IN WITNESS WHEREOF, WATERFRONT XX CONDOMINIUM ASSOCIATION, INC., has caused these Articles of Amendment to be executed in accordance with the authority hereinabove expressed this 1st day of October, 2011.

(CORPORATE SEAL)   WATERFRONT XX CONDOMINIUM
                          ASSOCIATION, INC.

ATTEST:

_____   By: _____
Secretary   President

STATE OF FLORIDA   )
COUNTY OF PINELLAS   )

     On this 15th day of October, 2011, personally appeared Joseph A. Jones, President, and acknowledged before me that he executed this instrument for the purposes herein expressed.

                           _____

                           Notary Public

                           My commission expires:

WATERFRONT XX CONDOMINIUM ASSOCIATION, INC.
A Corporation Not-for-Profit

NOTICE OF AMENDMENT
TO CONDOMINIUM DOCUMENTS

TO: MEMBERS, WATERFRONT XX
                CONDOMINIUM ASSOCIATION, INC.

FROM: SECRETARY,
                BOARD OF ADMINISTRATION

NOTICE IS HEREBY GIVEN that amendments to the Declaration of Condominium were adopted at the annual meeting of members of September 30, 2011, and recorded with the Clerk of the Circuit Court of Pinellas County, Florida, in O.R. Book 900, Page 1001, on October 15, 2011. The amendments became effective upon recording and a copy of the recorded amendments accompany this notice of their adoption.

DATED this 23rd day of October, 2011.

WATERFRONT XX CONDOMINIUM
ASSOCIATION, INC.

By: _____
      Secretary

Enclosures.

A RESOLUTION BY THE BOARD OF ADMINISTRATION OF WATERFRONT XX CONDOMINIUM ASSOCIATION, INC., ESTABLISHING RULES FOR THE INSTALLATION OF HURRICANE SHUTTERS

THAT WHEREAS, Section 718.113(5), Florida Statutes, authorizes any unit owner to install hurricane shutters in accordance with specifications approved by the Board of Administration, and

WHEREAS, the Condominium Act allows for such specifications to be adopted by the Board concerning the color, style and other relevant factors of such installations.

NOW THEREFORE BE IT RESOLVED by the Board of Administration of Waterfront XX Condominium Association, Inc., that the specifications governing the right of unit owners to install hurricane shutters shall be as follows:

1.   Any installation of hurricane shutters by a unit owner shall comply with the building code of Waterfront, Florida. Any contract for such installation shall be in writing and shall be with a properly licensed contractor.

2.   An owner installing hurricane shutters shall be responsible for any damage to the common elements or another unit as a result of such installation.

3.   No hurricane shutter shall be installed that is not white in color and is not fully retractable when not in use.

4.   Prior to commencement of installation of any hurricane shutter(s), the unit owner shall give written notice to the Board of Administration of the owner's intention to make such installation. The owner shall additionally provide the Board with a copy of the agreement for the installation, the color and specifications of the shutter(s), and an estimated work schedule for the installation.

ADOPTED by the Board of Administration this 5th day of October, 2011.

Hurricane Shutter Specifications FORM 9.05

10

Association Authority and Responsibility

MANAGEMENT FORMS

10.1 General. The condominium association is responsible for the operation of the affairs of the condominium and, as such, the association may operate more than one condominium.[1] The association's authority arises out of its defined purpose as the condominium's management entity and no unit owner has the authority to act for the association due to his or her status as a unit owner.[2] The powers and duties that the association may exercise in carrying out its role include all those powers granted to corporations in Florida by statute, except as otherwise limited by the Condominium Act or the condominium association's own charter.[3]

The general grant of powers to corporations in Florida is extremely broad. It includes the power to sue and be sued; the power to purchase or otherwise acquire real and personal property; to sell, mortgage, pledge or otherwise dispose of all or any part of its property and assets; to make contracts, incur liabilities, borrow money, and invest its funds; to elect officers and define their duties; and to exercise all powers necessary and convenient to effect the corporation's purpose.[4] The condominium association possesses all of these inherent corporate powers although their use and exercise is restricted to the purposes for which the corporation is organized and the limits imposed by the Condominium Act.[5]

10.2 Management and Maintenance. The primary responsibility of the association is to manage and maintain the condominium. This includes the responsibility to keep the property in a state of good condition, and to repair and replace portions of the property when necessity and circumstances dictate.[6] The responsibility includes care of the common elements in all circumstances, and it may also include the care of limited common elements[7] and portions of the individual units.

Although care of limited common elements and portions of the units may be part of the association's responsibility, the cost for carrying

---

[1] § 718.111 (1)(a), F.S. and § 718.405, F.S.
[2] § 718.111 (1)(c), F.S.
[3] § 718.111 (2), F.S.
[4] § 617.0302, F.S.
[5] § 718.111 (2), F.S.
[6] *Holiday Out in America at St. Lucie, Inc. v. Bowes,* 285 So.2d 63, 65 (Fla. 4th DCA 1973); *Baum v. Coronado Condominium Ass'n, Inc.,* 376 So.2d 914 (Fla. 3rd DCA 1979). 526 § 718.503, F.S.
[7] *Cedar Cove Efficiency Condominium Ass'n, Inc. v. Cedar Cove Properties, Inc.,* 558 So.2d 475 (Fla. 1st DCA 1990).

out this part of the responsibility is generally not considered a common expense and the costs are borne by the benefiting unit owner or owners.[8] Examples include care of individual parking spaces, balconies, patios and other similar property components used exclusively by a single owner, but in which all owners have a common interest such as the preservation of a uniform quality of appearance.[9]

To carry out its management and maintenance responsibilities, the association has the authority to hire a manager and to contract for all or a portion of the required needs of the condominium community.[10] When an association serves more than ten (10) units or has an annual budget exceeding $100,000, individuals or companies providing management services for the association must comply with the licensing provisions of Florida law.[11]

All contracts for maintenance and management services entered into by the association must specify the obligations of the party contracting to provide maintenance or management services, as well as the costs to be incurred for each of the services. The frequency of each service and the number of personnel to be employed for the purpose of providing the services to the association must also be specifically stated.[12] Any services or obligations not specifically enumerated in the contract are unenforceable.[13] Further, any financial or ownership interest a board member, developer, or other party has in the contractor providing maintenance or management services to the association must be fully disclosed or the contract is not valid or enforceable.[14] (See 10.3).

10.3 Contracting for Products and Services. The authority of associations to contract for products and services is restricted in certain circumstances by the provisions of the Condominium Act. Contracts for the purchase or lease of materials or equipment that cannot be fully performed within one (1) year must be in writing. All contracts for services, except for legal and accounting services, must also be in writing. When the aggregate amount of the contract requires payment by the association of more than 5% of the total annual budget of the association including reserves, the

---

[8] § 718.111 (3) and (4) and § 718.113 (1), F.S.
[9] *Cedar Cove Efficiency Condominium Ass'n, Inc. v. Cedar Cove Properties, Inc., supra* note 7.
[10] *Trafalgar Towers Ass'n #2, Inc. v. Zimet,* 314 So2d 595 (Fla. 4th DCA 1975).
[11] § 468.431 through § 468.437, F.S
[12] § 718.3025 (1), F.S.
[13] § 718.3025 (3), F.S.
[14] § 718.3025 (1)(d), F.S.

association must obtain competitive bids for the materials, equipment, or services.[15]

The association is not required to accept the lowest bid if prudent judgment dictates otherwise, and in emergency circumstances competitive bidding may also be dispensed with. The requirement for competitive bidding does not apply when the business entity with which the association desires to contract is the only source of supply within the county serving the association.[16]

Contracts which make services available for the convenience of individual unit owners, such as coin-operated laundry facilities, food and soft drink vendors, telephone services, retail store operators, communication service providers or similar vendors, are not subject to the requirements for competitive bidding and they are not restricted in their content or format.[17] Contracts for the services of an attorney, an engineer, an architect and a landscape architect, and contracts with employees of the association, including managers licensed pursuant to Section 468.431, Florida Statutes, are also exempt from the bidding requirements.[18]

Condominium associations governing less than ten (10) units may be granted an exemption from the requirements of competitive bidding and the other provisions of Section 718.3026, Florida Statutes, if the members of the association approve. An affirmative vote of two-thirds of the unit owners is required to opt out of these contracting requirements.

Any contract or other transaction between the association and a director or an entity in which a director has a financial interest is subject to special restrictions under the Condominium Act. Such transactions are permitted provided that a full financial disclosure is made to the board of administration and the disclosure appears in the written minutes of the meeting where the contract or transaction is approved.[19] Approval of such a contract or transaction must be by a vote of two-thirds (2/3) of the board members present at the meeting, and the transaction must be disclosed at the next regular or special meeting of the membership. The membership may cancel the contract by majority vote of the members present at the meeting.[20]

---

[15] § 718.3026 (1), F.S.
[16] § 718.3026 (2), F.S.
[17] § 718.3025 (4), F.S.
[18] § 718.3026 (2)(a) 1., F.S.
[19] § 718.3026 (3)(a) and (b), F.S.
[20] § 718.3026 (3)(c) and (d), F.S.

10.4   Representation of the Unit Owners. In its capacity as the entity responsible for the management and maintenance of the condominium property, the condominium association also serves as the representative of the owners of the commonly owned property for a variety of purposes.[21] The association may file a petition on behalf of individual owners before the Property Appraisal Adjustment Board when the taxable value of units and the common property is being contested, provided that the property appraiser determines that the units are substantially similar in their physical makeup.[22] The association is the entity responsible for insuring the condominium on behalf of the association members and is the collection and disbursement agent of the common funds of the members.[23]

The association may represent unit owners in court proceedings by bringing class action suits on behalf of the unit owners where controversies affect matters of common interest.[24] (See 12.13). The association may also sue or be sued in its own name involving matters of interest to the overall community.[25] When a governmental authority seeks to condemn portions of the common elements, the condominium association may defend actions in eminent domain on the unit owners' behalf. The association also has the limited power to convey portions of the common elements to a condemning authority for the purpose of providing utility easements, right-of-way expansion, or other public purposes.[26] The association may additionally bring inverse condemnation actions as the representative of the unit owners notwithstanding the fact that the association technically does not own title to the property being condemned.[27]

10.5   Liabilities of the Association. The condominium association is liable for its acts or its failure to act, and may pass this liability on to unit owners if it arises in connection with the common elements. The extent of each unit owner's liability is limited to the owner's proportionate ownership interest in the common elements. In no case may an individual owner's liability exceed the value of the unit itself. Whenever the association

---

[21] § 718.111 (3), F.S.
[22] § 194.011 (3)(e), § 194.013 (1), and § 194.034 (6), F.S.
[23] § 718.111 (4) and (11)(a), F.S.
[24] Rule 1.221, Florida Rules of Civil Procedure; *Trintec Construction, Inc. v. Countryside Village Condominium Ass'n, Inc.*, 992 So.2d 277 (Fla. 3rd DCA 2008).
[25] § 718.111 (3), F.S.
[26] § 718.111 (7)(b) and § 718.112 (2)(m), F.S.
[27] § 718.111 (3) and (10), F.S.

is exposed to liability through legal action in excess of the association's insurance coverage, the association must give notice of the deficiency in insurance coverage to each unit owner. After receiving notice, each owner has the right to intervene and defend in the legal action.[28]

When the association is responsible for maintaining a portion of the condominium property and it fails to do so and an injury results, the association may be negligent and responsible for the resulting injury.[29] To avoid liability, when the association has knowledge of an unsafe condition, the association must proceed to repair the problem without unnecessary delay. Since the condominium association is the designated agent for unit owners, notice to the association of defects in the common areas is deemed to be notice to the unit owners.[30]

The association may also be liable for interference with a contractual relationship when its conduct or actions are improper. When a unit owner enters into a contract for the sale or lease of the owner's unit and the condominium association denies the approval of the transfer, it must do so correctly. (See 13.17). If the denial is based upon improper criteria and the unit owner suffers damages as a result of the association's action the requisite elements for "tortuous interference" with the unit owner's contract relationship arises. If the improper actions can be proven, the association becomes liable for the unit owner's damages.[31]

10.6 Owning and Leasing Real Property.

The condominium association has the general power to acquire title to real property and to otherwise hold the property for the use and benefit of its members in the manner provided in the declaration of condominium.[32] If the declaration does not provide a procedure then the approval of 75 % of the total voting interests is required. The association has specific authority to purchase any land or recreational lease with the prior approval of the unit owners in the same percentage required to amend the condominium documents. The association may also purchase units in the condominium at foreclosure sale without restriction, and lease, mortgage, and re-convey them.[33] Property

---

[28] § 718.119 (2) and (3), F.S.
[29] *Winston Towers 100 Ass'n, Inc. v. DeCarlo,* 481 So.2d 1261 (Fla. 3rd DCA 1986).
[30] § 718.111 (3), F.S.
[31] *Barnett and Klein Corporation v. President of Palm Beach—A Condominium, Inc.,* 426 So.2d 1074 (Fla. 4th DCA 1983).
[32] § 718.111 (7), F.S.
[33] § 718.111 (8) and (9), F.S.

acquired by the association and held in the corporate name is correctly known as "association property" (see 1.8) and it is not "common elements" of the condominium.[34]

Condominiums created under long-term lease arrangements are authorized by the Condominium Act, and the leases themselves are valid and binding upon the association and its members.[35] Under current policy restrictions of the Act, however, the terms and content of long term lease agreements are severely restricted and any such lease must contain a purchase option for the benefit of the unit owners.[36] Prior to 1976, statutory restrictions on long term lease agreements did not appear in the Act and the content of leases entered into and the rights they established are not affected by the current statutory provisions.

When the terms of the recorded declaration of condominium grant the association the power to enter into agreements for leasehold interests or membership rights, the association may obtain these benefits or the use of such facilities for the enjoyment or recreation of unit owners even if the facilities are not contiguous to the lands of the condominium.[37] If the agreement or lease is not entered into within twelve (12) months following the recording of the declaration, however, the agreement or lease must be approved by an extraordinary vote of the unit owners.[38] The power to purchase or lease real property granted to a condominium association, when properly exercised, carries with it implicitly the right to assess individual unit owners for their proportionate share of the expenses incurred in the lease or purchase.[39]

10.7   Granting and Modifying Easements. Unless the declaration of condominium prohibits it, the condominium association has, by and through its board of administration, the authority to grant, modify, or move easements over and across the common elements. No vote or joinder by unit owners is required to ratify such actions. The association, however, may not grant, modify, or move any easement created in whole or in part for the use

---

[34] § 718.103 (3) and (8), F.S.
[35] § 718.104 (2) and § 718.401, F.S.
[36] § 718.401 (6), F.S.
[37] § 718.114, F.S.
[38] § 718.114 and § 718.113 (2), F.S.
[39] § 718.111 (4) and § 718.115 (1)(a), F.S.

or benefit of persons other than the unit owners without the consent of the persons affected by the association's actions.[40]

When the board deems it appropriate to grant, move or modify an easement, caution should be exercised to ensure that the action does not interfere with unit owners' rights in easements granted by the developer in the declaration of condominium.[41] When the declaration of condominium provides for an easement of access or ingress and egress, the actions of the association cannot impair the basic rights of owners, and the reasonable access intended by the documents must be preserved.

10.8   Right of Access to Units. The association is granted, by statute, the irrevocable right of access to each individual condominium unit. Such access must be during reasonable hours for the purpose of maintenance, repair, or replacement of common elements or any portion of the unit for which the association is responsible. As well, the association may have access to units to make emergency repairs which are necessary to prevent damage to the common elements or to another unit, such as to repair a broken water pipe which could cause water intrusion into other units.[42]

When the declaration of condominium requires a unit owner to provide a key to the condominium association so as to allow ready access to units, such requirement has been judicially upheld in Florida. The unit owner, not the condominium association, is responsible for any damage incurred in obtaining access to the unit if the access is not allowed by the unit owner.[43]

10.9   Smoking and the "Clean Indoor Air Act." In November of 2002, Floridians approved a constitutional amendment banning the smoking of all tobacco products in enclosed indoor locations where work is performed.[44] The definition of "work" includes all indoor meetings of the board of administration, committees of the board and meetings of the membership, and accordingly, no smoking is permitted at these meetings. The definition is also sufficiently broad to include all indoor common areas of the condominium where any work or service is performed by an officer, director, manager, employee, contractor or volunteer, and the simple cleaning

---

[40] § 718.111 (10), F.S.
[41] § 718.104 (4)(n), F.S.
[42] § 718.106 (3) and § 718.111 (5), F.S.
[43] § 718.303 (1), F.S.
[44] § 2, Article X, *Constitution of Florida;* § 386.204, F.S.

or maintenance of the enclosed common areas is sufficient to impose a ban on smoking within these areas.[45]

It is the responsibility of the board of administration to establish appropriate policies prohibiting smoking in enclosed indoor workplaces within the condominium, and policies may include the posting of "no smoking" signs as the board deems appropriate.[46] Persons violating the Clean Indoor Air Act are subject to a $100 fine for the first occurrence and a $500 fine for each subsequent occurrence.[47]

10.10 Keeping the Property Insured. The condominium association is required to use its best efforts to obtain and maintain adequate insurance to cover the replacement cost of the property improvements, and an independent insurance appraisal on the replacement cost must be done at least every thirty-six (36) months.[48] This insurance must cover the association, the association property, and the condominium property in the following respects: all hazard policies must be issued to protect fixtures, installations, or additions which are part of the building within the unfinished interior surfaces of the perimeter walls, floors, and ceilings of the individual units. Such fixtures and parts of the building must be those which were initially installed by the developer or their replacements when they are of similar kind and quality.[49]

The law permits the insurance policies maintained by the association to provide for reasonable deductible amounts. In determining what constitutes a reasonable deductible, the board of administration may consider the industry standards and prevailing practices for similar communities, the available cash in the reserve accounts of the association to cover the amount of the deductible, and the board may also rely on its assessment authority to cover the deductible amount.[50] When the deductible is based upon either available cash or the assessment authority of the association, the decision should be made at a properly notice meeting of the board, and the specific resources to be used for the deductible should be identified and recorded in the minutes of the meeting.[51]

---

[45] § 386.203 (5) and (12), F.S.
[46] § 386.206,(2), F.S.
[47] § 386.208, F.S.
[48] § 718.111 (11)(a), F.S.
[49] § 718.111 (11)(f), F.S.
[50] § 718.111 (11)(c), F.S.
[51] Notice must be mailed or hand-delivered to all unit owners at least fourteen (14) days prior to the meeting. § 718.111 (11)(c) 3., F.S.

Beginning in 2007, insurance policies obtained from a commercial self-insurance fund approved by the Office of Insurance Regulation[52] are deemed to be adequate insurance by terms of the Condominium Act.[53] Participation in a commercial self-insurance fund may involve a commitment to contingent assessments by the association,[54] and any contingent assessment should be authorized and approved under procedures required for other special assessments and with the assistance of the association's legal counsel. (See 8.7).

Association insurance coverage does not include the floor coverings, wall coverings, or ceiling coverings within individual units or electrical fixtures, appliances, air conditioners, heating equipment, water heaters and filters, built-in cabinets and countertops, or window treatments located within individual units.[55] Insurance for this portion of the property located within the boundaries of a unit is the responsibility of the individual unit owner.[56] The insurance policies maintained by individual unit owners must include "special assessment" coverage of no less than $2,000 per occurrence,[57] and this component of the coverage serves as the basis for the board's reliance on the assessment authority of the association when determining the deductible amounts for the master insurance policy of the association.[58]

Insurance policies which are obtained by the association are official records of the association and must be made available for inspection by unit owners at reasonable times.[59] Unit owners shall be considered additional insureds under all association policies. When obtaining insurance, the association must comply with the requirements for competitive bidding when the costs for the coverage exceed five percent (5%) of the association's annual budget.[60] (See 10.3).

---

[52] Self-insurance funds must be approved by the Office of Insurance Regulation and comply with the provisions of §§ 624.460 through 624.488, F.S.

[53] § 718.111 (11)(a) 1. and 2., F.S.

[54] § 718.115 (1)(f) and § 718.116 (10), F.S.

[55] § 718.111 (11)(f) 3., F.S.; see also *Costa Del Sol Ass'n, Inc. v. Department of Business Regulation, Division of Florida Land Sales, Condominiums, and Mobile Homes,* 987 So.2d 734 (Fla. 1st DCA 2008)..

[56] *Id.*

[57] § 627.714, F.S.

[58] § 718.111 (11)(g), F.S.

[59] § 718.111 (11)(a) and (12)(a) 8., F.S.

[60] § 718.3026 (1), F.S.

10.11 Borrowing Money. In conjunction with its powers to manage, maintain, and operate the condominium property and repair and replace the common elements, the association has the power to borrow necessary funds.[61] More specifically, the association may contract and incur liabilities, borrow money at such rates of interest as it may deem appropriate, and secure any of its obligations by mortgaging or pledging any or all of its property or income.[62] Thus, any assessment which is levied could be used to collateralize a loan to the association in connection with its duties and responsibilities for maintenance, repair, and replacement of common elements. The association also has the authority to purchase units in the condominium and, in connection therewith, to mortgage such units.[63]

10.12 Exercising All Necessary and Convenient Powers. The condominium association, as a Florida corporation either for-profit or not-for-profit, has and may exercise all powers which are necessary or convenient to the purpose for which the corporation is organized.[64] The purposes of the association are set forth in the declaration of condominium, the association's articles of incorporation, and the Condominium Act, and the powers that can reasonably be inferred as necessary to carry out those duties are inherent with the corporation even if they are not expressly stated in those documents.[65]

Examples include the authority to comply with the requirements for elevator safety when the community is served by elevators;[66] the authority to comply with the requirements governing public lodging establishments when transient occupancy is permitted in the community;[67] and the authority and responsibility to comply with the special provisions of the Florida Vacation Plan and Timesharing Act when there are timeshare estates in the condominium community.[68] Each association also has the authority to take all actions necessary to comply with laws, ordinances, and regulations concerning building and zoning in conjunction with the association's primary responsibilities.[69]

---

[61] § 617.0302 (7), F.S.
[62] § 718.111 (7), F.S.
[63] § 718.111 (9), F.S.
[64] § 617.0302 (15), F.S.
[65] § 718.111 (2), F.S.
[66] § 399.02 (5) and (8), F.S. and § 399.125, F.S.
[67] § 509.242 (1)(c), F.S.
[68] § 721.03, F.S.
[69] § 718.507, F.S.

10.13 Responding to Unit Owner Inquiries. When a unit owner in the community, following proper procedures, makes an inquiry of the board of administration, the owner is entitled to a written response from the association within thirty (30) days.[70] The unit owner's inquiry must be made in writing and by certified mail, and the board of administration must provide a substantive response or notify the inquiring owner that the association has sought a legal opinion or the advice of the Division of Florida Condominiums, Timeshares, and Mobile Homes within the required thirty-day time period.[71]

When the board of administration requests advice from the Division, the board is required to provide a substantive response to the unit owner within ten (10) days of receipt of the Division's advice. When the board seeks a legal opinion, it must provide a substantive response to the unit owner within sixty (60) days after receipt of the owner's inquiry. The failure of the association to provide a substantive response to the inquiring unit owner as required precludes the association from recovering attorney's fees and costs in any subsequent litigation, administrative proceeding, or arbitration arising out of the complaints. The board of the association may adopt reasonable rules and regulations regarding the frequency and manner of responding to unit owner inquiries, one of which may be that the association is only obligated to respond to one written inquiry per unit in any given thirty-day period.[72]

The association is not required to respond to requests for information about the condominium or the association from a prospective purchaser or a lienholder other than requests for copies of the condominium documents or for an assessment certificate as provided for in the Act. (See 8.9 and 13.17.). The association, at its option, may provide the requested information, however, and may charge the prospective purchaser or lienholder a reasonable fee not to exceed $150 plus the costs of photocopying and any attorney's fees incurred in providing responses.[73]

10.14 Fire Sprinkler Systems. In a condominium building initially constructed without a fire sprinkler system, unit owners may avoid the

---

[70] § 718.112 (2)(a) 2., F.S. See also *Seagull Townhomes Condominium Ass'n, Inc. v. Edlund,* 941 So.2d 457 (Fla. 3rd DCA 2006).

[71] § 718.112 (2)(a) 2., F.S.

[72] *Id.*

[73] § 718.111 (12)(e), F.S.

requirement to retrofit the building with a sprinkler system upon an affirmative majority vote of all the voting interests in the affected condominium. The vote to forego retrofitting must occur prior to December 31, 2016, and in a community where the vote to waive the requirement has not occurred, the condominium association must initiate an application for a building permit for the required system by that date.[74]

Unit owners voting to forego the sprinkler system retrofit must do so personally by ballot or by limited proxy at a properly called membership meeting or by the execution of a written consent. The results of the vote are effective upon the recording of an affidavit in the public records of the county where the condominium is located, and the association must notify each owner in writing of the vote by certified mail within twenty (20) days after the vote. When a unit is sold or rented in the condominium, a copy of the affidavit must be provided to the renter or new unit owner.[75] The association must also report the vote to the Division of Florida Condominiums, Timeshares, and Mobile Homes.[76]

10.15 Alternative Power Source and Emergency Plan. Each building in the condominium that is at least seventy-five (75) feet high and is served by one or more public elevators is required to have at least one (1) public elevator that is capable of operating on an alternative power source for emergency purposes. The alternative power source must be available for unit-owner access for a specified number of hours each day over a five-day period following a natural disaster, manmade disaster or other emergency that disrupts the normal supply of electricity to the building.[77] The alternative power source for the elevator operation must be sufficient to power the fire alarm system in the building and provide the fire alarm system in the building and provide emergency lighting for the interior lobbies and hallways of the building.[78]

The condominium association must also prepare and maintain a written emergency operations plan that details the sequence of operations before, during and after a natural or manmade disaster or other emergency situation. The plan must provide for the evacuation of the property, the

---

[74] § 718.112 (2)(l) 1., F.S.
[75] *Id.*
[76] § 718.112 (2)(l) 3., F.S.
[77] § 553.509 (2)(a), F.S.
[78] § 553.509 (2)(b), F.S.

maintenance of the electrical and lighting supply to the building, and provide for the health, safety and welfare of the unit owners in the condominium. In addition, the association must keep written records of any contracts for the emergency power generation equipment on site for verification, post quarterly inspection records of the emergency safety equipment, and keep a key for the power generation equipment in a lockbox posted at or near the emergency power generator.[79]

If a condominium building with the qualifying height is not initially equipped with the required alternative power supply to operate the elevator and lighting systems in the building, the board of administration must provide for retrofit and installation of these items.[80] The community may forego the requirement to retrofit the power source for the elevator and lighting systems, however, upon an affirmative vote of a majority of the voting interests in the affected condominium.[81]

10.16 Emergency Powers. During times of a declared emergency in the locale in which the condominium is located,[82] the Condominium Act vests emergency powers in the condominium association to protect the property and residents of the condominium. Pursuant to the special powers, the board of administration can implement an emergency disaster plan; require evacuation of the property; shut down the elevators, electricity, and other utility systems on the property; and declare the condominium unavailable for entry and occupancy.[83] The emergency powers authorize the board to mitigate further damage to the property by removing debris and water-damaged components of the building, and the powers permit the board to contract for services to prevent further damage to the condominium and make emergency repairs to the property.[84]

The Act also provides for administrative flexibility during times of a declared emergency. Meetings can be canceled and rescheduled, and meeting notices are required only as practicable and may be given by alternative means.[85] The association is permitted to relocate its principal

---

[79] § 553.509 (2)(d), F.S.
[80] § 553.509 (2)(b), F.S.
[81] § 718.112 (2)(l) 4., F.S.
[82] The emergency must be declared by the Governor under § 252.36, F.S.
[83] § 718.1265 (1)(g), (h) and (i), F.S.
[84] § 718.1265 (1)(j), (k) and (m), F.S.
[85] § 718.1265 (1)(a) and (b), F.S.

administrative office and appoint special officers to function during the state of emergency,[86] and the board may levy special assessments and borrow funds to carry out its functions during the declared emergency.[87]

The special emergency powers must be exercised in good faith, with prudent care, and in the best interests of the association.[88] The duration of the emergency powers is limited to the time reasonably necessary to protect the health and safety of the occupants of the condominium, to mitigate further damage to the property, and to make emergency repairs as appropriate.[89]

10.17 Automated External Defibrillator. The condominium association is permitted to maintain an automated external defibrillator device in the community for use in medical emergencies, and the association is immune from liability when the device is used as long as it is properly maintained, appropriate training has been provided to association employees, and the local emergency medical services director has been notified of the placement of the device in the community.[90] If the defibrillator device is placed in the community, the association's insurer may not require the association to purchase medical malpractice insurance and cannot exclude the use of the device from coverage under the association's general liability insurance coverage.[91]

10.18   Termination of the Condominium. Once created by the recording of the declaration of condominium, the condominium form of ownership and the restrictions and covenants governing the property and the unit owners continue until the condominium is terminated. Termination occurs when a "plan of termination" is approved by not less than 80% of the unit owners, and the plan is recorded with the Clerk of the Circuit Court in the county where the condominium is located.[92]

The plan of termination is required to separately state the valuation of each unit in the condominium, as well as the value of the common elements and other assets of the association at their respective market values. The plan must identify the termination trustee, customarily

---

[86] § 718.1265 (1)(c) and (d), F.S.
[87] § 718.1265 (1)(k) and (m), F.S.
[88] § 617.0830, F.S.
[89] § 718.1265 (2), F.S.
[90] § 768.1325 (3), F.S.
[91] § 768.1325 (6), F.S.
[92] §§ 718.117 (3) and (9), F.S.

the condominium association, and state the individual interests of each unit owner in the proceeds from the liquidation of the assets of the condominium upon termination.[93] A copy of the proposed plan of termination must be provided to each unit owner in the community at least fourteen (14) days prior to the meeting at which the plan is to be considered in the same manner that notice is given to owners for the annual meeting of the membership.[94]

Once approved by the required number of unit owners, title to the property vests in the termination trustee, and notice of the plan's adoption must be delivered by certified mail to each owner and mortgagee within thirty (30) days of the recording of the plan in the official records.[95] Within ninety (90) days after effective date of the plan, a certified copy of the recorded plan of termination must be provided to the Division of Florida Condominiums, Timeshares, and Mobile Homes.[96]

The Condominium Act also provides an additional, optional method to terminate the condominium when the costs to restore, construct or repair the property after a catastrophic loss exceeds the fair market value of the condominium after completion of the construction or repairs, or when it is impossible to reconstruct the physical configuration of the condominium because of the current zoning and land use regulations. In such circumstances, a majority of the voting interests is sufficient to approve the plan of termination following the same procedural steps otherwise required for terminating the condominium.[97]

---

[93] § 718.117 (10), F.S.
[94] § 718.117 (9), F.S.
[95] § 718.117 (15)(a), F.S.
[96] § 718.117 (15)(b), F.S.
[97] § 718.117 (2), F.S.

GRANT OF EASEMENT

THIS INDENTURE, made this 30th day of September, 2011, between WATERFRONT XX CONDOMINIUM ASSOCIATION, INC., a Florida corporation not-for-profit, on behalf of the owners of the below described property under the authority granted by Section 718.111 (10), F.S., party of the first part and the CITY OF WATERFRONT, 100 Main Street, Waterfront, Florida, party of the second part.

WITNESSETH, that the said party of the first part, for and in consideration of the sum of Ten Dollars ($10.00) and other good and valuable consideration to them in hand paid by the said party of the second part, the receipt whereof is hereby acknowledged, does hereby grant and release unto the said party of the second part, a perpetual easement

for the purposes of a drainage and utility easement over, under and across the following described property, lying in the County of Pinellas, Florida, to wit:

A portion of the common elements as described in the Declaration of Condominium for WATERFRONT XX CONDOMINIUM, recorded in O.R. Book 800, Page 100, Public Records of Pinellas County, Florida, being more particularly described as follows:

The westerly 5.0 feet along the western boundary of the condominium property as described in said Declaration of Condominium.

TO HAVE AND TO HOLD the same unto the party of the second part forever. The party of the first part does covenant to and with the party of the second part that it is acting on behalf of the lawful owners of the said property, that it is free from all encumbrances, that it has good right to grant the easement as aforesaid, and that it does warrant and will defend the grant of the said easement hereby made, unto the said party of the second part, against the lawful claims and demands of all persons whomsoever.

IN WITNESS WHEREOF, the party of the first part has caused these presents to be duly executed in its name by its President and its corporate seal to be hereto affixed, attested by its Secretary, this 30th day of September, 2011.

(CORPORATE SEAL)   WATERFRONT XX CONDOMINIUM
                        ASSOCIATION, INC.
ATTEST:

_____   By: _____
Secretary   President

STATE OF FLORIDA)
COUNTY OF PINELLAS   )

    Before me, the undersigned authority, this day personally appeared Marc Wesley and Nancy Jones to me well known and known to me to be the individuals in and who executed the foregoing instrument as its President and Secretary, respectively, of the corporation named in the foregoing instrument, and they severally acknowledged to and before me that they executed said instrument on behalf of and in the name of said corporation as such officers, that it was affixed thereto by due and regular corporate authority, that they are duly authorized by said corporation to execute said instrument, and that said instrument is the free act and deed of said corporation.

    IN WITNESS WHEREOF, I have hereunto set my hand and affixed my official seal this 30th day of September, 2011.

_____
Notary Public

My Commission Expires:

CERTIFICATE OF CORPORATE BORROWING RESOLUTION

I, NANCY SMITH, President of WATERFRONT XX CONDOMINIUM ASSOCIATION, INC., do hereby certify that at a duly held meeting of the Board of Administration of the condominium association held on September 30, 2011, by a unanimous vote of the Board, the following resolution was adopted:

BE IT RESOLVED that the President of WATERFRONT XX CONDOMINIUM ASSOCIATION, INC., is authorized to sign a $25,000.00 line of credit to the Florida Bank secured by association receivables. Any individual draw against the line must be signed by any two of the following officers and board members of this Association:

> NANCY SMITH, President
> SUE DAVIS, Secretary
> MATTHEW MARSHALL, Treasurer

BE IT FURTHER RESOLVED that WATERFRONT XX CONDOMINIUM ASSOCIATION, INC. authorized its legal counsel to furnish Florida Bank an Assignment of Interest in the Association's Assessments. The Assignment to be limited to no more than $25,000.00 or the amount of any outstanding loan to Florida Bank.

Signed this 30th day of September, 2011.

(CORPORATE SEAL)   WATERFRONT XX CONDOMINIUM
                          ASSOCIATION, INC.

ATTEST:

_____   By:_____
Secretary   President

11

Rights and Responsibilities of the Unit Owner

FORMS GOVERNING UNIT OWNERS' RIGHTS

11.1 Quiet Enjoyment of the Unit. Each unit owner is entitled to the exclusive use and possession of his or her unit, free of unnecessary nuisances but subject to the association's right of access for maintenance and repair of the condominium property.[1] The use that an owner makes of the unit, however, should not be an unreasonable source of annoyance to the other unit owners nor should it interfere with the peaceful and proper use of the property by any other condominium unit owner.[2]

Unit occupancy must be consistent with the condominium concept established by the declaration of condominium and its exhibits, and separate agreements attempting to grant special privileges or conditions to an owner different from those of other unit owners does not bind the association or the other owners.[3] Each owner, as a condition of ownership and occupancy of a condominium parcel, gives up a certain degree of freedom that he or she might otherwise enjoy in a separate, privately owned home, for the benefit of the health, happiness and peace of mind of a majority of all unit owners. (See 1.4).

11.2 Use of the Common Elements. Ownership of a condominium parcel includes ownership of an undivided portion of the common elements.[4] This ownership interest includes the right to use the common elements and the association property in accordance with the purposes for which they are intended,[5] unless the use rights have been suspended because an owner is delinquent in financial obligations to the association.[6] (See 8.12).

The common elements, common areas, and recreational facilities are available for use by every unit owner, and their invited guests; however, the use is subject to reasonable restrictions imposed by the board[7] and no use by an owner or group of owners may hinder or encroach upon the lawful rights of other unit owners.[8] Likewise, the rights of the common owners

---

[1] § 718.106 (3), F.S.; see also *Baum v. Coronado Condominium Ass'n, Inc.,* 376 So.2d 914 (Fla. 3rd DCA 1979).

[2] *Candib v. Carver,* 344 So.2d 1312 (Fla. 3rd DCA 1977).

[3] *Clearwater Key Ass'n—South Beach, Inc. v. Thacker,* 431 So.2d 641 (Fla. 2nd DCA 1983).

[4] § 718.103 (12), F.S.

[5] § 718.106 (3), F.S.

[6] § 718.303 (3), F.S.

[7] *Hidden Harbour Estates, Inc. v. Norman,* 309 So.2d 180 (Fla. 4th DCA 1975).

[8] "Prohibiting those types of assembly which will have a particularly divisive effect on the condominium community is a reasonable restriction." *Neuman v. Grandview at Emerald Hills, Inc.,* 861 So.2d 494 (Fla. 4th DCA 2003).

of an easement may not be exercised at the expense of the rights of other common owners,[9] and exclusive occupancy of a portion of the common elements may not be undertaken unless the other owners having a right to use the property also consent.[10]

The right of a unit owner to use the common property includes the right to peaceably assemble in the common facilities and the right to invite public officers or candidates for public office to appear and speak on the common facilities.[11] The condominium association may impose reasonable rules and regulations on the use of the common elements and the association property. It may not, however, impose a fee or charge upon any unit owner for the use of such property unless the charges are authorized by the declaration of condominium or by a majority vote of the condominium association's membership or unless the charges relate to expenses incurred by a unit owner having exclusive use of the common elements or the association property.[12]

Any unit owner prevented from exercising the rights guaranteed by the Act for use of the common elements or association property may bring a civil action to enforce those rights and may recover attorney's fees and costs if the action is successful.[13] Unit owners are also entitled to have reasonable access to public beaches adjacent to their condominium property, and the access cannot be denied by city or county ordinance.[14]

11.3 Appurtenances to Unit Ownership. The owner of a condominium parcel enjoys numerous rights and benefits from the covenants contained in the recorded condominium documents as appurtenances to ownership.[15] They may vary significantly based upon the language of an individual community's documents, but each owner is entitled to rely upon the content of the documents and the benefits conferred in them concerning the use of the condominium property.[16] The property rights, benefits, and

---

[9] *Sweetwater Oaks Condominium Ass'n, Inc. v. Creative Concepts of Tampa, Inc.,* 432 S.2d 654 (Fla. 2nd DCA 1983).

[10] *Enright v. Sea Towers Owners' Ass'n,* 370 So.2d 28, (Fla. 2nd DCA 1979)

[11] § 718.123 (1), F.S.

[12] § 718.111 (4), F.S.

[13] § 718.303 (1) and § 718.123 (2), F.S., F.S.

[14] § 718.106 (5), F.S.

[15] § 718.106 (2), F.S.

[16] See *Tower House Condominium, Inc. v. Millman,* 410 So.2d 926, 930 (Fla. 3rd DCA 1981) describing appurtenant interest in the condominium property and Beau Monde, Inc. v. Bramson, 446 So.2d 164, 167 (Fla. 2nd DCA 1984) holding that appurtenances include recreational and garage lease and long-term maintenance agreement.

obligations appurtenant to ownership cannot be changed or modified in a manner that is adverse to the interest of individual owners except in the manner, and with the formality, required by the Condominium Act and the declaration of condominium.[17]

While some rights and covenants conferred by the declaration of condominium cannot be changed without the consent of all affected owners, owners are presumed to know that substantial portions of the declaration of condominium may be lawfully amended after they acquire their ownership interests. Accordingly, many of the rights and covenants created by the condominium documents as appurtenances to unit ownership are subject to change or modification.[18] (See 9.1 and 9.8).

The rights appurtenant to ownership that cannot be changed or modified without the consent of the affected owners are those that are vested by the declaration as part of the condominium parcel and its ownership. Changes requiring individual owner consent to be effective are those to the unit boundaries, those changing the percentage of ownership in the common elements, and those changing the percentage allocation of the common expenses. Membership rights in the condominium association, membership rights in a master association,[19] ownership in the common surplus, and the right of exclusive use of the limited common elements or such portion of the common elements as may be provided in the declaration are also appurtenances to unit ownership that cannot be impaired without the consent of the affected owner.[20]

11.4   Access to Communication Services and Cable Television.

Every unit owner is entitled to access to communication services and cable television when there is available service from a duly franchised cable television operator. An owner cannot be denied access to the cable and communication services by the association, and cannot be required to pay anything of value to obtain the services except for those charges normally paid by single-family homeowners.[21] When the services are provided under a bulk contract with the association, the cost for the service is a common expense, and it cannot be avoided by a unit owner unless the owner receives

---

[17] § 718.110, F.S.
[18] *Everglades Plaza Condominium, Ass'n, Inc. v. Buckner,* 462 So.2d 835 (Fla. 4th DCA 1984).
[19] *Scott v. Sandestin Corporation,* 491 So.2d 334 (Fla. 1st DCA 1986).
[20] § 718.110 (4), F.S.
[21] § 718.1232, F.S.

supplemental security income or food stamps or is legally blind or hearing impaired.[22] (See 8.5).

The Telecommunication Act of 1996 also assures access by unit owners to certain television service provided over "direct broadcast satellite" by use of a satellite dish.[23] In response to this mandate from Congress, the Federal Communications Commission has adopted a rule prohibiting the enforcement of condominium covenants which impair the ability of an occupant of the condominium to receive video programming services over a satellite antenna which is less than one (1) meter in diameter or an antenna that is designed to receive television broadcast signals.[24]

11.5 Membership and Voting Rights in the Association. Every owner is entitled to membership in the condominium association designated in the declaration as the managing entity for the condominium, together with full voting rights pertaining to membership.[25] Unless the condominium documents provide otherwise, membership in the association extends to each owner of a unit having multiple owners, although co-owners of a unit may not serve as members of the board at the same time.[26] (See 4.7). The "voting interest" appurtenant to membership in the association shall be the voting rights as defined and distributed to the members by the declaration of condominium, the articles of incorporation, and the bylaws of the association.[27]

The association shall not deny or abridge the voting rights appurtenant to a unit, but it may place reasonable restrictions on the manner of exercising the right to vote in association affairs.[28] The voting interest of a unit owned by the association, however, may not be exercised or counted for any reason.[29] The voting interests of all other units may be voted by ballot and by limited proxy, and the voting rights of an owner may only be suspended for the

---

[22] § 718.115 (1)(d), F.S.
[23] § 207, Telecommunications Act of 1996.
[24] § 25.104, Rules of the Federal Communications Commission.
[25] § 718.106 (2)(d), F.S.
[26] § 718.112 (2)(d) 1., F.S.
[27] § 718.103 (30), F.S.
[28] § 61B-23.002 (5) and (6), F.A.C.
[29] § 718.112 (2)(b) 2., F.S.

non-payment of monetary obligations due to the association.[30] (See 8.12). Each owner is entitled to receive notice of all meetings and to have it posted conspicuously on the condominium property.[31]

Membership affords access to the records of the condominium association at all reasonable hours and permits a unit owner the right to make handwritten notes from the records or to obtain actual copies of the records at a reasonable cost.[32] (See 4.21). Each unit owner is entitled to receive annually a complete financial report of the association's actual receipts and expenditures. (See 7.14 and 7.15). Each member is also entitled to receive, upon request and within fifteen (15) days, an estoppel certificate from the association stating all assessments and money owed to it by the member. (See 8.9).

11.6 Participation in Association Affairs. No unit owner may act on behalf of the association simply by reason of being an owner,[33] but each owner has the right to participate in the association's decision-making processes. Notice must be provided to owners for all membership meetings and all meetings of the board. The notices must identify all items of business to be considered at the meetings. (See 3.6 and 4.17). Unit owners may participate in debate at meetings of the membership,[34] and may speak at all meetings of the board of administration and committees of the board.[35] Members may also petition to have items added to the agenda of a meeting of the board of administration.[36] (See 6.11 and 6.12).

The single exception concerning the right of individual unit owners to attend and participate board or committee meetings is when the board or committee is receiving advice from the association's legal counsel concerning pending or threatened litigation. Such meetings may be held in executive session and unit owners may be excluded from the meeting. (See 4.17).

Any unit owner is authorized by the Condominium Act to tape record

---

[30] § 718.303 (5), F.S.
[31] § 718.112 (2)(c) and (d), F.S.
[32] § 718.111 (12)(c), F.S.; *Winter v. Playa del Sol,* 353 So.2d 598, 599 (Fla. 4th DCA 1977).
[33] § 718.111 (1)(c), F.S.
[34] § 718.112 (2)(d) 6., F.S.
[35] § 718.112 (2)(c), F.S.
[36] *Id.*

or videotape meetings of the board of administration[37] and membership meetings of the association.[38] The right to record such meetings may be subject to reasonable restrictions provided that the restrictions have been adopted in advance by the board or the unit owners as written rules. Under such rules, an owner wishing to record a meeting may be required to install the recording equipment prior to the meeting. The owner may also be required to provide advance notice of his or her intention to record the meeting, and may be prohibited from moving around the meeting room during the recording process. The right to tape record or videotape meetings is restricted to equipment that does not produce distracting sound or light emissions.[39]

11.7 Fundamental Rights and Due Process. The condominium concept established by statute imposes a fiduciary duty upon the governing body of the association to afford due process and equal protection to each of its members.[40] Each unit owner is entitled to adequate notice of the restrictions being imposed during membership in the association and is further entitled to have the condominium covenants and restrictions uniformly applied and enforced.

When a unit owner can demonstrate that the condominium association is being arbitrary or selective in its enforcement policies, the actions of the association can be restrained or halted.[41] If a unit owner relies on a course of conduct by the board of administration and the board later attempts to change its position or commences enforcement proceedings, the unit owner may rely on the condominium association's initial representations.[42]

No owner may be treated differently from other owners in the obligation to pay proportionate shares of the common expenses of the condominium.[43] Rules of the board of administration may not be arbitrary or capricious, and they must relate to the health, happiness and enjoyment of

---

[37] *Id.*

[38] § 718.112 (2)(d) 7., F.S.

[39] § 61B-23.002 (10), F.A.C.

[40] § 718.111 (1)(a), F.S.

[41] *White Egret Condominium, Inc. v. Franklin,* 379 So.2d 346, 351 (Fla. 1979). See also *Prisco v. Forrest Villas Condominium Apartments, Inc.,* 847 So.2d 1012, 1014 (Fla. 4th DCA 2003).

[42] *Plaza Del Prado Condominium Ass'n, Inc. v. Richman,* 345 So.2d 851, 852 (Fla. 3rd DCA 1977).

[43] § 718.116 (9)(a), F.S.

the various association members.[44] (See 9.2). Provisions of the condominium documents are not permitted to abrogate the fundamental constitutional rights of a unit owner. The declaration of condominium and exhibits constitute an elaborate contract between the unit owners and the governing association, and each owner is protected from the unconstitutional impairment of the contract rights that have been granted by the condominium documents.[45]

When an owner has an inquiry or a complaint concerning the board of administration or the association, the owner is entitled to file it by certified mail with the board.[46] The board is required to act on the inquiry or complaint in a timely manner, and must respond to the inquiring unit owner concerning the action taken within thirty (30) days. (See 10.13).

11.8 Compliance with the Covenants and Restrictions. All provisions of the declaration of condominium are enforceable as equitable servitudes, and they are covenants and restrictions with which each unit owner and their guests must comply.[47] The uniqueness of condominium living and the resultant necessity for a greater degree of control over and limitation upon the rights of the individual unit owners than might be tolerated given more traditional forms of property ownership is one of the basic principles of condominium living. (See 1.4). An individual owner is not permitted to disrupt the integrity of the common scheme by violating the covenants and restrictions of the condominium no matter how well-intended the owner might be.[48]

Restrictions limiting the use of the condominium property and restrictions created for the benefit of unit owners are enforceable by every owner and the condominium association.[49] An owner who violates the covenants and restrictions of the condominium documents may be fined if the declaration of condominium or the bylaws permit.[50] An owner may also be subject to an action for damages or injunctive relief, or both, for failure to comply with the provisions of the Condominium Act, the

---

[44] *Hidden Harbour Estates, Inc. v. Norman,* 309 So.2d 180, 182 (Fla. 4th DCA 1975).

[45] U.S. Const., art. I, § 10; Fla. Const., art. I, § 10.

[46] § 718.112 (2)(a) 2., F.S.

[47] § 718.104 (7) and § 718.303 (1), F.S.

[48] *Sterling Village Condominium, Inc. v. Breitenbach,* 251 So.2d 685, 688 (Fla. 4th DCA 1971).

[49] § 718.303 (1), F.S.

[50] § 718.303 (3), F.S.

declaration of condominium, or the articles of incorporation and bylaws of the association.[51]

11.9 Financial Obligations. Every unit owner, regardless of how the owner's title has been acquired, including a purchaser at a judicial sale, is liable for all assessments that come due while he or she is the unit owner.[52] No unit owner may be excused from payment of a proportionate share of the common expenses unless all unit owners are likewise excused,[53] and liability for assessments may not be avoided by waiver of use of the common elements or by abandonment of the unit for which the assessments are made.[54]

The liability of the owner of a unit for common expenses is limited to the amounts properly assessed against the unit by the condominium association. Once assessed, the condominium association has a lien on each condominium parcel for any unpaid assessments and for attorney's fees and costs incurred by the association that are incident to the collection of the assessment or the enforcement of the lien. (See 8.12). The lien rights of the association relate back to the time of the filing of the declaration and are superior to the constitutional homestead rights of the unit owner.[55]

The owner of a unit may have additional financial responsibility for expenses incurred in the maintenance of limited common elements that are reserved for the exclusive use of the unit owner. When the declaration of condominium provides for other benefits for the owner from the association, the owner may be responsible for reimbursing the association for expenses incurred on the unit owner's behalf.[56] The owner of a unit may be personally liable for the acts or omissions of the condominium association in relation to the use of the common elements, but only when the liability is shared proportionately based upon the ownership in the common elements and in no event may that liability exceed the value of the unit.[57]

A unit owner is additionally responsible to the condominium association for any willful or malicious damage to the common elements or association property caused by the owner's minor children. The association is entitled to recover from the parents the total actual damages caused by

---

[51] § 718.303 (1), F.S.
[52] § 718.116 (1)(a), F.S.
[53] *Clearwater Key Ass'n—South Beach, Inc. v. Thacker, supra* note 3.
[54] § 718.116 (2), F.S.
[55] *Bessemer v. Gersten,* 381 So.2d 1344, 1348 (Fla. 1980).
[56] § 718.113 (1), F.S.
[57] § 718.119 (2), F.S.

the minor child, as well as the costs of any court proceedings which are necessary to collect the damages.[58]

Property taxes and special assessments by governmental authorities imposed on the condominium property are assessed separately against the individual condominium parcels and not upon the condominium property as a whole.[59] Each owner is separately responsible for payment of taxes and special assessments that come due against the condominium parcel which he or she owns, and failure to pay the obligation results in a tax lien only upon the delinquent parcel and not upon the other portions of the condominium property.[60]

11.10 Maintenance and Upkeep of the Property. Traditionally, the normal maintenance responsibilities of the condominium association are defined and identified in the declaration of condominium as a direct result of the descriptions of the units and the common elements. While maintenance responsibilities for the common elements belong to the condominium association by statute, maintenance responsibilities for the unit belong to the condominium unit owner together with the responsibility for those improvements that are designated as part of the unit or as part of the unit owner's responsibility by the declaration of condominium. Such items may include doors, windows, air conditioning, and heating systems, or other similar improvements that are designated as a part of the unit or for the exclusive use by a particular unit owner.[61]

An owner is responsible for damage that is intentionally or negligently caused to the condominium property by the unit owner.[62] The owner of a condominium parcel may not neglect his or her maintenance responsibility in a way that would adversely affect the safety or the soundness of the common elements or any portion of the condominium property that is to be maintained by the association.[63] In limited circumstances, the owners of a condominium unit may take reasonable steps to protect their unit and its furnishings from further damage when the condominium property is in a state of disrepair. The reasonable steps may include alterations to the

---

[58] § 741.24 (1) and (2), F.S.
[59] § 718.120, F.S.
[60] § 718.120 (2), F.S.
[61] § 718.106 (2)(b) and § 718.113 (1), F.S.
[62] § 718.111 (11)(j) 1., F.S.
[63] § 718.113 (3), F.S.

condominium property on a temporary basis.[64]

11.11 Alterations to the Condominium Property. A unit owner may not make any alterations or additions to the common elements or the limited common elements except in the manner permitted by the declaration of condominium, although the association may not refuse to permit the attachment of a religious object to the door frame of the owner's unit that does not exceed three (3) inches in width and six (6) inches in height.[65] Further, no unit owner may make any alteration to the unit itself which would result in a change to or infringement upon the common elements or which would adversely affect the safety or soundness of the common elements or any portion of the condominium property which is to be maintained by the association.[66] Unauthorized additions, modifications, or alterations are subject to removal and the condominium property being restored to its original condition and appearance at the expense of the unit owner.

When the declaration of condominium allows a unit owner to make alterations to the condominium property, the conditions for making the alterations or modifications must be specifically complied with by the owner.[67] If approval of the board of administration is required before the alterations are permitted, the approval cannot be unreasonably withheld. (See 9.13). When the approval for unit alterations has been received from the board, other unit owners may not object to the alterations.

The failure of the board of administration or the management company to respond to a request by a unit owner to make alterations to the condominium property is not the same as giving consent for the alterations. The lack of response does not operate as an estoppel or as a waiver of the condominium association's right to object once the actual work is started by the unit owner.[68]

The installation of hurricane shutters and other hurricane protection is a right of every unit owner, and the board is required to provide appropriate specifications to govern their installation. (See 9.14). Any owner may

---

[64] *Schmeck v. Sea Oats Condominium, Ass'n, Inc.,* 441 So.2d 1092, 1096 (Fla. 5th DCA 1983).

[65] § 718.113 (7), F.S.; *Curci Village Condominium Ass'n, Inc. v. Santa Maria,* 14 So.3d 1175 (Fla. 4th DCA 2009).

[66] § 718.113 (2) and (3), F.S.; *Schmidt v. Sherrill,* 442 So.2d 963 (Fla. 4th DCA 1983).

[67] § 718.113 (2), F.S.; *Fountains of Palm Beach Condominium, Inc. v. Farkas,* 355 So.2d 163 (Fla. 4th DCA 1978).

[68] *Id.*

display one (1) portable, removable United States flag in a respectful manner regardless of any provision in the declaration of condominium or rule of the association.[69] An owner may also display a service flag of the Army, Navy, Air Force, Marine Corps or Coast Guard on Armed Services Day, Memorial Day, Flag Day, Independence Day, and Veterans Day. The service flag may not exceed four and one-half (4 1/2) feet by six and one-half (6 1/2) feet in size.[70]

11.12 Sale and Transfer of the Condominium Parcel. The condominium parcel must be transferred as a whole, and the common elements and other appurtenances cannot be separated from the condominium unit at the time of transfer.[71] The declaration of condominium may also impose a variety of restrictions on the sale, lease, or transfer of the condominium units, and such covenants are enforceable against the unit owner. (See 13.17 and 13.18). The fact that the condominium unit may be less desirable and hence less valuable than it would be if it were not subject to the transfer restrictions, does not constitute an unreasonable restraint on the sale or lease of a unit. So long as the covenants restricting unit transfers are equally applicable to all owners and are not arbitrary or discriminatory in their application, they may be enforced against each unit owner.

Restrictions on the transfer of condominium units, both on the sale and rental of units, are recognized as a valid means for insuring that the condominium association has the ability to control the composition of the condominium as a whole. They may also serve to ensure that the owner's financial obligation to the condominium association is maintained. When board approval must be obtained prior to a lease or rental, it is reasonable for the board to withhold such approval from an owner who is in default on monthly assessments.[72] If permitted by the condominium documents, the association may require a security deposit as a prerequisite to renting or leasing to protect against damages to the common elements or association property.[73]

---

[69] § 718.113 (4), F.S. See also Pub. L. 109–243, July 24, 2006, 120 Stat.572 and *Gerber v. Longboat Harbour North Condominium, Inc.,* 724 F. Supp. 884 (M.D. Fla. 1989).
[70] § 718.113 (4), F.S.
[71] § 718.107 (2), F.S.
[72] § 718.116 (4), F.S.
[73] § 718.112 (2)(i), F.S.

Prior to the sale of a unit, prospective owners must be advised about the condominium, its restrictions and its finances. Each prospective buyer is entitled to receive, at the seller's expense, a current copy of the annual financial report, a governance form explaining the association operations, the Frequently Asked Questions and Answers document, and the declaration of condominium and its exhibits.[74] Any contract for the resale of a residential condominium unit is required to contain a special clause where the purchaser acknowledges the receipt of the condominium documents, as well as an opportunity of at least seven (7) days to review them prior to entering a binding agreement.[75] At the time a unit is sold, both the grantee and the grantor are jointly liable for all unpaid assessments attributable to the unit up until the time of the transfer.[76]

11.13 Public Participation and SLAPP Suit Protection. The Condominium Act provides unit owners with special protections to exercise their rights of free speech before institutions of government on matters related to the condominium association and from "strategic lawsuits against public participation," known as SLAPP suits, when unit owners engage in the participation.[77] SLAPP suits by any individual or business organization against a unit owner are prohibited,[78] and a condominium association is specifically prohibited from using association funds to prosecute a SLAPP suit against a unit owner.[79]

When a SLAPP suit is filed against a unit owner, the owner is entitled to petition the court for an order dismissing the action.[80] The court is required to set a hearing on the dismissal request at the earliest possible time, and if the unit owner is successful, the judge may award treble damages to the prevailing owner, together with an award for attorney's fees and costs against the person or entity bringing the action in violation of the SLAPP suit prohibition.[81]

---

[74] § 718.503 (2)(a), F.S.
[75] § 718.503 (2)(b), F.S.
[76] § 718.116 (1)(a), F.S.
[77] § 718.1224 (1), F.S.
[78] § 718.1224 (2), F.S.
[79] § 718.1224 (4), F.S.
[80] § 718.1224 (3), F.S.
[81] *Id.*

A RESOLUTION BY THE BOARD OF ADMINISTRATION OF WATERFRONT XX CONDOMINIUM ASSOCIATION, INC., ESTABLISHING RULES GOVERNING THE RIGHT OF UNIT OWNERS TO SPEAK AT BOARD MEETINGS AND COMMITTEE MEETINGS

THAT WHEREAS, Section 718.112(2)(c), Florida Statutes, authorizes any unit owner to speak at meetings of the board of administration and committees of the Association, and

WHEREAS, the Association may adopt reasonable written rules governing the frequency, duration, and manner of unit owner statements at such meetings.

NOW THEREFORE BE IT RESOLVED by the Board of Administration of Waterfront XX Condominium Association, Inc., that the rules governing the rights of unit owners to speak at meetings of the Board and committees of the Association be as follows:

1.   Any unit owner desiring to speak at meetings of the Board or meetings of a committee of the Association shall be entitled to do so with respect to all designated agenda items. An owner does not have the right to speak with respect to items not specifically designated, but may do so at the discretion of the chair.

2.   Any unit owner desiring to speak before a meeting must file a written request with the chairman of the meeting prior to the commencement of the meeting. The request shall state the subject which the unit owner wishes to address.

3.   No unit owner may exceed more than three (3) minutes with respect to any subject upon which the unit owner is recognized to speak. At the conclusion of his or her remarks, an owner shall refrain from further comments or remarks as a courtesy to the next speaker.

ADOPTED by the Board of Administration this 5th day of October, 2011.

By:_____
Secretary of the Association

Rule Regarding Speaking at Board Meetings FORM 11.01

A RESOLUTION BY THE BOARD OF ADMINISTRATION OF WATERFRONT XX CONDOMINIUM ASSOCIATION, INC., ESTABLISHING RULES GOVERNING RECORDING AND VIDEOTAPING MEETINGS

THAT WHEREAS, Sections 718.112(2)(c) and (d), Florida Statutes, authorizes any unit owner to tape record or videotape meetings of the Board of Administration and the membership, and

WHEREAS, the Condominium Act and Rule 61B-23.002(10), Florida Administrative Code, by the Division of Florida Land Sales, Condominiums and Mobile Homes allows for reasonable restrictions to be imposed on a unit owner desiring to tape record or videotape a meeting.

NOW THEREFORE BE IT RESOLVED by the Board of Administration of Waterfront XX Condominium Association, Inc., that the rules governing the taping and videotaping of meetings of the Board and the membership be as follows:

1.   Any unit owner desiring to utilize audio or video equipment at meetings of the Board or membership shall notify the Board of Administration of such owner's intention at least twenty-four (24) hours prior to the meeting.

2.   All equipment shall be assembled and placed in position prior to the commencement of the meeting in the location designated, and no one videotaping or recording a meeting shall be permitted to move about the meeting room in order to facilitate the recording.

3.   No equipment shall be permitted that produces distracting sounds or light emissions.

ADOPTED by the Board of Administration this 5th day of October, 2011.

By:_____
               Secretary of the Association

12

The Condominium Developer and Transition

TRANSITION AND DEVELOPER FORMS

12.1　General. The developer is the person or entity that creates the condominium community by the recording of the declaration of condominium.[1] The developer is also the person or entity that offers the condominium parcels for sale or lease in the ordinary course of business.[2] Under most circumstances, the same developer both creates and markets the condominium unit. The definition of "developer," however, applies not only to those who do both functions but also to those persons or entities who do either and to those who act concurrently with someone who creates, sells, or leases condominium units in the ordinary course of business.

For purposes of the statutory definition, one is presumed to be in the "ordinary course of business" when the person or entity, within a one (1) year period, offers more than seven (7) condominium parcels for sale or lease. If the community contains less than seventy (70) total condominium units, then it shall be when the person or entity offers more than ten percent of the total condominium units for sale or lease.[3] One is also presumed to be engaged in the "ordinary course of business" of selling or leasing condominium units when such person or entity participates with another, other than by simply providing financial contribution, in a common promotional plan which offers more than seven (7) condominium parcels over a period of one (1) year or more.

12.2　Association Organization and Operation. The developer creates the association and appoints the first complete board of administration at the time that the condominium is created. The developer-board maintains and operates the condominium association until the community matures and control of the board of administration passes to the unit owners.[4] The Condominium Act makes no distinction in the operation of a developer-controlled board and an owner-controlled board, and developer-board members must follow proper meeting procedures, maintain appropriate association records, and all meetings must be properly noticed and open to unit owners' participation.

The developer-controlled board of directors adopts a budget for the association, and during the period of developer control, assessments cannot

---

[1] § 718.103 (16), F.S. and § 61B-15.007 (1), F.A.C.
[2] *First Federal Savings and Loan Association of Seminole County v. Department of Business Regulation*, 472 So.2d 494, 496 (Fla. 5th DCA 1985).
[3] § 61B-15.007 (2), F.A.C.
[4] § 718.111 (1)(a), F.S.

exceed 115 % of assessments for the prior fiscal year unless approved by a majority vote of all voting interests in the condominium.[5] The Condominium Act also makes no exception for the waiver of reserves when the association budget is proposed by the developer, and the developer-controlled board must comply with the requirements of the Act to implement such a waiver if it is desired. (See 7.9). The developer may waive the reserves only for the first two (2) years of the association's operations. After the initial two (2) years, the waiver can only occur upon a majority vote of non-developer voting interests.[6]

The developer-controlled board must establish the initial financial accounts for the association, and must maintain separate accounts as required by the Act. Accounts must be maintained so as not to commingle the funds of one association with the funds of another association or with the funds of the developer.[7] (See 7.2). The developer-controlled board must comply with the annual financial reporting requirements of the Condominium Act (see 7.14), and may waive the annual audit requirements during the first two (2) years of operation.[8] Thereafter, the developer-controlled board may not waive the audit requirements unless a majority of the voting interests other than the developer approve the waiver.

Absent a provision to the contrary in the bylaws, the board shall be organized with at least five (5) members and there shall be a president, secretary, and treasurer to perform the duties customarily assumed by such officers.[9] During the period of developer control, each board member and officer is appointed by and serves at the pleasure of the developer.

12.3   Limitations and Obligations of the Developer. The developer has the initial obligation to make a complete disclosure of all matters relating to the condominium to each person or entity that purchases or acquires a condominium unit.[10] Additionally, during the period of developer control there are specific restrictions on the authority of the board of administration controlled by the developer. These restrictions are designed to protect and preserve the rights of purchasers of units in the condominium and to

---

[5] § 718.112 (2)(e) 2., F.S.
[6] § 718.112 (2)(f) 2., F.S.
[7] § 718.111 (14), F.S.
[8] § 718.111 (13)(b), F.S.
[9] § 718.112 (2)(a), F.S.
[10] § 718.503, F.S.

ensure that the initial representations made to each owner are kept by the developer.[11]

The developer cannot start, compromise, or settle disputes involving construction defects in the condominium community.[12] A developer-controlled board cannot compromise commitments or promises that the developer has made to the owners. When a developer-controlled board of administration exercises its power to make contracts for the maintenance, management, or operation of the condominium, the authority to do so is subject to reconsideration by the unit owners. (See 12.10). The statute of limitations for actions in law or equity which the association may have do not begin until the unit owners have elected a majority of the members of the board of administration.[13]

During the time when the board of administration is controlled by the developer, violations of the Condominium Act or rules promulgated under the Act by the association are the responsibility of the developer.[14] The action or inaction by the developer or the developer-controlled board of administration cannot be used against the association in an attempt to establish selective or arbitrary conduct by the owner-controlled board of the association. Finally, during the time of developer control, the association shall not vote to use reserves for purposes other than that for which they were intended without the approval of a majority of all non-developer voting interests.[15]

12.4   Rights and Privileges of the Developer. The developer has all of the rights appurtenant to ownership of a condominium parcel for each unit titled in the developer's name.[16] The developer is also entitled to the special rights and privileges that are allowed by the Condominium Act or which are reserved to the developer in the condominium documents.[17] By reservation in the condominium documents, the developer, under certain circumstances, may unilaterally amend the condominium documents without further consent of other unit owners.[18] The developer may also be exempted

---

[11] § 61B-18.007, F.A.C.
[12] § 718.111 (3), F.S.
[13] § 718.124, F.S.
[14] § 718.301 (5) and (6), F.S.
[15] § 718.112 (2)(f), F.S.
[16] § 718.106 (2), F.S.
[17] *Mayfair Engineering Co. v. Park,* 318 So.2d 171 (Fla. 4th DCA 1975).
[18] § 718.110 (2) and § 718.403 (1), F.S.

from the payment of common expenses of the condominium coming due on units owned by the developer under specific authority of the Condominium Act. (See 12.6).

The developer is entitled to representation on the board of administration of the association for as long as units are held and offered for sale in the ordinary course of business.[19] While the developer holds a unit or units for sale in the condominium, the condominium documents may be amended by the required procedure; however, copies of the documents must be filed with the Division and provided to all purchasers prior to closing or within ten (10) days of the amendment. (See 9.9).

For purposes of disclosure, if a developer has attempted to comply with the requirements of the Condominium Act in good faith and the developer's efforts have resulted in substantial compliance, nonmaterial errors or omissions in the disclosure materials and condominium documents shall not be actionable.[20]

12.5 "Frequently Asked Questions and Answers" and Governance Form.

In addition to the prospectus, the developer is responsible for furnishing each buyer a separate page of information entitled "Frequently Asked Questions and Answers." This page must inform prospective owners concerning their voting rights, their financial obligations, the liabilities of the association and the restrictions governing the use of the units.[21] Its content and format must comply with the requirements established by the Division of Florida Condominiums, Timeshares, and Mobile Homes.

The Division also provides a form summarizing the governance of the condominium property by the condominium association, and the form must be provided to all prospective purchasers of a condominium unit by the seller.[22] The governance form is intended to explain the responsibility and role of the board of administration; the financial and compliance obligations of the unit owners and the board; and the rights of unit owners to participate in the affairs of the condominium association.[23]

---

[19] § 718.301 (1)(d) 2., F.S.
[20] § 718.505, F.S.
[21] § 718.504, F.S.
[22] The form is required for all transaction on or after January 1, 2009. § 718.503 (2)(a), F.S.
[23] § 718.503(2)(a) 1.-11., F.S.

12.6 Assessment Responsibilities of the Developer. From the time of creation of the condominium and until the sale of units to a purchaser, the developer is the unit owner.[24] As a unit owner, the developer is liable for all assessments that come due while title is held by the developer regardless of how title is acquired unless excused under the provisions of the Condominium Act.[25] The obligation of the developer to pay a proportionate share of the common expenses applies to both assessments and special assessments even when a portion of the monies is being used to pay for a lawsuit against the developer. Efforts to excuse the developer-owned units from liability for payment of expenses by special terms in the declaration of condominium are ineffective, and the statutory obligation to pay assessments prevails in such circumstances.[26]

The developer may be excused from payment of common expenses only after meeting conditions specified in the Act.[27] The conditions under one alternative provide that the developer may be excused for a stated period of time subsequent to the recording of the declaration of condominium. The period must terminate no later than the first day of the fourth calendar month following the month in which the sale of the first condominium unit occurs, and the developer must pay the portion of the common expenses incurred during the period which exceed the amount assessed against other unit owners.

Under the second alternative, the developer is excused from payment if the common expenses for all other unit owners are guaranteed not to increase, and the developer agrees to pay all common expenses not produced from the other unit owners. Under either alternative, funds collected for reserves as capital contributions or as start-up funds and other non-assessment revenue may not be used for the payment of common expenses by the developer or by the developer-controlled association.[28]

During the period that a developer guarantees the common expenses for the condominium association, the guarantee does not extend to uninsured losses resulting from a natural disaster or an act of God, provided

---

[24] *Hyde Park Condominium Ass'n v. Estero Island Real Estate, Inc.,* 486 So.2d 1 (Fla. 2nd DCA 1986).

[25] § 718.116 (9)(a), F.S.

[26] *Palm Bay Towers Corp. v. Brooks,* 466 So.2d 1071 (Fla. 3rd DCA 1984).

[27] § 61B-22.004, F.A.C.

[28] § 718.116 (9)(b), F.S. and § 61B-22.004 (4), F.A.C.

that the developer-controlled association has obtained and maintained the required insurance for the condominium. When a loss occurs under these circumstances, each unit owner, including the developer, assumes a proportional share of the uninsured loss to the condominium property.[29] Failure by the developer-controlled association to exercise due diligence and maintain adequate insurance coverage for the condominium is a breach of the fiduciary responsibility by the developer-members of the board of administration.[30]

So long as the developer holds units for sale in the ordinary course of business, no assessments for capital improvements may be made against any developer-owned unit without the developer's written approval. Likewise, the association may not take any action detrimental to the sale of units owned by the developer although an increase in assessments for common expenses without discrimination against the developer is not considered detrimental to the sale of units.[31]

12.7 Transition Members' Meeting. Within seventy-five (75) days from the time that unit owners are entitled to control the board of administration (See 4.3), a meeting of the membership must be called by the developer-controlled association to allow the unit owners to elect the members of the board of administration.[32] Notices for the meeting and procedures for the transition election are the same as those required for the regular elections for the board of administration.[33] (See 3.8). If the developer-controlled board fails or refuses to call the transition meeting, it may be called and the notice given by any member of the association.[34]

Unless the meeting should happen to coincide with the association's annual members' meeting, it is a special meeting, and business is limited to that which is set forth in the meeting notice. Except for the election of members of the board of administration, the statute provides for no other formal business to come before the transition meeting for membership action.

Once the new board has been elected and control of the association

---

[29] § 718.116 (9)(a), F.S.
[30] § 718.111 (11), F.S.
[31] § 718.301 (3), F.S.
[32] § 718.301 (2), F.S.
[33] § 718.301 (2), F.S. and § 61B-23.0021 (1), F.A.C.
[34] § 718.301 (2), F.S.

has passed to the unit owners, the developer thereupon relinquishes control of the association and all of the records and property of the association. Within ten (10) business days of the election of the first unit owners other than the developer to the board of administration, the developer must forward to the Division of Florida Condominiums, Timeshares, and Mobile Homes in writing the name and mailing address of each unit owner member of the board.[35]

After control of the board passes to the owners, the developer remains entitled to at least one (1) representative on the board of administration as long as the developer continues to sell units in the ordinary course of business and continues to own at least 5% of the total units in the condominium. If the condominium has five hundred (500) units or more, the right of the developer to have at least one (1) member of the board continues as long as the developer owns at least 2% of the total units in the condominium and continues normal sales activities. The members of the board of administration serving as representatives of the developer are not subject to recall by the unit owners. Developer representatives may be removed only by the developer or under the requirements of transition of control of the board.[36]

12.8 Delivery of Documents, Building Report and Financial Report. Simultaneously with the transfer of control of the board of administration, the developer must deliver to the association all of the property of the unit owners and association which is held or controlled by the developer or the developer-controlled board of administration. The developer shall be responsible for any expenses incurred in providing the documents and property to the association.[37] The required documents include the original or a photocopy of the recorded declaration of condominium and all amendments thereto, and the formal documents creating the association together with the resignation of all officers and board members.

The developer must transfer all tangible personal property and must provide an inventory of that property. The developer must also deliver the insurance policies, copies of the certificates of occupancy, other applicable governmental permits for the condominium property, and all written

---

[35] § 61B-23.003 (5), F.A.C.
[36] § 61B-23.0026 (1)(c), F.A.C.
[37] § 718.301 (4), F.S. and § 61B-23.003 (4), F.A.C.

warranties of the contractors, sub-contractors, suppliers, and manufacturers, if any, that are still effective.[38]

The transition materials must include a report attesting to the maintenance requirements, useful life, and estimated replacement costs for enumerated improvements on the condominium property. The report must be prepared and sealed by an architect or engineer, and it must include the building structure, roof, electrical, and plumbing systems, drainage and irrigation systems, parking area, and other major components on the property.[39] In addition to the report, the transition materials must include a copy of the plans and specifications utilized in the construction or remodeling of the improvements in the condominium together with a certificate, in affidavit form, from the developer or an architect or engineer to the effect that such plans and specifications represent those actually used in construction.[40]

A complete roster of unit owners including their addresses and their telephone numbers, if known, must be provided at the time of transition. Copies of all other agreements and contracts to which the association is a party must also be provided including leases of the common elements, employment contracts, service contracts, and all other agreements in which the association or the unit owners have an obligation or responsibility, directly or indirectly, to pay some or all of the fee or charge of the person performing the services. Finally, the developer must deliver all of the financial records, including financial statements of the association and source documents since the incorporation of the association through the date of transition. Together with these records, the developer must also turn over all of the association funds.[41]

The financial records of the association must be audited by an independent certified public accountant who may not be an employee of the developer and who is professionally independent of the control of the developer as determined by the policies established by the Florida State Board of Accountancy.[42] The audit must cover a period which begins with

---

[38] § 718.301 (4), F.S.
[39] § 718.301 (4)(p), F.S.
[40] § 718.301 (4), F.S.
[41] *Id.*
[42] *Alternative Development, Inc. v. St. Lucie Club and Apartment Homes Condominium Ass'n, Inc.*, 608 So.2d 822, 826–827 (Fla. 4th DCA 1992).

the date of incorporation through the date of transfer of association control to unit owners other than the developer. The audit must accurately state the amounts of monies paid by the developer towards common expenses of the association, whether direct or indirect, and shall specify the purpose for such expenditures. The expense for the audit and the work of the independent certified public accountant is the responsibility of the developer.[43]

The developer or the developer's agent is responsible for obtaining a receipt for transfer of the condominium records to the owner-controlled association. The receipt shall include, but shall not be limited to, a listing of all of the items required under the Condominium Act for each condominium managed by the association. The receipt shall contain the date that the records were transferred, and it shall be signed by both the developer and a non-developer unit owner board member. A copy of the receipt shall become a permanent part of the condominium association's official records.

The receipt and its execution does not constitute a waiver by the condominium association of any of its rights with respect to the completeness and accuracy of the transfer of the condominium documents or preclude administrative remedies which are available under the Condominium Act.[44]

12.9 Organization of Owner-Controlled Board. The newly elected members of the board of administration must be prepared to select their own officers and assume their duties and control of the association immediately. (See 5.2). The new board members will receive and acknowledge control of the association property, records, and funds simultaneously with the acceptance of control, and their responsibilities for the operation of the condominium begin immediately.[45] The act of acknowledging receipt of the records and property of the association does not bind the board on the issues of completeness and accuracy of the information being received.

One of the primary duties of the new board following its organization is to determine both the completeness and accuracy of the building report, financial audit and other records and property received from the developer. If the transition requirements have not been fully met by the developer, the new board should be prepared to enforce the association's rights as allowed under the Act.[46]

---

[43] § 718.301 (4)(c), F.S. and § 61B-23.003 (4), F.A.C.
[44] § 718.301 (4), F.S. and § 61B-23.003 (6), F.A.C.
[45] § 718.301 (4), F.S.
[46] § 718.302 (6), F.S.

As part of their organizational duties and responsibilities, the board should attempt to identify potential legal causes of action which the association may have against other parties. The statute of limitations for any actions in law or equity which the association may have does not begin to run until the transfer of control of the board of administration is complete; but once control is accomplished, the time period begins to run.[47] The association's right to cancel agreements for the management and maintenance of the condominium property made by the developer also expires within eighteen (18) months of transition.[48]

Attention to warranty rights is also important since claims under the statutory warranties may be restricted to the first year following transition.[49]

The new board of administration must finally be prepared to assume its role in the enforcement of the condominium documents. Prior conduct by the developer cannot be used against the association in an attempt to show selective or arbitrary enforcement policies of the use restrictions in the documents. The board of administration controlled by the unit owners must be prepared to establish the uniform enforcement procedures of the association once transfer occurs if the enforceability of the condominium documents is to be preserved.[50]

12.10 Contracts of the Developer-Controlled Board. Any contract providing for the operation, maintenance, or management of a condominium association or the property serving the unit owners that is made by the association prior to transition of control of the board of administration is subject to cancellation by the unit owners.[51] The right of cancellation applies to any grant or reservation made by the declaration of condominium, lease, other document, and any contract providing for maintenance or management services. All agreements serving the condominium association or the unit owners must be fair and reasonable, and after 1976, public policy prohibits the inclusion or enforcement of escalation clauses in management contracts that are based upon a nationally recognized consumer price index.[52]

---

[47] § 718.124, F.S.

[48] § 718.302 (2), F.S.

[49] § 718.203 (1)(e), F.S.

[50] *Ladner v. Plaza Del Prado Condominium Ass'n, Inc.*, 423 So.2d 927 (Fla. 3rd DCA 1982).

[51] § 718.302 (1), F.S.; *Tri-Properties, Inc. v. Moonspinner Condominium Ass'n, Inc.*, 447 So.2d 965, 967 (Fla. 1st DCA 1984); *Comcast of Florida, L.P. v. L'Ambiance Beach Condominium Ass'n, Inc.*, 17 So.3d 839 (Fla. 4th DCA 2009).

[52] § 718.302 (5), F.S.

To unilaterally cancel an agreement made by the developer-controlled association, the board must have the concurrence of the owners of not less than 75% of the voting interests of the association, excluding the voting interests owned by the developer. If both parties to the agreement concur with the termination, the concurrence of the individual voting interests is not required. Cancellation may also be made prior to the transition of control provided that unit owners other than the developer own not less than 75% of the total voting interests in the condominium.[53]

When a contract is canceled prior to transition, a majority of the voting interests in the condominium other than the developer shall make a new contract or otherwise provide for maintenance services at the direction of the owners of not less than a majority of the voting interests in the condominium, excluding the voting interests of the developer. When the contract for maintenance services covers property used and maintained by the owners of units in other condominiums, the agreement may not be canceled until the unit owners of all associations have assumed control from the developer. Thereafter, the cancellation may be made with the concurrence of the owners of not less than 75% of the voting interests in all of the condominiums.[54]

12.11 Statutory Warranties. By statute, the developer is deemed to have granted to the purchaser of each unit an implied warranty of fitness and merchantability for the purposes or uses intended as to each unit and as to the personal property and improvements for use by the unit owners.[55] Unless otherwise provided in the statute, all warranties granted by the developer are not limited to the initial purchasers of the units.[56] If the condominium is created by the conversion of existing improvements, the developer makes no implied warranties if the required conversion reserve accounts are established. If the reserve accounts are not established, the developer is deemed to have made the implied warranties of fitness and merchantability to the purchasers of units.[57]

The statutory warranty period for each unit and for the other improvements for use by the unit owner is for a period of three (3) years

---

[53] § 718.302 (1), F.S.
[54] *Id.*
[55] *Leisure Resorts, Inc. v. Frank J. Rooney, Inc.,* 654 So.2d 911, 914 (Fla. 1995).
[56] § 718.203, F.S.
[57] § 718.618, F.S.

commencing with the completion of the building containing the unit. The warranty period for personal property transferred with, or appurtenant to, the unit is for a one (1) year period commencing with the date of closing with the purchasers or the date of possession of the unit, whichever is earlier.

As to the roof and structural components of a building, the mechanical, electrical and plumbing units serving the building and the other improvements of the condominium, the statutory warranty is for a period of three (3) years from the completion of the building or for a period of one (1) year after the unit owners obtain control of the association, whichever occurs last, but in no event for a period of more than five (5) years.[58] After the owners assume control of the association, all warranties are conditioned upon performance of appropriate routine maintenance by the association.[59]

The contractor and all subcontractors and suppliers grant to the developer and to the purchaser of each unit implied warranties of fitness as to work performed or the materials supplied by them.[60] The warranty period is for three (3) years from the date of completion of construction for the roof, structural components, and the mechanical and the plumbing elements serving the building or improvement. For all other improvements, the warranty period is for one (1) year.[61] As to personal property, the warranty period shall be for the length of time provided by the manufacturer and it shall begin at the time of closing on the unit or upon possession of the unit, whichever is earlier.

The developer of the condominium is required to maintain a list of the names and addresses of all contractors, subcontractors, and suppliers. The list shall be available to unit owners or their representatives at all reasonable times, and the list shall be delivered to the association at the time of transition.[62]

12.12 Common Law Warranties. The developer of a condominium owes the eventual occupants of the units therein certain duties which arise by operation of law. These duties include implied warranties above and beyond the statutory warranties set forth in Section 718.203, Florida Statutes. By operation of law, a developer impliedly warrants that the plans

---

[58] § 718.203 (1), F.S.; *Turnberry Court Corp. v. Bellini,* 962 So.2d 1006, 1009 (Fla. 3rd DCA 2007).

[59] § 718.203 (4), F.S.

[60] *Leisure Resorts, Inc. v. Frank J. Rooney, Inc., supra* note 55.

[61] § 718.203 (2), F.S.

[62] § 718.301 (4)(g), F.S.

and specifications on file with the municipal authority will be followed,[63] and that the units and buildings will be built in accordance with industry standards.[64]

Implied warranties of fitness and merchantability extend from developers to first purchasers of condominium units.[65] The right to bring an action for an implied warranty claim belongs to the unit owners,[66] and the right may be exercised by the unit owners in the aggregate through their condominium association in matters of common interest.[67]

This implied warranty of fitness and merchantability requires that the premises meet ordinary, normal standards reasonably expected of living quarters of comparable kind and quality. The criteria to determine whether an implied warranty has been breached is an objective one, and the party asserting the breach of an implied warranty has the burden of establishing that a reasonable person would find the premises unfit for their ordinary or general purpose; a "personal satisfaction" test is not sufficient.[68]

As to the common elements, if the implied warranties of fitness and merchantability are breached by the developer, the condominium association may recover damages equal to the sum necessary to correct the defective condition even though unit owners who did not purchase from the developer will benefit from the recovery.[69]

12.13 Construction Defects–Presuit Procedure. Construction defect claims against a developer, contractor or design professional for damages to a unit or the condominium must be submitted to expert evaluation and to presuit procedures before a claim can be filed in court. When the claim alleges a defect in design, construction, structural elements, or other components of the condominium property, the defect must be examined and certified by a licensed professional before the association presents the claim to the

---

[63] *David v. B & J Holding Corp.,* 349 So.2d 676 (Fla. 3rd DCA 1977).

[64] *Vantage View, Inc. v. Bali East Development Corp.,* 421 So.2d 728 (Fla. 4th DCA 1982).

[65] *Gable v. Silver,* 264 So.2d 418 (Fla. 1972); *Chotka v. Fidelco Growth Investors,* 383 So.2d 1169 (Fla. 2nd DCA 1980).

[66] *Rogers & Ford Construction Corporation v. Carlandia Construction,* 626 So.2d 1350, 1355 (Fla. 1993).

[67] *Charley Toppino & Sons, Inc. v. Seawatch at Marathon Condominium Ass'n, Inc.,* 658 So.2d 922, 924 (Fla. 1994).

[68] *Putnam v. Roudebush,* 352 So.2d 908 (Fla. 2nd DCA 1977).

[69] *Drexel Properties, Inc. v. Bay Colony Club Condominium, Inc.,* 406 So.2d 515 (Fla. 4th DCA 1981).

developer.[70] Following the examination and certification, the law provides specific procedures for the presentation of the defect claim to allow for an opportunity for the parties to resolve the dispute to the satisfaction of the condominium association or the affected unit owners by either correcting the defect or by the payment of a cash settlement.[71]

Notice of a construction defect claim must be served on the developer, contractor or design professional at least sixty (60) days before a court action is filed. The notice must describe the claim in sufficient detail to determine the nature of defect or the loss resulting from the defect.[72] Once the notice has been sent, the developer, contractor or design professional must be given an opportunity to inspect the defect and has thirty (30) days to provide a written response to the claim. The response is required to be in writing, and it may (1) offer to fix the defect at no cost to the owners; (2) offer to settle the claim by a monetary payment that will be paid within thirty (30) days after acceptance of the offer; or (3) dispute the claim and refuse to correct the alleged defect.[73]

If the developer, contractor or design professional will not settle the claim or correct the defect, or if the developer, contractor or design professional fails to respond within the required time, the unit owner or the association making the claim may proceed with an action in court.[74] The unit owner or the association making the claim may also reject the offer in writing and proceed in court without further notice.[75]

---

[70] § 718.301 (7), F.S.

[71] § 558.001, F.S.

[72] § 558.004 (1), F.S. Mailing written notice tolls the applicable statute of limitations. *Saltponds Condominium Ass'n, Inc. v. McCoy*, 972 So.2d 230, 233 (Fla. 3rd DCA 2007).

[73] § 558.004 (2)-(5), F.S. The time periods for claims in condominium buildings containing more than twenty (20) units are longer.

[74] § 558.001 through § 558.005, F.S.

[75] § 558.004 (7), F.S.

WATERFRONT XX CONDOMINIUM ASSOCIATION, INC.

A Corporation Not-for-Profit

NOTICE OF TRANSITION MEMBERS' MEETING FOR WATERFRONT XX CONDOMINIUM ASSOCIATION, INC.

NOTICE IS HEREBY GIVEN, in accordance with Section 718.301, F.S., and the Bylaws of the Association, that the transition members' meeting of WATERFRONT XX CONDOMINIUM ASSOCIATION, INC., will be held at the following date, time and place:

Date: September 30, 2011

Time: 7:00 p.m.

Place: Clubhouse, Waterfront XX Condominium

100 Waterfront Drive

Waterfront, Florida 33444

The purpose of the meeting will be to elect members of the Board of Administration and to accept control of the Association.

The Agenda for the meeting will be as follows:

1. Calling of roll and certifying of proxies.
2. Proof of notice of meeting.
3. Election of inspectors of election.
4. Election of board members.
5. New Business.
6. Adjournment.

WATERFRONT XX CONDOMINIUM
ASSOCIATION, INC.

By: _____

Secretary

Dated: 1st day of August, 2011

Notice of Transition Members' Meeting FORM 12.01

WATERFRONT XX CONDOMINIUM ASSOCIATION, INC.
100 Waterfront Drive
Waterfront, Florida 33444

September 30, 2011

Board of Directors
Waterfront XX Condominium Association, Inc.
100 Waterfront Drive
Waterfront, FL 33444

Re: Control of Association Records and Property

Dear Board of Directors:

In accordance with the requirements of Florida's Condominium Act, accompanying this correspondence please find the following items to be delivered from the developer-controlled Board of Administration to the unit owner-controlled Board of Administration at the time of transition:

1.   The original or a photocopy of the recorded Declaration of Condominium and all its amendments. If a copy is provided, it must be certified by an affidavit from the developer or an officer or agent of the developer stating that it is a complete copy of the actual recorded declaration.

2.   A certified copy of Association's Articles of Incorporation.

3.   Copy of Bylaws.

4.   The minute books, including all minutes, and other books and records of the association, if any.

5.   Any house rules and regulations which have been adopted.

6.   Resignation of officers and members of the board of administration who are required to resign because the developer is required to relinquish control of the association.

7.   The financial records, including financial statements of the Association, and source documents from the incorporation of the

Association through the date of turnover. The records must be audited from the incorporation of the Association or if the records have been audited each fiscal year since incorporation, the audit must be from the date of the last audit.

8. Actual Association funds or control over the funds.

9. All personal property that is the property of the Association, which is part of the common elements or which is alleged to be a part of the common elements, and an inventory of that property.

10. A copy of the plans and specifications used in conjunction and/or remodeling pursuant to Section 718.301 (4)(f), F.S.

11. A list of all the names and addresses of all contractors, subcontractors, and suppliers used in construction or remodeling, and in the landscaping of the condominium or Association property.

12. Insurance policies.

13. Copy of all certificates of occupancy issued for the condominium property.

14. Any other permits issued by governmental bodies that are in force or were issued within 1 year prior to turnover.

15. All written warranties in effect.

16. A roster of the unit owners, their addresses and telephone numbers, if known.

17. Leases.

18. Employment contracts or service contracts.

19. All other contracts to which the Association is a party.

20. Building Inspection Report

Please acknowledge receipt by having a member of the Board of Administration sign below. The signing of this receipt shall not constitute a waiver of individual unit owner or Association rights with respect to completeness and accuracy of the documents being transferred or preclude administrative remedies available to the Division of Florida Condominiums, Timeshares, and Mobile Homes.

Receipt of Documents FORM 12.02

WATERFRONT XX DEVELOPMENT CORPORATION

By: _____

Receipt of the foregoing materials is hereby acknowledged this 30th day of September, 2011.

WATERFRONT XX CONDOMINIUM ASSOCIATION, INC.

By: _____

WATERFRONT XX CONDOMINIUM ASSOCIATION, INC.
100 Waterfront Drive
Waterfront, Florida 33444

October 5, 2011

Division of Florida Condominiums, Timeshares, and Mobile Homes

725 South Bronough Street,

Tallahassee, FL 32301

Re: Waterfront XX Condominium Association, Inc.

(Notice of Unit Owner Elections)

The undersigned developer does hereby provide notice to the Division that the following individuals were elected as unit owner board members on September 30, 2011.

Matthew Marshall
102 Waterfront Drive
Waterfront, FL 33444

David Smith
104 Waterfront Drive
Waterfront, FL 33444

Marc Wesley
105 Waterfront Drive
Waterfront, FL 33444

Sara Harris
103 Waterfront Drive
Waterfront, FL 33444

Joseph A. Jones
101 Waterfront Drive
Waterfront, FL 33444

Transfer of control of the Association Board of Administration has occurred as a result of the election of these unit owner board members.

Respectfully,

WATERFRONT XX CONDOMINIUM
ASSOCIATION, INC.

By: _____
President

Notice of Election of Owner-Board Members FORM 12.03

FREQUENTLY ASKED QUESTIONS AND ANSWERS

_____   As of _____

Name of Condominium Association

Q: What are my voting rights in the condominium association?
A:

Q: What restrictions exist in the condominium documents on my right to use my unit?
A:

Q: What restrictions exist in the condominium documents on the leasing of my unit:
A:

Q: How much are my assessments to the condominium association for my unit type and when are they due?
A:

Q: Do I have to be a member in any other association? If so, what is the name of the association and what are my voting rights in this association? Also, how much are my assessments?
A:

Q: Am I required to pay rent or land use fees for recreational or other commonly used facilities? If so, how much am I obligated to pay annually?
A:

Q: Is the condominium association or other mandatory membership association involved in any court cases in which it may face liability in excess of $100,000? If so, identify each such case.
A:

NOTE: THE STATEMENTS CONTAINED HEREIN ARE ONLY SUMMARY IN NATURE. A PROSPECTIVE PURCHASER SHOULD REFER TO ALL REFERENCES, EXHIBITS HERETO, THE SALES CONTRACT, AND THE CONDOMINIUM DOCUMENTS

13

Enforcing the Documents and Resolving Disputes

ENFORCEMENT FORMS

13.1 General. The declaration of condominium and other documents governing the community set the standards for the residential character of the condominium and control the composition and conduct of its residents.[1] Effective enforcement of the declaration and other documents preserves the common scheme and the long-term community goals and standards. Enforcement procedures may also take away rights and limit individual freedoms. A delicate balance exists between enforcement procedures that protect the overall integrity of the common scheme and those that unreasonably restrict the individual freedoms of unit owners.[2]

The principles of condominium ownership require that rights of individuals yield, in some degree, to the ownership goals of the majority. Compromise for the common scheme is an essential ingredient in the condominium concept of property ownership.[3] Enforcing the documents preserves that concept, protects the architectural integrity of the property, and controls the manner in which individuals may use the condominium property.

Enforceability of the documents is dependent, in large measure, on the level of approval given by the residents and the reasonableness, uniformity and consistency exercised by the board of administration. In the overall management and operation of the condominium, enforcing the documents is perhaps the most difficult part of condominium living for both the enforcing authority and those against whom enforcement is sought.

13.2 Association's Obligation to Enforce. Leadership in maintaining the community scheme comes from the condominium association.[4] The condominium documents and the Condominium Act give the association the right and impose the obligation to maintain and preserve the condominium property and the condominium concept.[5] To do this properly, timeliness and uniformity in the association's actions are important to the enforcement procedures.

---

[1] "A declaration of condominium is more than a mere contract spelling out mutual rights and obligations of the parties thereto—it assumes some of the attributes of a covenant running with the land, circumscribing the extent of and limits of the enjoyment and use of real property." *Pepe v. Whispering Sands Condominium Ass'n, Inc.,* 351 So.2d 755, 757 (Fla. 2nd DCA 1977).

[2] *Hidden Harbour Estates, Inc. v. Basso,* 393 So.2d 637, 640 (Fla. 4th DCA 1981).

[3] *Hidden Harbour Estates, Inc. v. Norman,* 309 So.2d 180 (Fla. 4th DCA 1975).

[4] The association is granted broad authority by statute and the declaration to regulate the use of the common elements and limited common elements. *Juno By The Sea North Condominium Ass'n, Inc. v. Manfredonia,* 397 So.2d 297, 302 (Fla. 4th DCA 1981).

[5] § 718.111 (3) and §718.303 (1), F.S.

The declaration of condominium and the covenants that it embraces promote the health and happiness for a majority of the community. These documents designate the board of administration as the entity responsible for carrying out the association's enforcement authority. In carrying out this authority, the board is responsible for preserving the continuity and character of the community that is established when the declaration of condominium is initially recorded.[6] The obligation of the board to preserve the common scheme includes enforcement of the use restrictions, preservation of the architectural integrity, and maintenance of the safety and soundness of the common property.

The failure to enforce restrictions in a timely manner results in the forfeiture of the enforcement right through principles of equitable estoppel. The failure to enforce restrictions in a uniform manner will destroy their enforceability through conduct considered capricious and discriminatory.[7] The failures in enforcement resulting from inaction or improper action by the board of administration can be considered malfeasance or nonfeasance. It may also be considered a breach of the board's fiduciary responsibility to the unit owners of the community.

13.3   Unit Owner's Right to Enforce. Each unit owner benefits from the declaration of condominium and each owner may enforce its terms. This includes the right to bring an enforcement action against a neighboring unit owner when the neighboring owner does not comply with the declaration of condominium or its exhibits.[8] It also includes the right to bring an action against the association for its failure to maintain the property,[9] for its failure to provide access to and to properly maintain the records, or for its violation of the covenants and conditions in the documents. These rights permit each owner to protect his or her property values and to preserve the use and enjoyment of their unit as promised by the declaration of condominium.

An owner may seek to resolve a disagreement through the use of available mediation or nonbinding arbitration procedures, or may maintain an action for damages or for injunctive relief against another owner or the association in appropriate circumstances.[10] An individual owner may also

---

[6] *Sterling Village Condominium, Inc. v. Breitenbach,* 251 So.2d 685 (Fla. 4th DCA 1971).
[7] *White Egret Condominium, Inc. v. Franklin,* 379 So.2d 346 (Fla. 1979).
[8] *Candib v. Carver,* 344 So.2d 1312 (Fla. 3rd DCA 1977).
[9] *Baum v. Coronado Condominium Ass'n, Inc.,* 376 So.2d 914 (Fla. 3rd DCA 1979).
[10] § 718.1255 and § 718.303 (1), F.S.

seek the assistance of the Division of Florida Condominiums, Timeshares, and Mobile Homes. The owner may do so by filing a formal complaint or request for the Division to intervene and exercise its enforcement authority where it has jurisdiction.[11]

The declaration of condominium and the other documents governing the community are basically an elaborate set of contract terms. Each owner is protected by the contract and may insist on the enforcement of the terms of the condominium documents that protect the individual owner's rights.[12]

13.4 Knowledge and Clarity of the Documents. Understanding the documents and restrictions is an essential ingredient to successful enforcement. Restrictions found in the originally recorded declaration of condominium and attached exhibits are clothed with a strong presumption of validity because each owner purchases with the knowledge of their existence.[13] Each owner receives the offering circular or prospectus and a copy of the annual financial report prior to purchase and is presumed to have knowledge of their content.[14]

The board of administration extends this presumed knowledge of the documents' content to each successive purchaser by maintaining copies of all of the documents and the annual financial report available for review by prospective purchasers.[15] Each purchaser must acknowledge receipt of the condominium documents and the annual financial report prior to the time of purchase, and this acknowledgement must appear in the contract for sale. (See 11.12). Knowledge of each new amendment or rule can be assured of all existing unit owners if the board of administration will provide notice of their adoption prior to any attempted enforcement. (See 9.4 and 9.9).

Unit owners are entitled to clarity in the provisions of the documents that guide them in their actions on the condominium property. The covenants and restrictions must be certain and definite to ensure consistency within the condominium scheme. Lack of clarity or ambiguity in the covenants jeopardizes successful enforcement and permits the common scheme to

---

[11] § 718.501 (1), F.S.
[12] § 718.111 (3) and § 718.303 (1), F.S.
[13] *Hidden Harbour Estates, Inc. v. Norman, supra* note 3.
[14] § 718.504, F.S.
[15] § 718.111 (12)(c), F.S.

deteriorate.[16] The board of administration should be prepared to supplement unclear provisions of the declaration of condominium with supplemental rules or by recommending that clarifying amendments be adopted by the membership. (See 9.1).

13.5 Notice of Violation and Uniform, Timely Enforcement.

When a violation of the documents occurs, the desired result is voluntary correction of the situation by the violator. To accomplish this goal, the first step is notice of the violation. Notice is given by the board of administration. It should consist of a standard format, which includes a clear statement of the act or alleged violation and specific reference to the rule or paragraph prohibiting the conduct. The notice of violation should also state a specific deadline for compliance, allowing the non-conforming unit owner an opportunity to correct the deficiency.

Uniform treatment of community residents is essential to successful enforcement. The enforcement procedures of the condominium must be uniform and consistent or they can be attacked as discriminatory and capricious and enforcement will be unsuccessful.[17] It is not permissible to create different classes for selective treatment, whether it is between renters and owners or between different classes of owners.[18]

Knowledge of a violation and inaction by the board of administration may permanently prejudice the community's ability to enforce a rule or covenant under the legal principle of equitable estoppel. Equitable estoppel is a basic concept of fairness that results in a forfeiture of the enforcement rights when they are not used in a timely fashion.[19] Once knowledge of a violation is obtained, enforcement procedures must be implemented without unreasonable delay.

There is no specific definition for "timely enforcement," and the facts of each case will determine whether the response by the enforcing authority was timely and reasonable under the circumstances. For example, following transition, when the association has consistently precluded further violations of the documents following lax enforcement by the developer,

---

[16] *White Egret Condominium, Inc. v. Franklin, supra* note 7.
[17] *Id.* See also *Sockolof v. Eden Rock Point North Condominium Ass'n, Inc.,* 487 So.2d 1114, 1115 (Fla. 3rd DCA 1986).
[18] *Pearlman v. Lake Dora Villas Management, Inc.,* 479 So.2d 780 (Fla. 5th DCA 1985).
[19] *Quality Shell Homes and Supply Co. v. Riley,* 186 So.2d 837, 840 (Fla. 1st DCA 1966).

it will not be prejudiced by the developer's prior conduct.[20] To avoid the issues of estoppel and untimely enforcement, procedures for prompt notice of violations and subsequent enforcement should be adopted and followed by the board of administration.[21]

13.6 Documenting the Violation. From the time that a potential violation surfaces, detailed information of the offending conduct must be maintained by the board of administration if formal enforcement is to be successful. When voluntary compliance is not achieved, the detailed information of the offending conduct becomes the foundation for an arbitration petition or a formal enforcement complaint. The documentation should include the date, time and the nature of each violation. It should also include the names of those who observed the violation as it occurred. The information should be in written form and available for future reference as evidence in support of the community's enforcement actions.

The documented violation becomes the essential ingredient for the association and its attorney when a formal case must be brought against the violator. When a record of the violations has not been properly maintained and it becomes necessary to implement formal enforcement proceedings, new monitoring of the specific conduct will be necessary and enforcement will be delayed. To be prompt and successful with formal enforcement, the community must document the violation with clear and concise evidence.

13.7 Authority for Fines, Penalties and Suspension. The Condominium Act gives associations limited fining authority as a tool in the enforcement process. No fine may exceed $100.00 per violation, although a fine may be levied on the basis of each day of a continuing violation provided that the aggregate does not exceed $1,000.00. Fines may be levied against an owner of the unit, an occupant of the unit, or a guest of the unit owner, but it cannot become a lien against the unit. No fine may be levied unless the violator has been afforded reasonable notice and the opportunity to be heard.[22]

If fines and financial penalties are used as a part of the association's enforcement policies, the specific conditions and amounts of the fines should

---

[20] *Ladner v. Plaza Del Prado Condominium Ass'n, Inc.,* 423 So.2d 927 (Fla. 3rd DCA 1982) and *Constellation Condominium Ass'n, Inc. v. Harrington,* 487 So.2d 378 (Fla 2nd DCA 1985).

[21] *Chattel Shipping and Investment, Inc. v. Brickell Place Condominium Ass'n, Inc.,* 481 So.2d 29 (Fla. 3rd DCA 1985).

[22] § 718.303 (4), F.S.

be clearly documented. Before a fine or suspension can be imposed against an owner, occupant or guest, the condominium association must provide at least fourteen (14) days' written notice of the impending sanction, and an opportunity for a hearing must be afforded to the alleged violator. The hearing must be held before a committee of unit owners, and if the committee does not approve the fine or suspension, it may not be imposed.[23]

The notice and hearing requirements do not apply to fines, to the suspension of use rights, or to the suspension voting rights of unit owners when the owner is more than ninety (90) days delinquent in any financial obligation due to the association. In such circumstances, the Act provides that the fine or suspension may be imposed at a properly noticed meeting of the board of administration, followed by the delivery of written notice to the unit owner or the unit's occupant by mail or hand delivery.[24] (See 8.12).

13.8 Formal Enforcement Actions. When efforts to achieve voluntary compliance are unsuccessful and the internal enforcement mechanisms do not succeed in stopping a violation, formal enforcement becomes the appropriate remedy. Formal enforcement may take one of three forms: (1) voluntary mediation with mediators provided by the Division or through Citizen Dispute Settlement Centers,[25] (2) mandatory nonbinding arbitration under procedures established by the Division of Florida Condominiums, Timeshares, and Mobile Homes,[26] or (3) by the filing of formal legal proceedings in Circuit Court.[27] Each owner and the association may pursue the use of one of these methods when a violation of the Act or the documents occurs in the condominium.

Citizen Dispute Settlement Centers are not readily available in all parts of Florida, but the program does exist in most of the state's more populous areas. The Centers are forums for the mediation and settlement of disputes, and they present an opportunity for unit owners and association officials to resolve disagreements quickly and without the more structured proceedings found in other forums.[28] The Clerk of the Circuit Court will

---

[23] The committee must consist of unit owners who are not a member of board or reside in the household of a board member. § 718.303 (3), F.S.

[24] § 718.106 (2)(d), F.S.

[25] § 44.201, F.S.

[26] § 718.1255, F.S.

[27] § 718.303 (1), F.S.

[28] § 44.201, F.S.

be able to advise parties to a disagreement concerning the availability of a Dispute Center and the procedures to follow in order to engage in the voluntary mediation process.

Use of mandatory nonbinding arbitration must be used in most disputes between a unit owner and the association[29] before the matter can be presented to a court.[30] Following arbitration, either party may take the dispute to Circuit Court, but if a suit is not filed in court within thirty (30) days of the decision by the arbitrator, the decision becomes final. The final decision of the arbitrator may be enforced in the Circuit Court.[31] The Circuit Court is also the forum for formal enforcement proceedings concerning disputes where arbitration is not applicable. (See 13.10).

13.9 Notice of Intended Arbitration.

Mandatory nonbinding arbitration before an arbitrator from the Division of Florida Condominiums, Timeshares, and Mobile Homes is a dispute resolution forum available to governing boards and unit owners in a residential condominium under a variety of circumstances.[32] The bylaws of every community must include a provision for arbitration. If they do not, the Condominium Act deems that such a provision shall be included for purposes of resolving internal disputes arising from the operation of the condominium.[33]

Before a petition for nonbinding arbitration is filed with the Division, however, it must be preceded by a notice to the opposing party in the intended arbitration. The notice of intended arbitration must include a demand for relief and a reasonable opportunity for the other party to comply with the request or to provide other appropriate relief. Finally, the notice must state that if the relief is not granted, then an arbitration petition or other legal action will be filed. The petition for arbitration must recite that the required notice has been given to the other party in the dispute, and a copy of the notice or supporting proof that it has been given must be attached to

---

[29] *National Ventures, Inc. v. Water Glades 300 Condominium Assín*, 847 So.2d 1070, 1073 (Fla. 4th DCA 2003).

[30] § 718.1255 (4)(a), F.S.

[31] § 718.1255 (4)(e), F.S.

[32] *United Grand Condominium Owners, Inc. v. The Grand Condominium Ass'n, Inc.*, 929 So.2d 24, (Fla. 3rd DCA 2006).

[33] § 718.112 (2)(l), F.S.

the petition when it is filed with the Division.[34]

13.10 Arbitration. The Division of Florida Condominiums, Timeshares, and Mobile Homes employs full-time arbitrators to conduct hearings, and their jurisdiction extends to disagreements concerning the authority of the board, under any law or the condominium documents, to require any owner to take an action or to refrain from any action involving an owner's unit. Jurisdiction further extends to disputes concerning the board's authority to alter or add to a common area or to the common elements. It also covers disputes where the board has failed (1) to provide proper notice for meetings or other actions where notice to members is required; (2) to properly conduct elections; (3) to properly conduct meetings of either the board or the membership; or (4) has failed to allow inspection of the association's books and records.[35] Arbitration petitions challenging the election of any director must be handled by the Division on an expedited basis.[36]

Arbitration jurisdiction does not extend to disputes concerning the title to a unit or the common elements; disputes involving the interpretation or enforcement of warranties; disagreements concerning the levy or collection of a fee or assessment by the board of administration; the eviction or removal of a tenant from a unit; the alleged breach of fiduciary duty; or claims based on the alleged failure of the association to maintain the common elements or the association property. Disputes between individual unit owners and not involving the association are also not eligible for arbitration.[37]

The Division has promulgated special rules which allow parties to the arbitration proceedings to subpoena witnesses and evidence and to make inquiries under oath or through sworn statements.[38] The arbitration hearings are held in the area of the residence of the individuals involved or at the most convenient location for all parties.[39] An attorney may be used in the arbitration proceedings by either side, but individuals or representatives of the association may represent themselves if the individual is properly qualified to do so in the opinion of the arbitrator.[40] The arbitrator also has

---

[34] § 718.1255 (4)(b), F.S.
[35] § 718.1255 (1)(a) and (b), F.S.
[36] § 718.1255 (5), F.S.
[37] § 718.1255 (4)(a), F.S. and § 61B-45.013, F.A.C.
[38] § 718.1255 (4)(b), F.S. and § 61B-45.001 through § 61B-45.048, F.A.C.
[39] § 61B-45.033, F.A.C.
[40] § 61B-45.004, F.A.C.

the authority to refer any pending dispute to mediation.[41]

The intended purpose of mandatory nonbinding arbitration is to provide for swift, equitable and inexpensive decisions when disputes arise within the condominium community.[42] Although it is a relatively new forum, arbitration must be considered when formal enforcement of the documents becomes necessary. In disputes where arbitration jurisdiction applies, the parties are required to petition for mandatory nonbinding arbitration prior to instituting proceedings in court.[43] The final decision of the arbitrator is not binding on the parties, however, if one of them wishes to pursue the matter further in the Circuit Court. Should a court proceeding ensue, the final decision of the arbitrator is admissible as evidence.[44]

13.11 Voluntary Mediation. In 1997, changes to the Condominium Act provided comprehensive new procedures for the mediation of disputes among unit owners and between a unit owner and the condominium association.[45] Either party to an arbitration proceeding may now request mediation after a petition has been filed with the Division. Once the request for mediation has been received by the arbitrator, the arbitrator is required to promptly contact all parties to determine if they agree that mediation would be appropriate. Even if all parties do not agree, however, the arbitrator may still refer the dispute to mediation.

When the matter is referred to mediation, the parties must select a mutually acceptable mediator. The arbitrator is required to provide the parties with a list of volunteer and paid mediators to assist with the selection process. Mediation is conducted in accordance with the Florida Rules of Civil Procedure, and the process is intended to provide the parties with an opportunity to resolve the underlying dispute with a minimum expenditure of time and resources. The parties in a mediation are required to share the expenses equally, unless they agree otherwise.[46]

13.12 Enforcement in Court. Arbitration proceedings are not a

---

[41] § 718.1255 (4)(e)—(h), F.S.
[42] § 718.1255 (3), F.S.
[43] § 718.1255 (4), F.S.
[44] § 718.1255 (4)(a), F.S.
[45] § 718.1255 (4)(e)—(h), F.S.
[46] § 718.1255 (4)(f), F.S.

prerequisite to entering the judicial process, and the Circuit Court is the appropriate forum when (1) a condominium dispute involves the levy and collection of fees or assessments; (2) when the matter involves the enforcement or interpretation of warranties; (3) when the status of legal title to a unit or the common elements is in question; (4) when the claim is the eviction or removal of a tenant from a unit; (5) when breach of fiduciary duty is alleged; or (6) when the claim is based upon the alleged failure of the association to maintain the common elements or the condominium property.[47]

In addition, where arbitration is required when a disagreement arises, any party dissatisfied with the decision of the arbitrator may proceed into Circuit Court for a new trial, or trial de novo, on the merits of the dispute. The evidence and testimony must be resubmitted in the judicial proceeding, and the court is not bound by the prior decision of the arbitrator. The filing for a trial de novo must be made within thirty (30) days from issuance of the arbitrator's written decision. If no filing is made within thirty (30) days, the decision is final. Once the decision becomes final, any party to the arbitration proceeding may file a petition in Circuit Court to enforce the terms of the arbitrator's decision.[48]

When engaged in formal enforcement action in Circuit Court, the association is compelled to use legal counsel when bringing the action and presenting its case or defenses. An individual owner may represent himself in court proceedings, but it is rarely, if ever, advisable to do so.

13.13 Fees and Costs. In mediation proceedings, the parties are required to share the expenses equally, unless they agree otherwise.[49] In arbitration proceedings, attorney's fees and costs may be awarded in the discretion of the arbitrator. When efforts to resolve a dispute by mediation or arbitration are unsuccessful and it becomes necessary to resort to a formal court action[50] or when arbitration proceedings are not available and formal court proceedings are necessary, the Condominium Act allows the prevailing or successful party to recover reasonable attorney's fees and the costs incurred

---

[47] § 718.1255 (1)(b), F.S.; § 718.116 (6), F.S.; and § 718.303 (1), F.S.
[48] § 718.1255 (4), F.S. and § 61B-45.045, F.A.C.
[49] § 718.1255 (4)(f), F.S.
[50] § 718.1255 (4)(c) and (d), F.S.

in the court proceedings.[51]

Caution must be exercised by a party seeking relief in the court following an arbitration decision, however. If the party filing in court does not obtain a more favorable result, they become responsible not only for the other party's attorneys fees and court costs, but also the other party's original arbitration costs, including investigation costs and expenses for expert testimony.[52]

Finally, any party to an arbitration proceeding may enforce the arbitration award by filing a petition in a court having jurisdiction over the parties and the dispute. If the petition for enforcement is granted, the petitioner is entitled to recover reasonable attorney's fees and costs incurred in the proceedings. In a similar manner, a mediation settlement may be enforced in court proceedings, and any costs and fees incurred in enforcing the settlement agreement must be awarded to the prevailing party in the action.[53]

13.14 Upkeep of the Condominium Property. Maintenance of the common elements is the responsibility of the condominium association.[54] The responsibility is mandated by the documents and a failure to comply with the mandate gives rise to rights of enforcement by both owners and the association. From the association's perspective, it has the right to enforce the maintenance standards against each owner who refuses to comply with them. It also extends to actions preventing conduct which impairs the soundness or quality of maintenance of the condominium property.[55]

When the board of administration fails to carry out its mandated duties to repair and maintain the condominium property, an individual owner has the right to maintain an action against it for its failure to do so.[56] The responsibility to maintain the common elements carries with it the affirmative obligation to take all reasonable actions necessary to repair damage in a timely way and to protect the condominium property from

---

[51] *Mainlands of Tamarac by the Gulf No. Four Ass'n, Inc. v. Morris,* 388 So.2d 226 (Fla. 2nd DCA 1980). See also *Sorrentino v. River Run Condominium Ass'n,* 925 So.2d 1060 (Fla. 5th DCA 2006).

[52] § 718.1255 (4)(d), F.S.

[53] § 718.1255 (4)(m), F.S.

[54] § 718.111 (4) and § 718.113 (1), F.S.

[55] *Chattel Shipping and Investment, Inc. v. Brickell Place Condominium Ass'n, Inc., supra* note 21.

[56] § 718.303 (1), F.S.

further damage. The board may be liable for damages resulting from its initial failure to make the repairs in a timely fashion.

The upkeep of the condominium property should not be overlooked when consideration is given to enforcing the documents and preserving the condominium concept. Failure of the board to carry out this important function exposes the members of the board to a possible breach of their fiduciary responsibility to the individual owners. An individual owner may be liable to the association and to other individual owners for damages done by the owner to the condominium property or for improper maintenance to the owner's unit.[57]

13.15 Negligence by the Association. Under some circumstances, the failure of the board to carry out its maintenance responsibilities results in expanded financial exposure for the association. If the inaction of the board can be shown as negligent, the association's responsibility is expanded to include the damage and expenses that are incurred by individual unit owners as a result of the board's negligence. This responsibility is in addition to the obligation to repair or replace the damage to the common elements.

Three elements are necessary prerequisites to establish negligence by the board and the association. First, there must be a duty to carry out a specific responsibility (maintenance of the common elements); next, there must be knowledge that the action is necessary (knowledge that certain repairs are needed); and, finally, the failure to carry out the act must result in damage (failure to repair the common elements results in water damage to the interior of a condominium unit).

If the board of administration carries out its obligation to repair the common elements as soon as it has knowledge that the repairs are necessary, the board is not negligent and responsibility may be limited to the common element repair. If the board fails to make the repairs when it knows the repairs are required, then the board is responsible for all additional damage to the property of individual owners resulting from the board's inaction.

The board's first duty is to protect the condominium property and it may not be excused for its inaction when repairs are necessary to prevent further damage. Inaction cannot be justified because another party is responsible for the initial damage. The board must meet its responsibility

---

[57] *Winston Towers 100 Ass'n, Inc. v. DeCarlo,* 481 So.2d 1261 (Fla. 3rd DCA 1986).

first if it wishes to avoid the consequences of negligence for failure to carry out its responsibility. It may then look to others who may have some responsibility.

The damage or disrepair may be a result of defective workmanship by the original developer, improper repairs by an outside maintenance contractor, or damage caused by another unit owner. In each of these circumstances, the board of administration first has a responsibility to make the necessary repairs to protect the condominium property and prevent further damage. Then the board may seek payment or warranty claims from the party responsible for causing the damage or disrepair.

13.16 Architectural Standards. Common elements of the condominium, exterior surfaces of condominium units, and structural components of the condominium property are either owned by or are for the benefit of all the unit owners in the community. They may not be modified or changed except in the manner as provided in the Condominium Act or declaration of condominium as originally recorded.[58] This restriction also extends to the limited common elements of the condominium, such as porches, balconies, windows, and doorways.

Many condominium documents permit modifications and alterations to the condominium property. The permitted changes generally must preserve the architectural integrity of the exterior of the property and they must be approved by the board of administration or by a certain percentage of the unit owners before they can be made.

When the condominium documents or the Act permit alterations or modifications with the approval of the board, approval cannot be arbitrarily withheld.[59] To ensure consistency in the permitted alterations, the board should maintain a set of policy standards to judge all unit owners' requests. This helps to ensure that rejections are not arbitrary and that the changes will be in keeping with the uniform standards and architectural continuity of the community.

Notwithstanding the provisions of the condominium documents, some types of exterior alterations may be made by unit owners. The Condominium Act allows any unit owner to install hurricane shutters or

---

[58] § 718.110 (4), F.S.
[59] *Hidden Harbour Estates, Inc. v. Basso, supra* note 2.

other hurricane protections, provided the installations comply with the specifications adopted by the board of administration. (See 9.14). The board is required to adopt standards that may include specifications as to color, style, and other factors, and the specifications must comply with applicable building codes. The installation and maintenance of hurricane protections by a unit owner is not considered a material modification or alteration, and only approval by the board is required even though the condominium documents might provide otherwise.[60]

Another authorized modification to the exterior surfaces of condominium units is for direct broadcast satellite service. The rules of the FCC prohibit the enforcement of covenants which impair the ability to receive video programming services over a satellite antenna which is less than one (1) meter in diameter, and unit owners may make modifications to exterior surfaces in order to access services permitted by this rule.[61] (See 11.4).

A unit owner is permitted to install solar collectors and other energy-saving devices within the boundaries of the owner's condominium unit, and state law prohibits the enforcement of covenants that would restrict the unit owner's right to do so.[62] (See 9.13). The Condominium Act also provides that the association may not refuse the request of a unit owner to attach a religious object to the mantle or door frame of the unit that does not exceed three (3) inches wide, six (6) inches high, and one and a half (1.5) inches deep.[63]

Permission to alter or modify the common elements given by the developer and the standards established by the developer for granting such permission are not binding on the owner-controlled board of administration. The owner-controlled board of administration may enforce stricter standards from the condominium documents so long as they are not arbitrary or selective in their implementation. Many times a developer ignores the standards altogether. In such cases the board must reestablish the standards of architectural integrity for the condominium after the owners assume control.[64]

---

[60] § 718.113 (5), F.S.
[61] § 21.104, Rules of the Federal Communications Commission.
[62] § 163.04, F.S.
[63] § 718.113 (7), F.S.
[64] *Ladner v. Plaza Del Prado Condominium Ass'n, Inc., supra* note 20.

Unauthorized modifications or alterations have resulted in the removal of jalousy window enclosures,[65] storm shutters,[66] balcony enclosures,[67] terrace railings, patios,[68] roof shingles,[69] and the mandated restoration of original color and appearance. The failure of the board of administration to respond to a request is not the same as receiving affirmative permission.[70] Timely and consistent enforcement may be successfully maintained by either the board or by another unit owner against the unauthorized or nonconforming architectural changes to the condominium property. Any owner desiring to make a change or alteration must follow the required procedures and must obtain proper permission. Failure to do so may be an expensive mistake if the change must be undone.

When an alteration or improvement occurs as part of a repair to the common elements or is necessary to protect the common elements from further damage, the alteration or improvement may be made without seeking normal approvals required for material modifications or alterations.[71] Under such circumstances each owner must contribute the unit's proportionate share of the capital costs of the alterations or repairs.

13.17 Sale and Transfer Approval. Restrictions on the sale and transfer of condominium units are recognized and permitted by the Condominium Act and are commonplace in many declarations of condominium.[72] These restrictions are recognized as enforceable by Florida courts as long as they are for a lawful purpose and the restrictions are reasonable and clearly expressed in the declaration of condominium.[73] Unreasonable or arbitrary application of such restrictions violates individual civil rights and is an unlawful interference with individual property rights.[74]

---

[65] *Sterling Village Condominium, Inc. v. Breitenbach, supra* note 6.

[66] *Schmeck v. Sea Oats Condominium Ass'n, Inc.,* 441 So.2d 1092 (Fla. 5th DCA 1983).

[67] *Schmidt v. Sherrill,* 442 So.2d 983 (Fla. 4th DCA 1983).

[68] *Fountains of Palm Beach Condominium, Inc. No. 5 v. Farkas,* 355 So.2d 163 (Fla. 4th DCA 1978).

[69] *George v. Beach Club Villas Condominium Ass'n,* 833 So.2d 816 (Fla. 3rd DCA 2002).

[70] *Id.*

[71] *Ralph v. Envoy Point Condominium Ass'n, Inc.,* 455 So.2d 454, 455 (Fla. 2nd DCA 1984); *Cottrell v. Thornton,* 449 So.2d 1291 (Fla. 2nd DCA 1984); and *Tiffany Plaza Condominium Ass'n, Inc. v. Spencer,* 416 So.2d 823 (Fla. 2nd DCA 1982).

[72] § 718.104 (5), F.S.

[73] *Aquarian Foundation, Inc. v. Sholom House, Inc.,* 448 So.2d 1166, 1168 (Fla. 3rd DCA 1984).

[74] *Id.* See also *Camino Gardens Ass'n, Inc. v. McKim,* 612 So.2d 637 (Fla. 4th DCA 1993).

Sale and transfer restrictions are not necessarily designed to result in the disapproval of sales and such results are rare. The review process gives the new resident an opportunity to be advised of the nature of condominium living. Each prospective purchaser is entitled to a current copy of the condominium documents, as well as copies of the Frequently Asked Questions and Answers Sheet, governance form, and the annual financial report at the seller's expense. It is an opportunity for the new owner to understand the restrictions and responsibilities that the owner will assume when the purchase is complete.[75]

The review process informs the board of all new residents coming into the community. It gives the board the opportunity to advise new owners of financial responsibilities and the use restrictions which they face as residents of the condominium. The review process should be used by the board to ensure that each new resident has been provided a full set of the condominium documents and that the roster of unit owners for the association is kept current and up-to-date.

In rare instances when a disapproval of a sale or transfer is being considered, it should be approached with caution by the reviewing board. It would be improper to disapprove a transfer simply because the board anticipated that a future restriction might be violated by the new owner. Such an example would include rejection of a purchaser with a minor child when the community did not permit the child to be a permanent resident. The existence of the minor child is not a basis for disapproval. The violation would not occur by transfer of the unit, but only if the transfer occurred and if the child moved into the unit and became a permanent resident. Each act is separate and one is not necessarily dependent on the other.

It is equally improper to deny a sale or transfer of a condominium unit based on race, religion, national origin or other discriminatory criteria. To do so is a substantial infringement on basic constitutional rights and is not permitted. Disapprovals are rare and difficult to defend in almost all circumstances. Where the board agrees to purchase the unit at fair market

---

[75] § 718.503 (2), F.S.

value after it has disapproved a sale, the likelihood that the denial will be upheld is significantly increased.[76]

When enforcing sale and transfer restrictions, the board should be sensitive to the exceptions. Existing owners purchasing another unit are generally exempt and lenders obtaining title through foreclosure or a deed in lieu of foreclosure are also exempt. (A lender's resale to a new owner may be governed by the approval process.)

The association may charge a fee in conjunction with its screening process, but may do so only if the condominium documents require the approval of the sale or transfer and specifically authorize the fee. The fee may not exceed $100.00, and no fee is permitted when the application is for renewal of an existing lease.[77]

13.18 Lease and Rental Restrictions. The lease or rental of a unit is a type of transfer and may be subject to the same approval process as a sale.[78] Many documents contain separate restrictions for leases and rentals, however, that are even more stringent than those imposed on an outright sale.[79] The courts in Florida have upheld the enforcement of rental restrictions which permit an owner to rent only once during the owner's entire term of ownership. They have also upheld provisions which prohibit rentals for business or speculative purposes, and have permitted various restrictions setting minimum rental periods.[80]

Lease and rental restrictions that are clearly stated in the condominium documents and uniformly enforced promote the continuity of the residential character of the condominium community. It is this valid objective that allows restrictions on rentals and permits their enforcement.[81] When the rule or restriction is unclear or when it is improperly applied, the objective may be lost. If an otherwise valid lease is incorrectly rejected, the association may be liable for damages resulting from improper interference with the contract rights between the unit owner and the prospective tenant.

---

[76] *Chianese v. Culley,* 397 Fed. Supp. 1344 (USDC Fla. SD 1975); see also *Old Port Cove Condominium Ass'n One, Inc. v. Old Port Cove Holdings, Inc.,* 954 So.2d 742 (954 So.2d 742) and *Edlund v. Seagull Townhomes Condominium Ass'n, Inc.,* 928 So.2d 405, 407 (Fla. 3rd DCA 2006).

[77] § 718.112 (2)(i), F.S.

[78] *Id.*

[79] § 718.104 (5), F.S.

[80] *Seagate Condominium Ass'n, Inc. v. Duffy,* 330 So.2d 484 (Fla. 4th DCA 1976).

[81] *Id.*

If an owner is delinquent in the payment of an assessment at the time approval for a lease is sought, the delinquency is considered adequate reason to reject the application.[82] The actual character of other rental restrictions may be tailored to the community, and restrictions in the declaration of condominium reserving the exclusive rental rights to a developer in a travel trailer resort condominium have been upheld by the Florida courts.[83]

Rental restrictions, from the lax to the very stringent, are enforceable as long as the implementation is properly carried out by the board of directors. The key to maintaining successful rental restrictions is uniformity and fairness. Rental restrictions in the condominium may also be modified, but modified restrictions to the duration of the rental period apply only to the unit owners who approve the amendments and to owners who acquire their units after the effective date of the amendment.[84] (See 9.12).

Once a lease or rental has been permitted, restrictions creating different standards for owner-residents and rental-residents would be discriminatory. Restrictions attempting to make such distinctions are improper and are unenforceable. When a unit is leased, the tenant receives all of the use rights in the association property and common elements otherwise available to unit owners unless the rights of use are waived in writing by the tenant. The owner of the unit retains access rights to the unit as the landlord, but shall not have rights to use the common elements or association property except as a guest.[85]

If the documents permit, a fee not to exceed $100 may be charged in conjunction with the lease approval application.[86] The association is also permitted to adopt rules prohibiting the dual usage of the condominium property by the owner and the owner's tenant when the unit is leased.[87]

13.19 Guest and Occupancy Restrictions. A wide variety of occupancy restrictions is permitted as part of the inherent condominium concept. The restrictions are designed to promote the health, happiness and

---

[82] § 718.116 (4), F.S.

[83] *Holiday Out in American at St. Lucie, Inc. v. Bowes,* 285 So.2d 63 (Fla. 4th DCA 1973); *Outdoor Resorts of America, Inc. v. Outdoor Resorts at Nettles Island, Inc.,* 379 So.2d 471 (Fla. 4th DCA 1980).

[84] § 718.110 (13), F.S

[85] § 718.106 (4), F.S.

[86] § 718.112 (2)(i), F.S.

[87] § 718.106 (4), F.S.

peace of mind of a majority of owners living in close proximity with one another and sharing common properties and facilities. Occupancy restrictions prohibiting the use of alcoholic beverages on the common elements,[88] restricting use of units to their intended purpose,[89] and activities generating excessive noise are typical of those that have been recognized and upheld by the Florida courts.[90] The success of these occupancy restrictions and others is conditioned on their clarity and uniformity and establishing that the restriction serves a legitimate and lawful purpose for the community.

One of the most troublesome sets of occupancy restrictions involves the use of the condominium property by the "guest" of a unit owner.[91] Restrictions lacking a clear definition of the term "guest" and clear standards to govern the guest when visiting the condominium property offer opportunities for abuse. Some owners attempt to avoid the screening process for leasing and rentals by claiming that the occupant of the unit is a guest. Other owners will permit an excessive number of people to occupy a unit by claiming that they are guests and not permanent residents.[92] Such problems are a direct result of unclear occupancy restrictions and make enforcement extremely difficult.

"Single family" is also an occupancy restriction that is subject to multiple interpretations and difficult to enforce because of its inherent ambiguity. The definition of "single family" should be refined to state the maximum number of persons permitted to occupy the unit or clarified to describe the nature of the family unit allowed in the condominium. The wide variation in family relationships makes regulations based upon actual numbers of authorized residents easier to make and enforce than restrictions attempting to define the type of family members permitted to share the unit.[93]

The Condominium Act and the courts of Florida have allowed condominium communities great latitude to enforce guest and occupancy

---

[88] *Hidden Harbour Estates, Inc. v. Norman, supra* note 3.

[89] *Palm Beach Hotel Condominium Ass'n v. Rogers,* 605 So.2d 143 (Fla. 4th DCA 1992).

[90] *Candib v. Carver, supra* note 8.

[91] Occupancy of a unit by guests is not a transfer of the unit. See *Pacitti v. Seapointe Condominium Ass'n,* 584 So.2d 212 (Fla. 3rd DCA 1991

[92] *Beachwood Villas Condominium v. Poor,* 448 So.2d 1143 (Fla. 4th DCA 1984).

[93] "The word 'family' has been used to describe a number of different sets of relationships and there is no consensus as to exactly what a family is." *Franklin v. White Egret Condominium, Inc.,* 358 So.2d 1084 (Fla. 4th DCA 1978); see also *White Egret Condominium, Inc. v. Franklin, supra* note 7.

restrictions. For the enforcement to be successful, however, the board must ensure, either through rule promulgation or document amendment, that the occupancy restrictions are clear and concise.

The definitions of "guest" and "single family" should be accurately described, and the number of persons allowed to occupy a unit overnight should be stated in specific number. Guests may be restricted to visiting in a unit only when the owner is present, and prohibited from an overnight stay when the owner is not at home. Effective and enforceable guest and occupancy restrictions have a collateral benefit as a security tool for the community. They allow the board to know who has authority to be in the community and to identify those who are unauthorized intruders.

13.20 Age Limitations. Preserving the common scheme and continuity for a senior-adult community necessitates the enforcement of age restrictions that prohibit children from becoming permanent residents in the condominium. Age restrictions are not constitutionally prohibited unless they are unreasonably or arbitrarily applied.[94] Such restrictions are, however, governed by the Federal Fair Housing Act. The Fair Housing Amendments Act of 1988 prohibits discrimination based upon age unless occupancy is intended for and restricted to persons sixty-two (62) years of age or older, or unless occupancy is restricted to fifty-five (55) years of age or older and at least 80% of the units are occupied by at least one person fifty-five (55) years of age or over.[95]

A community claiming senior-adult status is required to register with the Florida Commission on Human Relations, stating that the community complies with the appropriate requirements to qualify for the status. The filing must be submitted in writing on the letterhead of the community and signed by the association president. The registration must be renewed biennially from the date of the original filing. The Commission is authorized to charge a registration fee, not to exceed $20.00 for the filing, and the filings are public records and available on the Commission's internet website. An administrative fine, not to exceed $500.00, may be imposed against a community that knowingly submits false information in its filing.[96]

As with the enforcement of all restrictions, uniformity and

---

[94] *Id.*; § 760.29, F.S.
[95] § 42 U.S.C. 3607(2).
[96] 760.29 (4)(e), F.S.

consistency are important. Because age restrictions clearly have the potential of excluding persons from the community, adequate notice and timely enforcement must be consistently provided. Careful compliance with the Federal Fair Housing Act is also essential if an adult community is to be successfully preserved; however, the condominium may forego the requirement to retrofit the common elements with handrails and guardrails by an affirmative vote of two-thirds of all the affected voting interests.[97]

13.21 Parking and Unauthorized Vehicles. Regulation of motor vehicles and motor vehicle traffic is often part of the scheme of restrictions for the condominium. It takes numerous forms. The regulations may assign one or more parking places for use by each unit owner and may set aside areas for visitor parking. Some restrictions control the flow and speed of traffic and restrict the type of vehicles and trailers that are permitted on the condominium property. Restrictions on parking, traffic control and unauthorized vehicles are enforceable like other restrictions in the documents as long as the correct standards and criteria are followed.

The most troublesome problems encountered when enforcing parking and vehicle restrictions result from an inherent ambiguity in the content of certain restrictions. The terms "commercial vehicle," "recreational vehicle," and "truck" are often used and rarely defined in such restrictions. Each term has a wide variety of meanings and, without further clarification, it is virtually impossible to successfully enforce restrictions using these terms alone. A narrower and more specific definition must be developed for inclusion in the documents or the rules. The specificity may be by size, weight or registration category with the Department of Highway Safety and Motor Vehicles. Restrictions may also limit the number of motor vehicles per unit or designate a particular area for vehicles over a certain size. "Commercial vehicles" can be further defined to mean those with visible, exterior identification or lettering above a certain size.

In some areas of parking and motor vehicle control, restrictions are frustrated by arbitrary or selective enforcement policies. When assigning or enforcing the assignment of individual parking spaces, procedures must be fair and uniform.[98] Parking spaces that have been set aside for visitors and

---

[97] § 718.1085, F.S.
[98] *Juno by the Sea North Condominium Ass'n, Inc. v. Manfredonia, supra* note 4.

guests should not be selectively appropriated by an individual unit owner who finds the proximity more convenient than the owner's assigned space. One owner may not be permitted to have an unauthorized vehicle while others cannot. As with other restrictions, vehicle restrictions must be applied equally to all owners.

Finally, the board must be sensitive to its authority over traffic control. The association has it within its ability to control traffic flow, vehicle speed, and the location for proper parking on the property. When making or enforcing rules that affect the safety of the residents of the condominium, the welfare and well-being of the residents are of paramount consideration.

13.22 Towing of Unauthorized Vehicles. The Florida Statutes impose specific requirements on a condominium association or its designated representative prior to the towing of an improperly parked motor vehicle if the association is to avoid liability for its acts.[99] The owner of the improperly parked vehicle must personally be notified that parking is not authorized, or the area must be prominently posted at each driveway access within five feet of the public right of way line giving notice to motorists that the area is a "tow-away zone."

The notice on the signs must have light-reflective letters on contrasting background at least two inches in height, and the words "tow-away zone" must be included on the signs in no less than four (4) inch letters. The sign structures must extend at least four (4) feet above ground level. If the association has a contract with a towing company, the name and telephone number of the company must also appear on the sign.[100]

When an unauthorized vehicle is actually removed from the condominium property, it must be stored at a site within ten (10) miles of the property in a county having a population of more than 500,000 people and within fifteen (15) miles in a county having a population of less than 500,000 people. The person towing the motor vehicle must notify the appropriate law enforcement officials within thirty (30) minutes of the towing and provide to them a description of the vehicle, the model, and license plate number.

If the owner of the vehicle arrives at the scene prior to towing of the motor vehicle, the vehicle must be disconnected and the owner shall be liable for the payment of a reasonable service fee. If the association causes

[99] §715.07 (2), F.S.
[100] §715.07 (2)(a), F.S.

a vehicle to be removed improperly, it is liable for the cost of removal, transportation, and storage as well as damages resulting from the removal of the vehicle including any attorney's fees and court costs.[101]

13.23 Pet Restrictions. A frequent compromise in the condominium scheme is the restriction on the size and number of pets or their outright prohibition on the condominium property. Covenants which restrict or prohibit pets are enforceable.[102] Such restrictions should reflect the desires of the community's residents although the desires of the majority will dominate the rights of individuals to maintain a pet. Pet restrictions cannot be selectively enforced,[103] and when pets may be maintained with the approval of the board of administration, the board must consider each application on its merits and may not unreasonably withhold permission from an owner who wishes a pet. When pets are allowed in the condominium they are the responsibility of both the board and their owner.

If the community determines that pets are a problem and unwanted, they may pass a restriction to prohibit them. The restriction may be enforced prospectively and may prohibit an existing pet owner from replacing the pet after its death or permanent removal from the community. The amendment cannot be applied retroactively, however. A unit owner who brought a pet to the community when the condominium documents permitted pets cannot be required to remove the existing pet.[104]

The close proximity of residents in a condominium makes it difficult to allow an unrestricted pet policy without infringing on the rights of some residents. Comprehensive pet restrictions should recognize the constraints of this close proximity.[105] They should address issues relating to the noise, the mess, the type of food and the number of pets that are appropriate for a unit in the community.[106] Thirty-five pet birds in a unit may be as much of a nuisance as a sixty-five pound pet dog. Too many pet cats may be as much of a problem as large parrots eating fruits and other foods that also attract rodents. Well-designed pet restrictions will consider the panorama of abuses

---

[101] §715.07 (4), F.S.
[102] *Zeskind v. Jockey Club Condominium Apartments, Unit II, Inc.,* 468 So.2d 1021 (Fla. 3rd DCA 1985).
[103] *Prisco v. Forest Villas Condominium Apartments, Inc.,* 847 So.2d 1012 (Fla. 4th DCA 2003).
[104] *Winston Towers 200 Ass'n, Inc. v. Saverio,* 360 So.2d 470 (Fla. 3rd DCA 1978).
[105] *Wilshire Condominium Ass'n, Inc. v. Kohlbrand,* 368 So.2d 629 (Fla. 4th DCA 1979).
[106] *Majestic View Condominium Ass'n, Inc. v. Bolotin,* 429 So.2d 438 (Fla. 4th DCA 1983).

and will temper them against the benefits and enjoyment of pet ownership.

13.24 Rules and Restrictions of the Board. While many use restrictions for the condominium property are found in the declaration of condominium and the other recorded governing documents, other restrictions are imposed by rules of the board of administration. (See 1.18). The Condominium Act grants specific authority to the board for rules concerning certain uses and activities on the condominium property. These include standards for the installation of hurricane shutters[107] and solar collectors;[108] restrictions on the recording of meetings[109] and speaking at meetings;[110] limitations on smoking on the property;[111] and the elements to be included in an emergency operations plan.[112]

Other rules of the board are promulgated based upon the authority of the governing documents to preserve the character of the community consistent with the wishes of the owners in the community. (See 9.2 and 11.2). If rules are properly adopted, uniformly applied, and not unreasonable,[113] they may be appropriately enforced by the condominium association. Rules banning the use and consumption of alcoholic beverages on the common elements;[114] rules prohibiting the use of the common elements for religious services;[115] rules designating and restricting uses in parking areas;[116] and rules authorizing fees for the use of a dock on the common elements[117] have been held to be reasonable in enforcement proceedings.

---

[107] § 718.113 (5), F.S.

[108] § 718.113 (6), F.S.

[109] § 61B-23.002 (10), F.A.C.

[110] § 718.112 (2)(c), F.S.

[111] § 386.208, F.S.

[112] § 553.509 (2)(d), F.S.

[113] *Woodside Village Condominium Ass'n, Inc. v. Jahren,* 806 So.2d 452 (Fla. 2002).

[114] *Hidden Harbour Estates, Inc. v. Norman, supra* note 3.

[115] *Neuman v. Grandview at Emerald Hills, Inc.,* 861 So.2d 494 (Fla. 4th DCA 2003).

[116] *Juno by the Sea North Condominium Ass'n, Inc. v. Manfredonia, supra* note 4.

[117] *Rosso v. Golden Surf Towers Condominium Ass'n,* 651 So.2d 787, 789 (Fla. 1995).

WATERFRONT XX CONDOMINIUM ASSOCIATION, INC.
A Corporation Not-for-Profit
100 Waterfront Drive
Waterfront, Florida 33444

October 5, 2011

Mr. Matthew Marshall
102 Waterfront Drive
Waterfront, Florida 33444
Re: Notice of Violation of Condominium Documents

Dear Mr. Marshall:

The condominium documents governing the community and its residents require that each owner, resident and guest comply with the rules and restrictions of the condominium.

Article XIX of the Declaration of Condominium prohibits pets over 25 lbs. in size. A German shepherd dog exceeding that weight is currently being kept in the unit by you.

This shall serve as formal notice of violation of the provisions of the condominium documents referenced above. The board requests that the violation cease immediately.

If the violation has not been corrected within fifteen (15) days from the date of this correspondence, the board will commence formal enforcement procedures in accordance with the documents and the Condominium Act. Any questions or responses must be submitted in writing to the association to the attention of the Board of Administration.

> Respectfully,
>
> WATERFRONT XX CONDOMINIUM
> ASSOCIATION, INC.
>
> By: _____

Notice of Violation FORM 13.01

WATERFRONT XX CONDOMINIUM ASSOCIATION, INC.
A Corporation Not-for-Profit

APPLICATION FOR SALE OR TRANSFER OF UNIT

TO: BOARD OF ADMINISTRATION
WATERFRONT XX CONDOMINIUM
ASSOCIATION, INC.

The undersigned submits this application for approval of the Board to acquire title to Unit _____, WATERFRONT XX CONDOMINIUM, and states that the following information is true and correct (any intentional misrepresentations shall be a basis for automatic disapproval):

1.   NAME OF PROPOSED OWNER(S):

_____

2.   PERMANENT ADDRESS (AFTER ACQUISITION):

_____

_____

3.   NAMES AND AGES OF PROPOSED UNIT OCCUPANTS:

_____

_____

4.   PURPOSE OF PURCHASE: _____

5.   TYPE AND NUMBER OF PETS TO BE IN UNIT:

_____

_____

6.   TYPE AND NUMBER OF MOTOR VEHICLES:

_____

_____

7.   CURRENT OWNERS:_____

_____

      The undersigned agrees to provide any further information that may be reasonably requested by the Board. The undersigned has received a copy of the Declaration of Condominium and exhibits and understands that its covenants impose responsibilities and restrictions on each unit owner at WATERFRONT XX CONDOMINIUM.

_____   _____

Print Name   Signature of Applicant

_____   _____

Current Address   Telephone Number

(IMPORTANT NOTE: If you have questions about completing the application or if you have not received a copy of the condominium documents, contact the Board of Administration.)

APPROVAL OF UNIT TRANSFER

STATE OF FLORIDA   )
COUNTY OF PINELLAS   )

WATERFRONT XX CONDOMINIUM ASSOCIATION, INC., by its Board of Administration, does give its approval to MATTHEW MARSHALL, a single man, to acquire title to the following condominium unit:

Unit 102, WATERFRONT XX, A CONDOMINIUM, according to the Declaration of Condominium recorded in O.R. Book 800, Page 100, and Condominium Plat Book 8, Page 10, Public Records of Pinellas County, Florida, together with an undivided 2.537% interest in the common elements appurtenant thereto.

Said approval is based upon the information submitted by the applicant and assumes its accuracy and truthfulness.

(CORPORATE SEAL)   WATERFRONT XX CONDOMINIUM
                          ASSOCIATION, INC.

ATTEST:

_____   By: _____
Secretary   President

SWORN to before me this 15th day of October, 2011.

_____

Notary Public

My commission expires:

WATERFRONT XX CONDOMINIUM ASSOCIATION, INC.
A Corporation Not-for-Profit

REQUEST TO MODIFY CONDOMINIUM PROPERTY

The undersigned requests permission to modify the condominium property and submits the following true and correct information in support of the request:

BRIEF DESCRIPTION OF PROPOSED MODIFICATION

_____

_____

DOES THE MODIFICATION CHANGE THE COLOR OR APPEARANCE OF THE CONDOMINIUM?

_____

DOES THE CHANGE INVOLVE ANY STRUCTURAL CHANGES TO THE CONDOMINIUM PROPERTY?

_____

_____

NAME AND ADDRESS OF PERSON DESIGNING PROPOSED MODIFICATION

_____

CONTRACTOR   ESTIMATED COST

_____   _____

Respectfully submitted this _____ day of February, 2011.

Unit #_____   _____
                              Signature of Owner

_____   _____
Print Owner's Name   Signature of Owner

(IMPORTANT NOTE: You are required to attach a sketch or drawing of the proposed modification. You are encouraged to submit any additional information supporting your case.)

WATERFRONT XX CONDOMINIUM ASSOCIATION, INC.
A Corporation Not-for-Profit

APPROVAL OF MODIFICATION OR ALTERATION

You are hereby notified that the Board of Administration has approved the proposed modification or alteration requested by you on February 15, 2011. This approval is limited strictly to the modification or alteration described in the plans and specifications submitted by you and must be performed by the contractor shown on your application.

This approval will be revoked immediately if a change is made in the contractor performing the work or if there is a departure from the approved plans and specifications.

In accepting this approval you shall assume responsibility for any damage resulting from the modification or alteration. You must restore the remaining condominium property to its original condition at the conclusion of the work authorized by this approval.

BY ORDER OF THE BOARD OF ADMINISTRATION

_____
Secretary

Dated: _____

14

Dispute Resolution and the Division of Florida Condominiums, Timeshares and Mobile Homes

DIVISION FORMS

14.1   General. During developer control and through turnover of the association to the unit owners, the Division of Florida Condominiums, Timeshares, and Mobile Homes of the Department of Business and Professional Regulation has the power to enforce and ensure compliance with the provisions of the Condominium Act and rules promulgated under the Act relating to the development, construction, sale, lease, ownership, operation, and management of residential condominiums.[1] Following turnover, the Division continues to have authority to investigate financial irregularities, election disputes, and unit owner access to the official records of the condominium association.[2] In the exercise of its authority, the Division has the power to make investigations, take testimony, and subpoena both witnesses and records. It may additionally institute enforcement proceedings and impose financial penalties when violations of the Act or the rules occur.[3]

The Division is responsible for maintaining educational programs and a toll-free telephone number accessible to condominium unit owners to help them with questions and information, and it provides periodic training programs for unit owners and association board members.[4] The Division also has a role in determining the applicability of provisions of the Condominium Act under specific circumstances, and it is presumed to have special expertise in such capacity. All findings of the Division, however, must be supported by competent, substantial evidence[5] and must be within the scope of the Division's authority or jurisdiction.

Under the provisions of the Act, the Division must annually provide each association with any changes to the Act, and with a summary of the declaratory statements and formal legal opinions issued by the Division which relate to the operation of condominiums.[6] The Division is additionally required to adopt uniform accounting principles and policies to govern the financial reporting requirements of residential condominium associations in Florida. (See 7.14 and 7.15).

---

[1] § 718.501 (1), F.S.; *Sans Souci v. Division of Florida Lands Sales and Condominiums,* 421 So.2d 623, 625 (Fla. 1st DCA 1982). Jurisdiction also extends to a bulk buyer or bulk assignee under Part VII of the Condominium Act.

[2] § 718.111 (12) and § 718.501 (1), F.S.

[3] § 718.501 (1)(a)-(d), F.S.

[4] § 718.501 (1)(h) and (k), F.S.

[5] *Tall Trees Condominium Ass'n, Inc. v. Division of Florida Land Sales and Condominiums,* 455 So.2d 1101, 1102 (Fla. 1st DCA 1984)

[6] § 718.501 (1)(h), F.S.

14.2 Jurisdiction of the Division of Florida Condominiums, Timeshares, and Mobile Homes.

The jurisdiction of the Division of Florida Condominiums, Timeshares, and Mobile Homes should always be considered as an alternative when the community is faced with a decision of enforcing the documents or resolving a dispute. On most occasions where enforcement is an issue, contact with the Division is through the Bureau of Compliance which is organizationally the part of the Division of Condominiums, Timeshares, and Mobile Homes of the Department of Business and Professional Regulation responsible for handling enforcement functions and case-related public education.[7] The Division also houses a Bureau of Standards and Registration that is responsible for all document examinations and billing functions, and the Customer Service Bureau that is in charge of complaint intake and inquiries as well as educational materials and information distribution.

The Division has the power to enforce compliance with the provisions of the Condominium Act and the rules of the Division. Its jurisdiction reaches to disputes involving the development, construction, sale, lease, ownership, operation, and management of residential condominium units during the period of developer control.[8] Thereafter, the Division jurisdiction is limited to disputes involving financial issues, elections, and records access. When the association or an owner seeks assistance from the Division, they may do so by filing a complaint alleging the violations with the Division offices in Tallahassee.[9] If the complaint is within the Division's jurisdiction, an investigator will be assigned to the complaint.

The jurisdiction of the Division is limited to matters that require enforcement of the Act and the rules of the Division. The Division does not have the authority to enforce the individual restrictions of the condominium documents, and it does not interpret ambiguous provisions of an individual community's documents.[10] The agency will refuse to accept jurisdiction of a complaint that requests an interpretation of unclear portions of a community's documents. It will also reject a complaint that seeks to have a document restriction enforced by the Division. Matters involving these types

---

[7] § 718.501 (1)(d), F.S.

[8] § 718.501 (1), F.S.

[9] § 61B-20.005, F.A.C.

[10] *Peck Plaza Condominium v. Division of Florida Land Sales and Condominiums,* 371 So.2d 152, 154 (Fla. 1st DCA 1979).

of disputes must be resolved through arbitration[11] or judicial proceedings. (See 13.10 and 13.12).

14.3 Enforcement Action. When the Division or its Bureau of Compliance has reasonable cause to believe that a violation of the Condominium Act or the rules promulgated under it has occurred, it may take formal action against the violator. The action may include proceedings against any developer or the association, or any of their agents, including their officers, directors and employees.[12] In pursuit of enforcement, the agency may make investigations, take sworn statements, accept evidence and subpoena both individuals and documentation. Association officers and directors, developers, community association managers, and management firms have an ongoing obligation to cooperate with Division investigations being conducted under the Act, and the Division is obligated to refer to local law enforcement authorities any person that the Division believes has destroyed or altered documents or impaired the availability of association records during an investigation.[13]

When it believes a violation has occurred, the agency may institute enforcement proceedings in its own name to stop the violation and seek compliance in one of four ways. First, compliance may be voluntary, and the violator may consent to the entry of an order stopping the improper activity without formal proceedings. Voluntary compliance is always the desired alternative when the Division finds it necessary to exercise its enforcement authority.

If voluntary compliance cannot be achieved, three formal enforcement alternatives remain at the agency's disposal. They include (1) the issuance of administrative orders to cease and desist from the unlawful practice;[14] (2) enforcement actions filed by the agency in the Circuit Court on behalf of unit owners to seek declaratory or injunctive relief;[15] and (3) the imposition of civil penalties by the Division for violation of the Act or rules in amounts up to $5,000 per violation.[16] The Division may impose civil penalties

---

[11] § 718.1255, F.S.

[12] § 718.501 (1)(d), F.S.

[13] § 718.501 (1)(n), F.S.

[14] § 718.501 (1)(d) 2., F.S.; *Suntide Condominium Ass'n, Inc. v. Division of Florida Land Sales and Condominiums,* 409 So.2d 65, 66 (Fla. 1st DCA 1982).

[15] § 718.501 (1)(d) 3., F.S.; *Sans Souci v. Division of Florida Lands Sales and Condominiums, supra* note 1.

[16] § 718.501 (1)(d) 4., F.S.; *Finst Development, Inc. v. Department of Business Regulation,* 456 So.2d 952, 953 (Fla. 3rd DCA 1984).

individually against any officer or board member of the association who willfully or knowingly violates the Condominium Act or a rule or final order of the Division. The Division may also remove an individual as an officer of the association or as a member of the board of administration and prohibit the individual from further service in either capacity.[17]

When the Division is presented with proof that a unit owner has been denied access to official records of the association after two (2) written requests by certified mail, the Division is obligated to issue a subpoena requiring the production of the requested records for the unit owner at the location where the records are maintained by the association.[18]

14.4   Penalty Guidelines. The Division of Florida Condominiums, Timeshares, and Mobile Homes has adopted, by rule, penalty guidelines for violations or categories of violations of the Condominium Act or Rules of the Division adopted pursuant to the Act. The Division was directed to specify a meaningful range of civil penalties based upon the nature of the violations and whether or not the violations are a repeat of earlier transgressions by the offending party.

The penalty guidelines take into consideration mitigating and aggravating circumstances, whether the association is developer or owner-controlled, the size of the community and other factors.

The rules distinguish minor violations from those that might endanger the health, safety or welfare of the condominium residents or other persons in the community. The new guidelines became effective on January 1, 1998, and they are set forth in sections 61B-20.006 and 61B-21.001 of the Florida Administrative Code.

14.5   Declaratory Statement. Prior to actual confrontation in the community, a potential problem can sometimes be presented to the Division and resolved through the agency's power to provide declaratory statements on the subject. The declaratory statement is requested by filing a formal petition with the Division. The petition seeks the Division's opinion on the applicability of the Condominium Act, the agency rules or agency orders to factual circumstances in the condominium community giving rise to the problem.[19]

---

[17] § 718.501 (1)(d), F.S.
[18] § 718.501 (1)(d) 5., F.S.
[19] § 120.59, F.S.

The jurisdiction of the Division to entertain and issue a declaratory statement covers the same subject matter as the jurisdiction for hearing formal complaints.[20] A petition requesting a declaratory statement may inquire about the applicability of new changes in the law to the community; it may request an interpretation of an existing provision in the statutes; or it may seek the application of the law to specific factual circumstances in the condominium. The request must involve questions relating to the Condominium Act, the administration rules developed under the Act, or orders from the Division. A petition for a declaratory statement cannot be used to resolve ambiguities in the condominium documents, to interpret a contract or to enforce individual restrictions in the documents.[21]

A declaratory statement is considered to be an order from the agency, and it may be appealed to the courts by any party affected by the declaratory statement. A declaratory statement is binding on the person or the board of administration obtaining it. The declaratory statement is not binding on individuals not directly involved in the petition; however, it has value in precedent for those who did not participate in the proceedings. It can be easily presumed that a similar question on similar circumstances will result in a similar declaratory result from the Division, and the Florida courts have recognized that the Division has special expertise in making such decisions.[22]

14.6   Condominium Ombudsman. In 2004, the Florida Legislature created the office of condominium ombudsman, and the ombudsman is empowered to assist with the resolution of disputes between unit owners and the association when the dispute is not within the jurisdiction of the Division.[23] The ombudsman also advises and makes recommendations to the Division, as well as to other government leaders.[24] The duties of ombudsman include a liaison role between the Division and condominium

---

[20] § 718.501 (1), F.S.
[21] *Lee v. Division of Florida Land Sales and Condominiums,* 474 So.2d 282, 284 (Fla. 5th DCA 1985); *Peck Plaza Condominium v. Division of Florida Land Sales and Condominiums, supra* note 8; and *Lennar Homes, Inc. v. Department of Business and Professional Regulation, Division of Florida Land Sales, Condominiums and Mobile Homes,* 888 So.2d 50 (Fla. 1st DCA 2004).
[22] *Sans Souci v. Division of Florida Lands Sales and Condominiums, supra* note 1.
[23] § 718.5012 (9), F.S.
[24] § 718.5012 (3), F.S.

owners and community leaders, and the office assists the Division with the preparation and adoption of educational and reference materials.[25] The office of the ombudsman is authorized to make recommendations to the Division concerning enforcement actions, new rules and procedures for resolving complaints, and to assist condominium communities in carrying out their duties and responsibilities under the Condominium Act.[26]

The ombudsman has the ability to assist communities with elections, and the office has the authority to appoint an election monitor to the conduct the annual election for the board of administration when fifteen percent (15%) of the total voting interests in the association request the assistance.[27] The request for assistance is made by petition on the form provided by the rules of the Division,[28] and the costs and expenses associated with the election monitoring process are paid for by the association.[29]

14.7 Division Educational Programs. To keep condominium communities current on the changes in the Condominium Act and the policies of the Division Florida Condominiums, Timeshares, and Mobile Homes, the Division is required to annually furnish each condominium association with updated versions of the Act and current rules of the Division.[30] Additionally, the Division has the authority to sponsor and provide educational and training programs that unit owners and community leaders can locate or access through the Division's website.[31]

Under a new program authorized the by the Legislature in 2008, the Division is also expected to review and approve education and training programs offered by other providers for community leaders and unit owners. Once approved, a current list of the approved providers and the program offerings is to be maintained by the Division and made available to board members and unit owners through the Division's website.[32]

---

[25] § 718.5012 (4), F.S.
[26] § 718.5012 (5) through (8), F.S
[27] § 718.5012 (9), F.S.
[28] § 61B-23.00215, F.A.C.
[29] § 718.5012 (9), F.S.
[30] § 718.501 (1)(h), F.S.
[31] § 718.501 (1)(j), F.S.
[32] *Id.*

STATE OF FLORIDA
DEPARTMENT OF BUSINESS REGULATION
DIVISION OF CONDOMINIUMS,
TIMESHARES, AND MOBILE HOMES

DATE July 20, 2011

IN RE:
WATERFRONT XX CONDOMINIUM
ASSOCIATION, INC.
RE: Section 718.112 (2)(1), Florida Statutes

PETITION FOR DECLARATORY STATEMENT

COMES NOW, WATERFRONT XX CONDOMINIUM ASSOCIATION, INC., ("WATERFRONT"), by and through its undersigned representative, and does file this Petition for Declaratory Statement based upon the following facts and circumstances, to wit:

1.   That the Petitioner, WATERFRONT XX CONDOMINIUM ASSOCIATION, INC., whose address is 100 Waterfront Drive, Waterfront, Florida 33444, is the governing association of WATERFRONT XX CONDOMINIUM. The Declaration of Condominium was recorded on October 23, 1997.

2.   That WATERFRONT seeks a Declaratory Statement on the applicability of the provisions of Section 718.112 (2)(1), Florida Statutes, as it relates to the condominium operated and managed by WATERFRONT. The section requires that a provision for mandatory non-binding arbitration be in the bylaws of all condominium associations.

3.   That WATERFRONT request a Declaratory Statement based upon the facts and circumstances as follows:

    a. Section 718.112 (2)(1), Florida Statutes, provides that all bylaws include a provision for arbitration of disputes in the condominium.

    b. WATERFRONT XX CONDOMINIUM was created prior to the change in the law requiring the inclusion of a provision for arbitration in the bylaws.

c. The bylaws of the Association do not contain a provision relating to the arbitration of disputes as required by Section 718.112 (2) (1), F.S.

4.   The Petitioner does not request a hearing and the Division may dispose of this Petition at its discretion without a hearing.

WHEREFORE, WATERFRONT respectfully requests that a Declaratory Statement be entered upon the above-cited facts and circumstances on the following question:

a. Are the provisions of Section 718.112 (2)(1), F.S., applicable to WATERFRONT XX CONDOMINIUM?

b. Must the community amend its bylaws to include a specific provision on the arbitration of disputes into the bylaws of the association if the new law is applicable to WATERFRONT XX CONDOMINIUM?

Respectfully submitted,

_____

Wayne J. Boyer, Esq.
Attorney for Waterfront XX
Condominium Association, Inc.
1968 Bayshore Boulevard
Waterfront, Florida 33444
Telephone: (813) 733–2154

Index

Here are some other books from Pineapple Press on related topics. For a complete catalog, visit our website at www.pineapplepress.com. Or write to Pineapple Press, P.O. Box 3889, Sarasota, Florida 34230-3889, or call (800) 746-3275.

The Law of Florida Homeowners Associations, 8th Edition, by Peter M. Dunbar and Charles F. Dudley. The only complete and practical guide to help ensure that a Florida homeowners association carries out its responsibility fairly and effectively under current Florida laws. Cross-referenced to the Florida Statutes. Includes sample forms, a table of cases, and complete subject index. (hb & pb)

The Homeowners Association Manual, 5th Edition, by Peter M. Dunbar and Marc Dunbar. This manual provides a step-by-step explanation of the requirements for meetings, membership voting, and the necessary parliamentary procedures. It serves as a guide to help ensure that the association carries out its responsibilities fairly and effectively. In addition to the comprehensive text, there are 28 forms and sample documents—all you need to run an effective homeowners association. (hb & pb)

Florida Law: A Layman's Guide, 5th Edition, by Gerald B. Keane. This practical guide is for anyone who needs to know the basics of Florida law. It covers property, family, business, and criminal law in an easy-to-read style. (pb)

Florida Divorce Handbook, 5th Edition, by Gerald Keane. This handbook offers an overview of the divorce process, introduces the basic vocabulary and legal concepts associated with divorce, and familiarizes you with what to expect if you are planning to divorce in Florida or if you are already divorced and have questions about your rights. (pb)

The Club Board Members Guide by John L. Carroll. Although written with private club members in mind, the common-sense solutions offered here apply to a much broader audience, especially those who oversee the running of a nonprofit organization. Learn what to expect as a club board member, what your legal responsibilities are, and how meetings should be handled. (pb)